That Time I Got Reincarnated as a SLIME

The Ways of the Monster Nation

3

Sho Okagiri Original Story: **FUSE** Character Design: **Mitz Vah**

The Story So Far

Rimuru, demon lord and leader of the nation of Tempest, has asked rabbitfolk girl Framea to write a guidebook for his fledgling country. With a little help from the locals, she checks out Tempest's forges, hot springs, and underground labyrinth—and thanks to a newly developed magical device called a "camera," the guidebook's really beginning to take shape.

Now that the book's launch is imminent, Rimuru decides to hold a gala event to celebrate...

Contents

Chapter 15 ▷ **Top-Shelf Sweets☆Three Stars!!** —————— 3

Chapter 16 ▷ **Sweets Coliseum☆Three Stars!!** —————— 27

Chapter 17 ▷ **Food Judging☆Three Stars!!** —————— 53

Chapter 18 ▷ **Kitchen Tour☆Three Stars!!** —————— 83

Chapter 19 ▷ **Class Visit☆Three Stars!!** —————— 107

Chapter EX ▷ **A Date With Shion☆Three Stars...?** —————— 131

GB ▷ *Tempest Guidebook* (Part 1) —————— 143

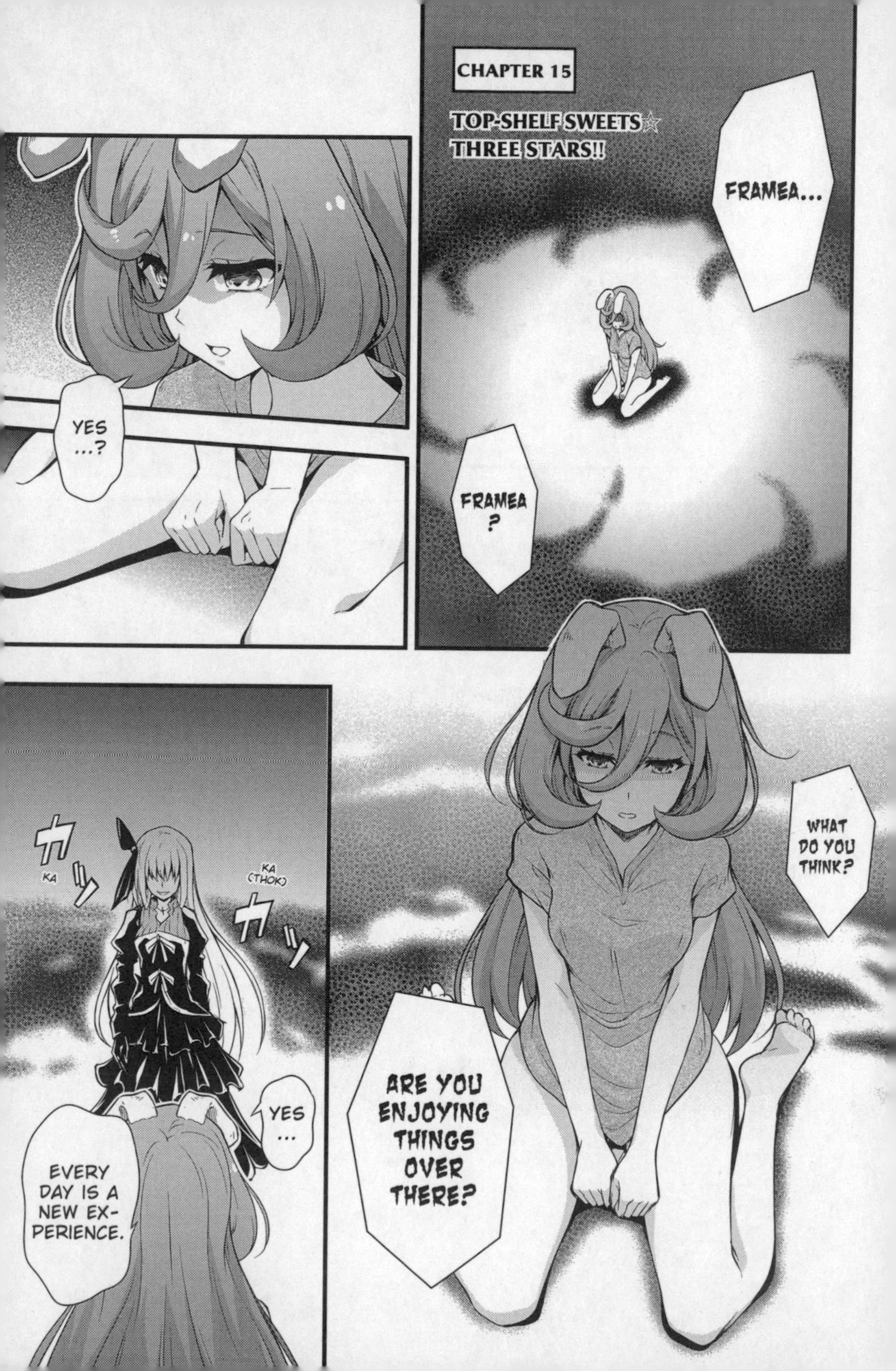
CHAPTER 15
TOP-SHELF SWEETS☆ THREE STARS!!
FRAMEA...
FRAMEA?
YES...?
WHAT DO YOU THINK?
ARE YOU ENJOYING THINGS OVER THERE?
KA (THOK)
KA
YES...
EVERY DAY IS A NEW EXPERIENCE.

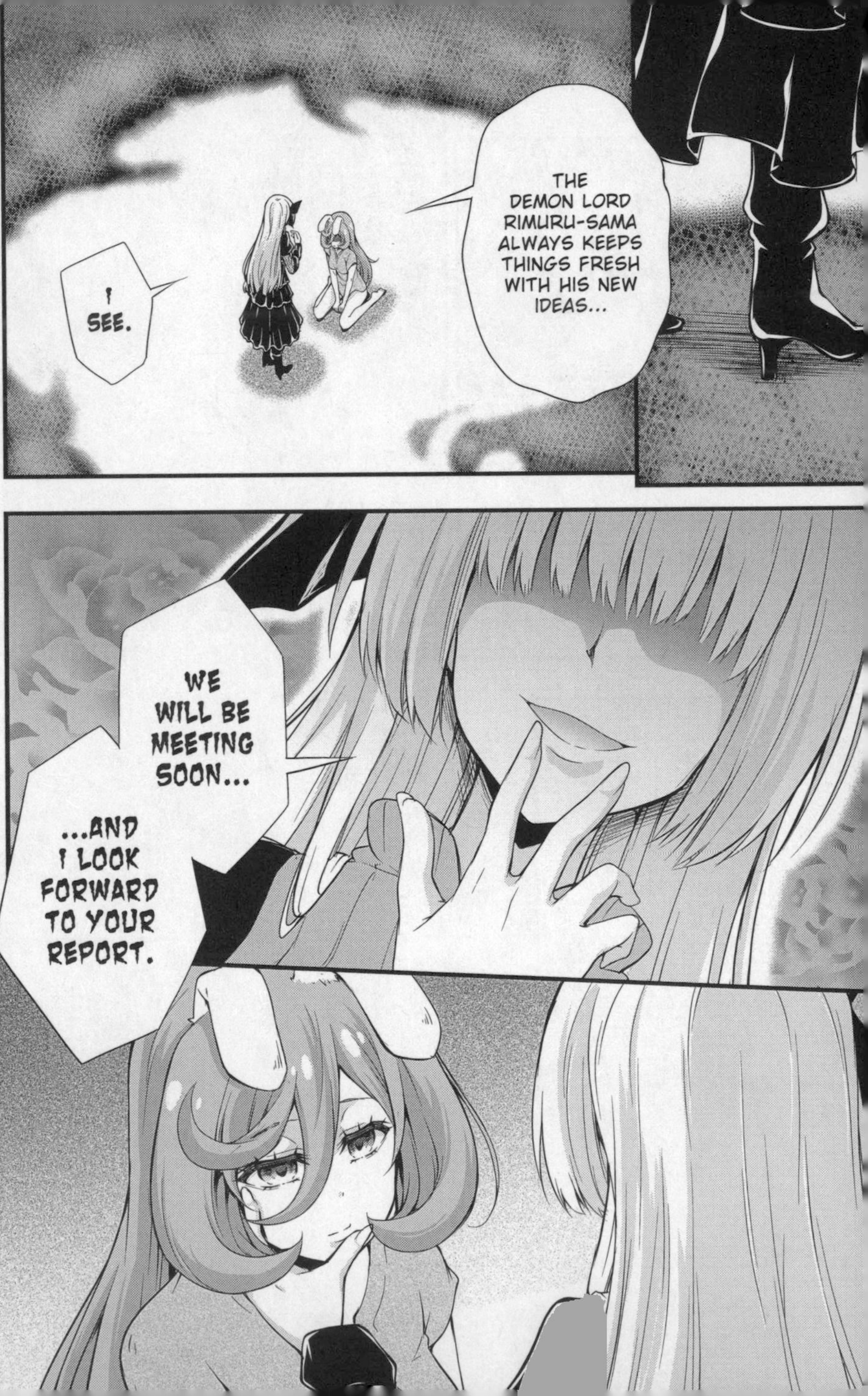
THE DEMON LORD RIMURU-SAMA ALWAYS KEEPS THINGS FRESH WITH HIS NEW IDEAS...
I SEE.
WE WILL BE MEETING SOON...
...AND I LOOK FORWARD TO YOUR REPORT.

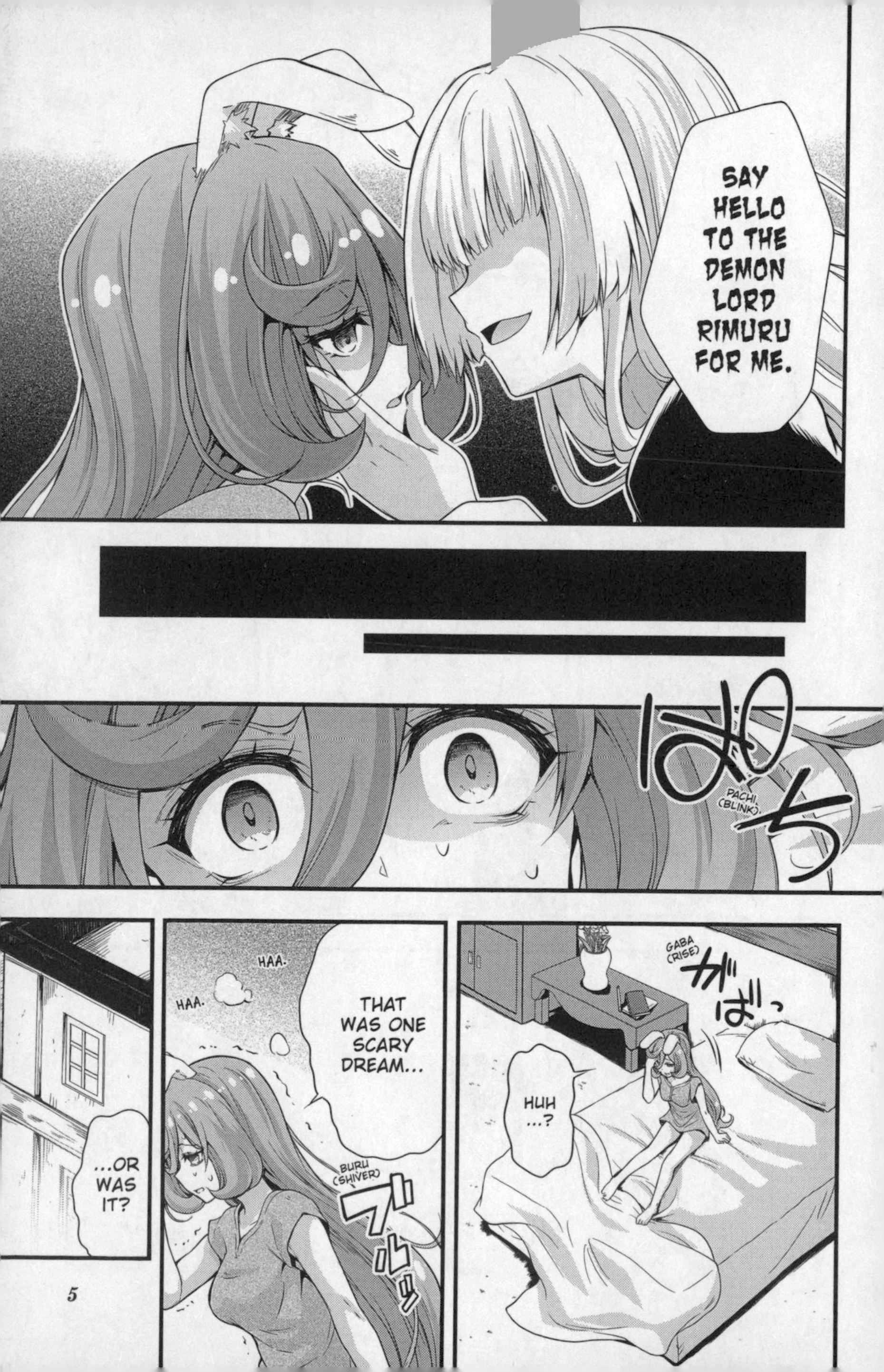
SAY HELLO TO THE DEMON LORD RIMURU FOR ME.
ぱち
PACHI (BLINK)
がばっ
GABA (RISE)
HUH ...?
HAA.
HAA.
THAT WAS ONE SCARY DREAM...
ブルッ
BURU (SHIVER)
...OR WAS IT?

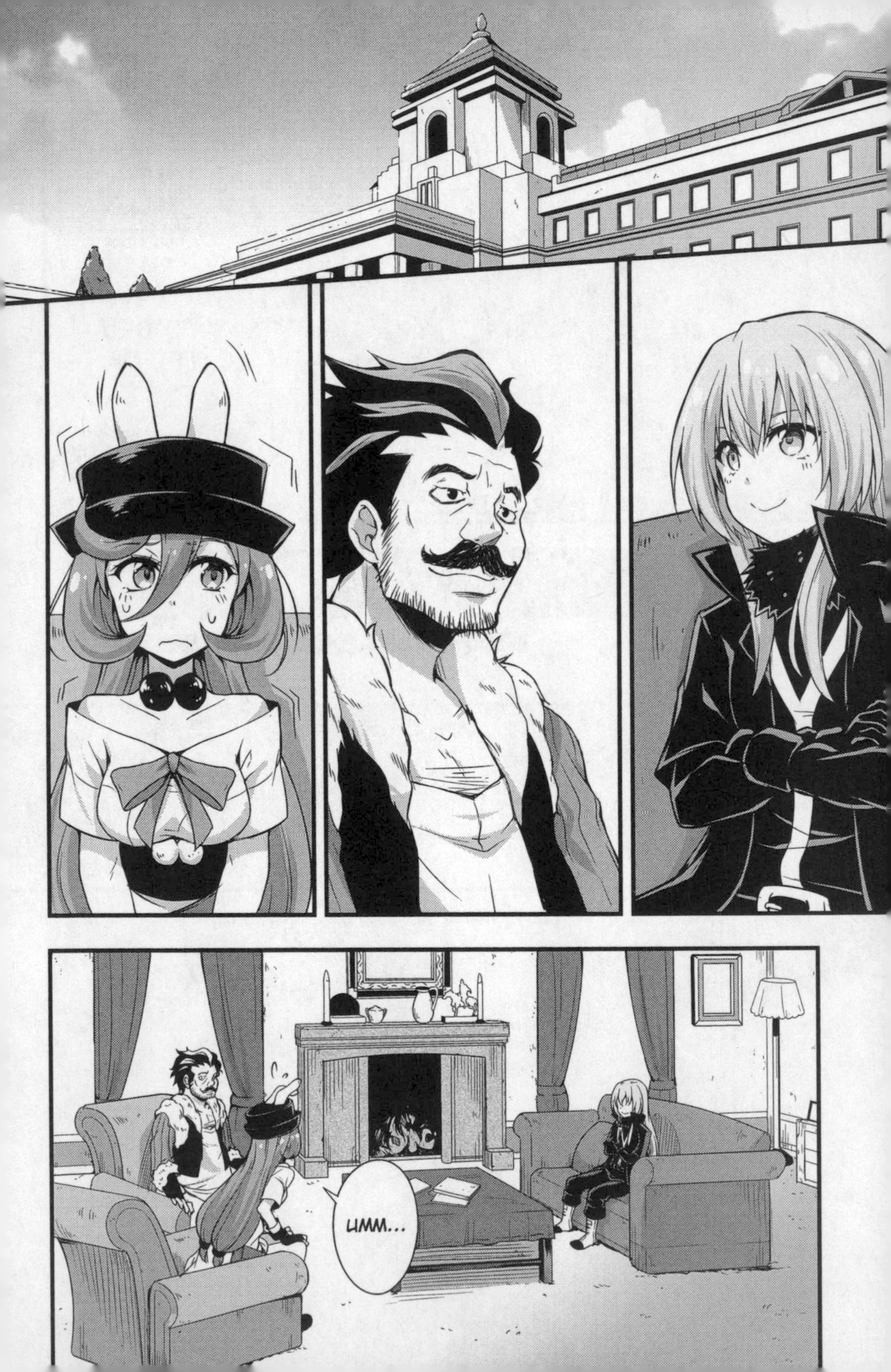
UMM...

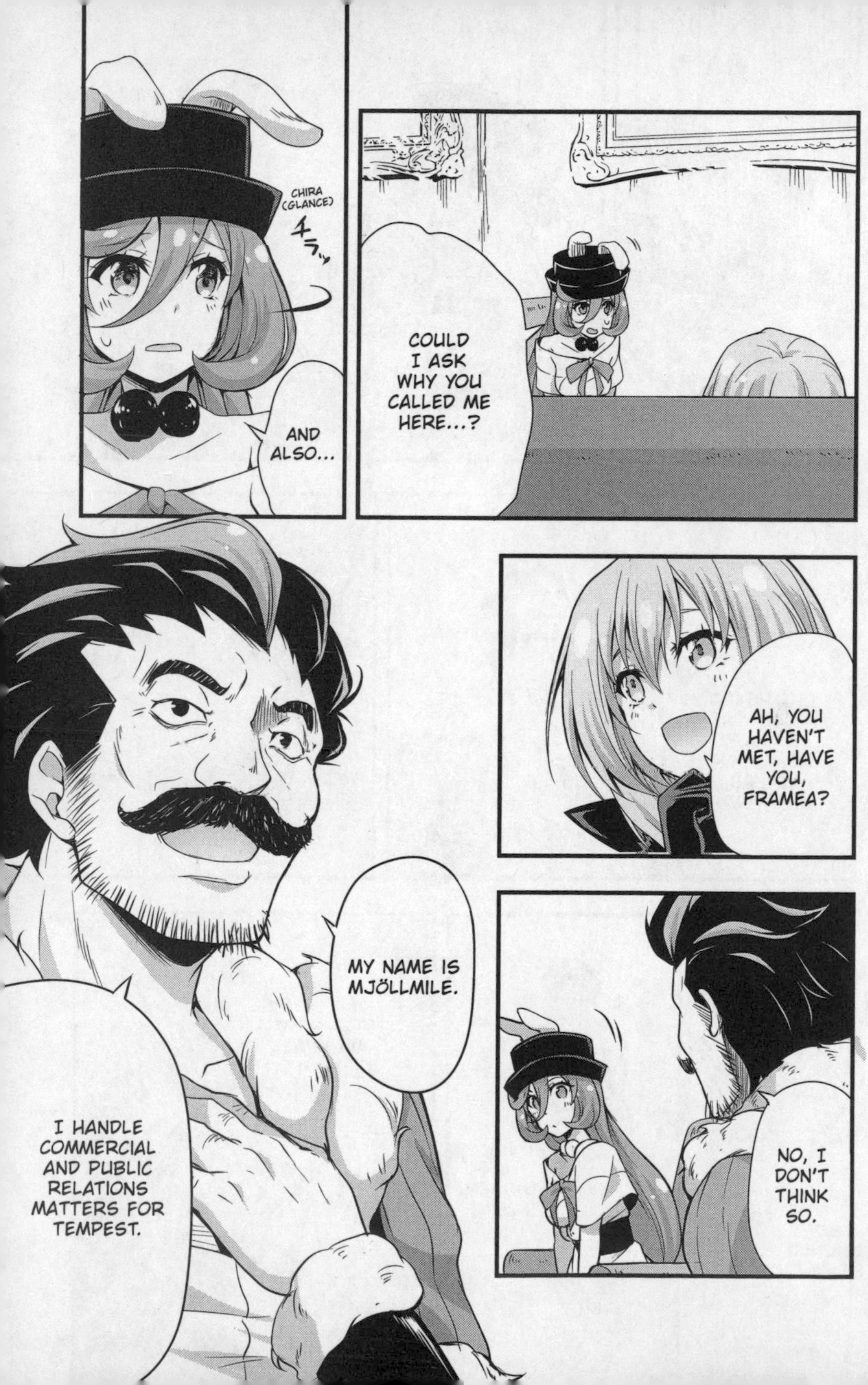
COULD I ASK WHY YOU CALLED ME HERE...?
CHIRA (GLANCE)
チラッ
AND ALSO...
AH, YOU HAVEN'T MET, HAVE YOU, FRAMEA?
NO, I DON'T THINK SO.
MY NAME IS MJÖLLMILE.
I HANDLE COMMERCIAL AND PUBLIC RELATIONS MATTERS FOR TEMPEST.

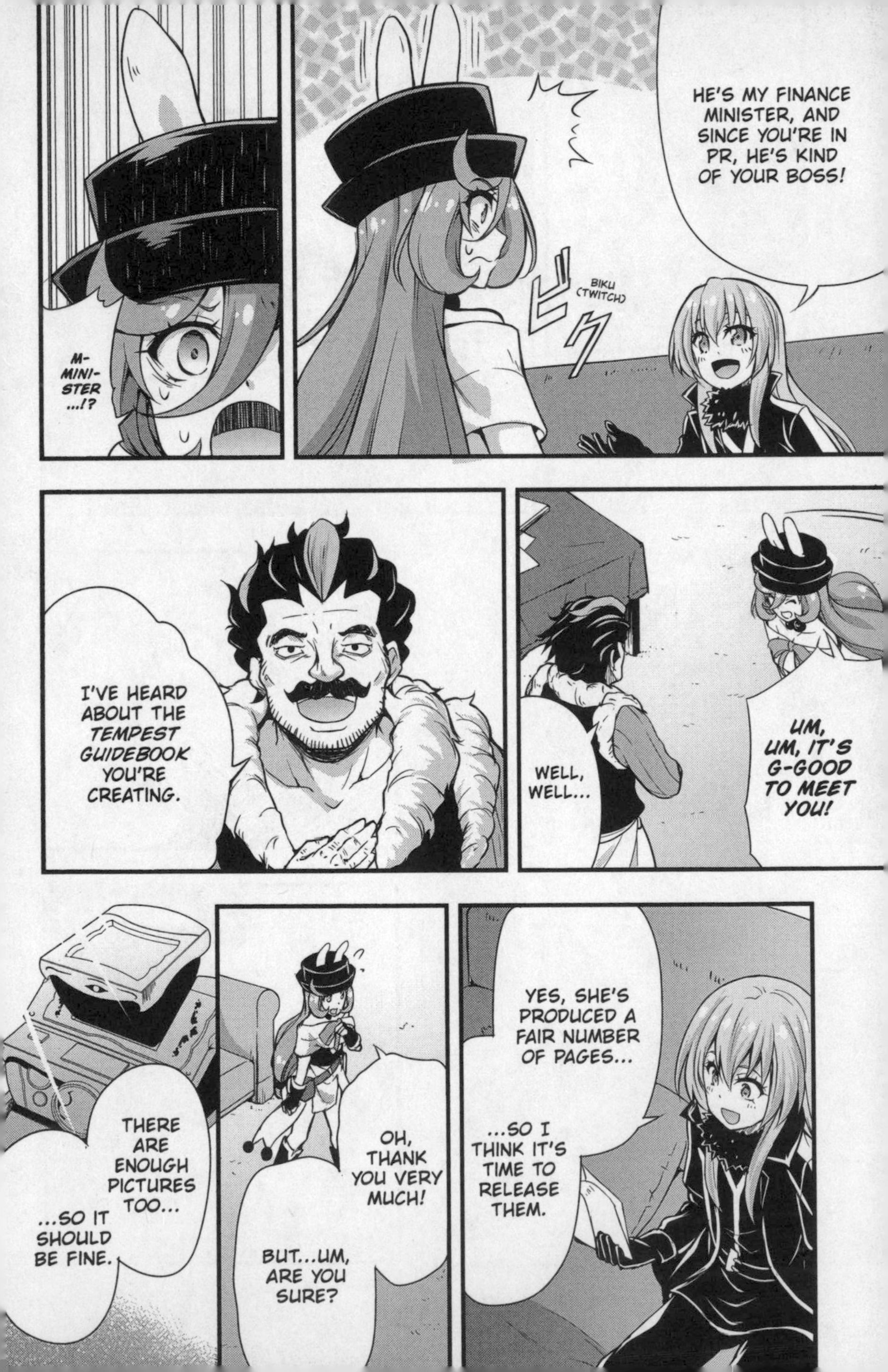
HE'S MY FINANCE MINISTER, AND SINCE YOU'RE IN PR, HE'S KIND OF YOUR BOSS!
BIKU (TWITCH)
M-MINISTER...!?
UM, UM, IT'S G-GOOD TO MEET YOU!
WELL, WELL...
I'VE HEARD ABOUT THE *TEMPEST GUIDEBOOK* YOU'RE CREATING.
YES, SHE'S PRODUCED A FAIR NUMBER OF PAGES...
...SO I THINK IT'S TIME TO RELEASE THEM.
OH, THANK YOU VERY MUCH!
BUT...UM, ARE YOU SURE?
THERE ARE ENOUGH PICTURES TOO...
...SO IT SHOULD BE FINE.

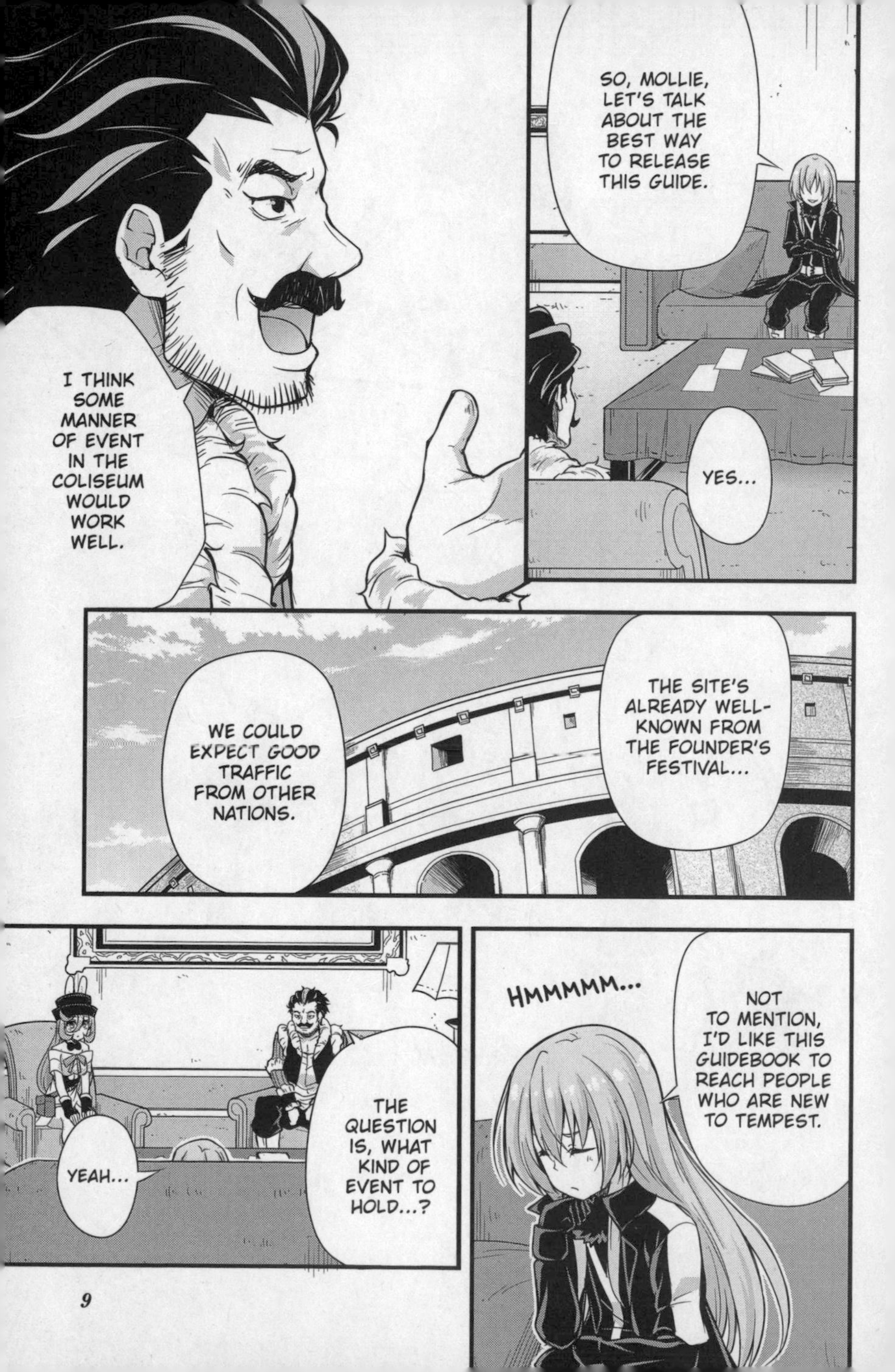
SO, MOLLIE, LET'S TALK ABOUT THE BEST WAY TO RELEASE THIS GUIDE.
YES...
I THINK SOME MANNER OF EVENT IN THE COLISEUM WOULD WORK WELL.
THE SITE'S ALREADY WELL-KNOWN FROM THE FOUNDER'S FESTIVAL...
WE COULD EXPECT GOOD TRAFFIC FROM OTHER NATIONS.
NOT TO MENTION, I'D LIKE THIS GUIDEBOOK TO REACH PEOPLE WHO ARE NEW TO TEMPEST.
HMMMMM...
THE QUESTION IS, WHAT KIND OF EVENT TO HOLD...?
YEAH...

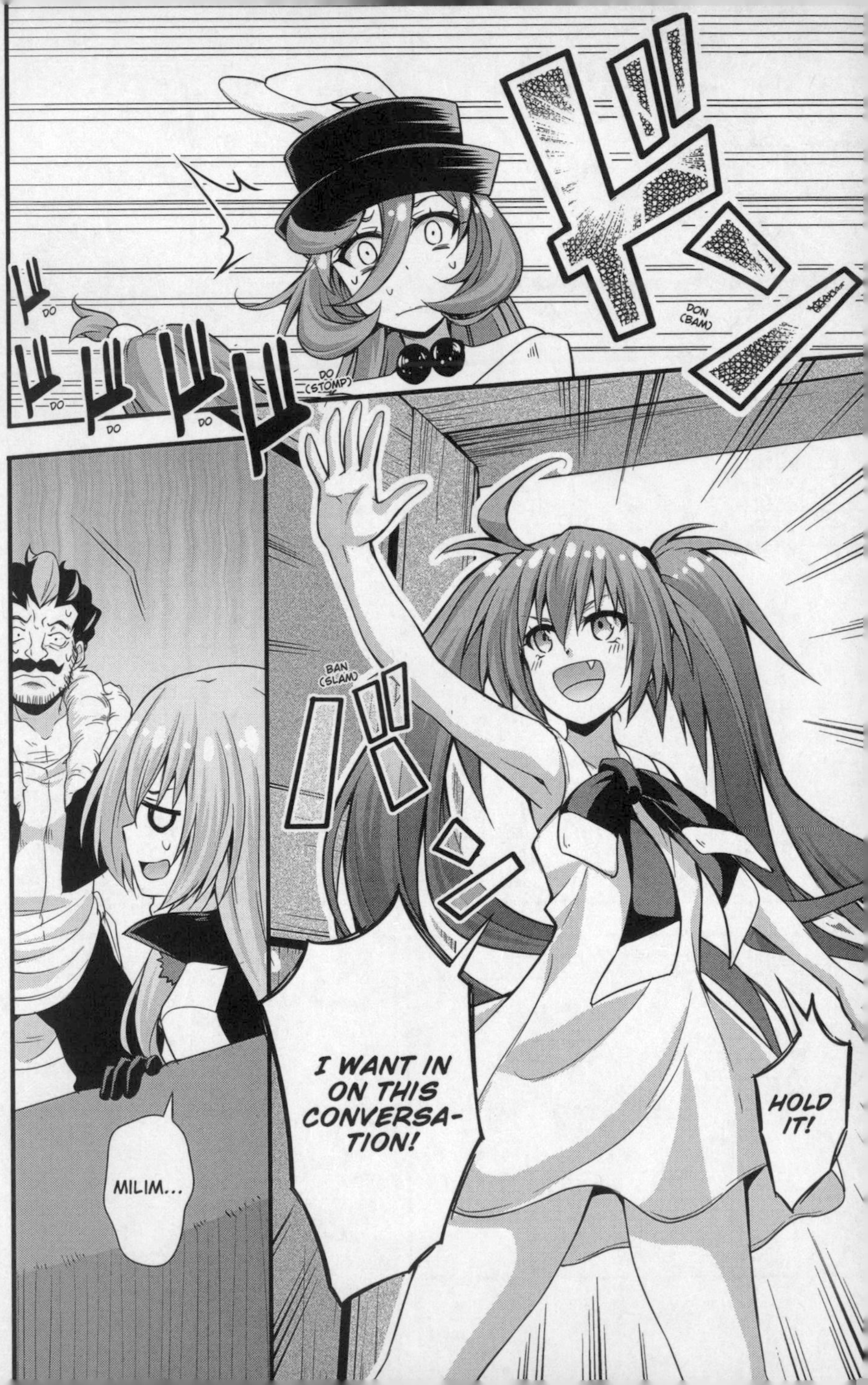
DON (BAM)
DO (STOMP)
DO
DO
DO
DO
HOLD IT!
I WANT IN ON THIS CONVERSA-TION!
BAN (SLAM)
MILIM...

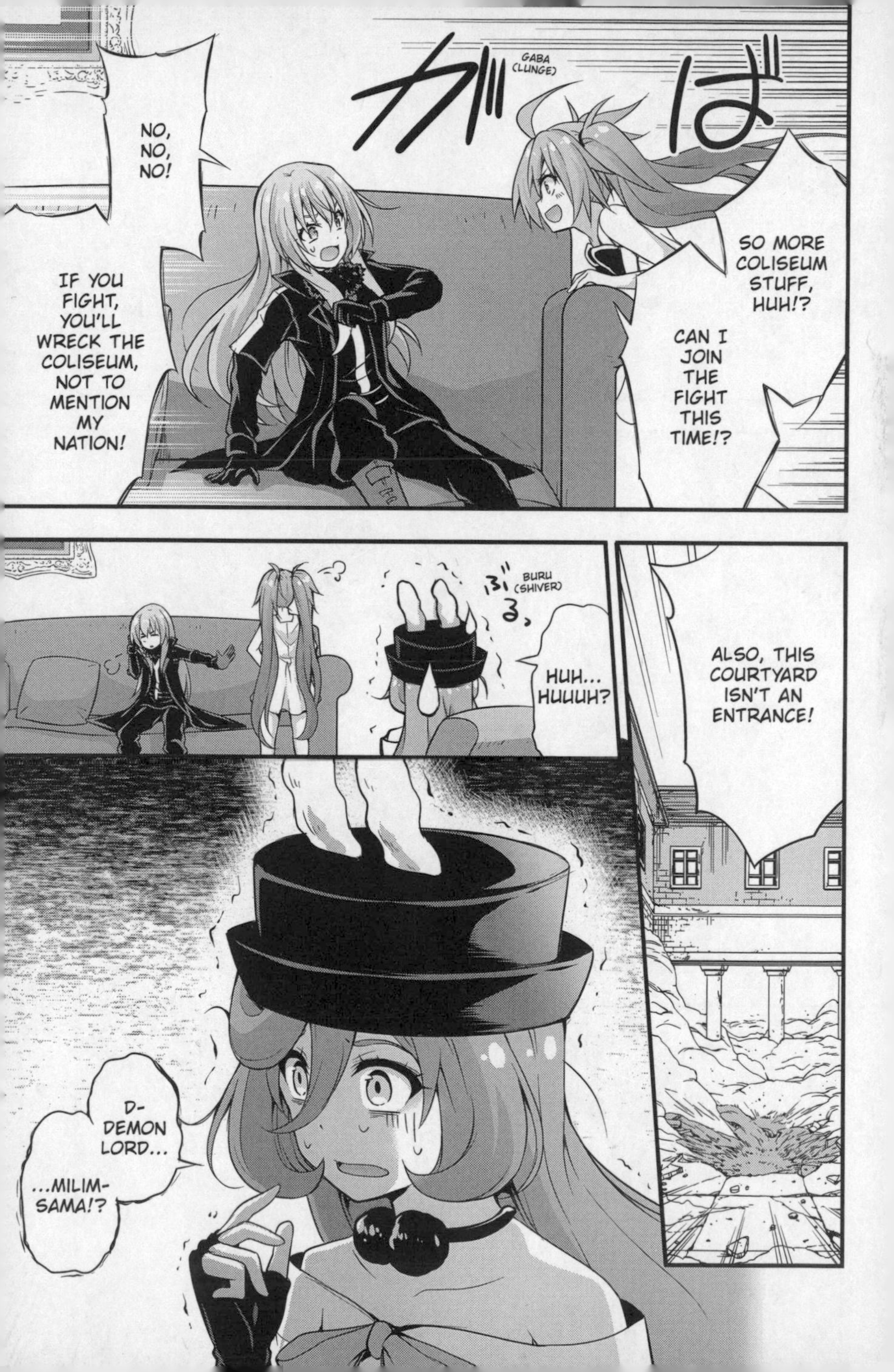
がば
GABA (LUNGE)
SO MORE COLISEUM STUFF, HUH!?
CAN I JOIN THE FIGHT THIS TIME!?
NO, NO, NO!
IF YOU FIGHT, YOU'LL WRECK THE COLISEUM, NOT TO MENTION MY NATION!
ALSO, THIS COURTYARD ISN'T AN ENTRANCE!
ぶる
BURU (SHIVER)
HUH... HUUUH?
D-DEMON LORD...
...MILIM-SAMA!?

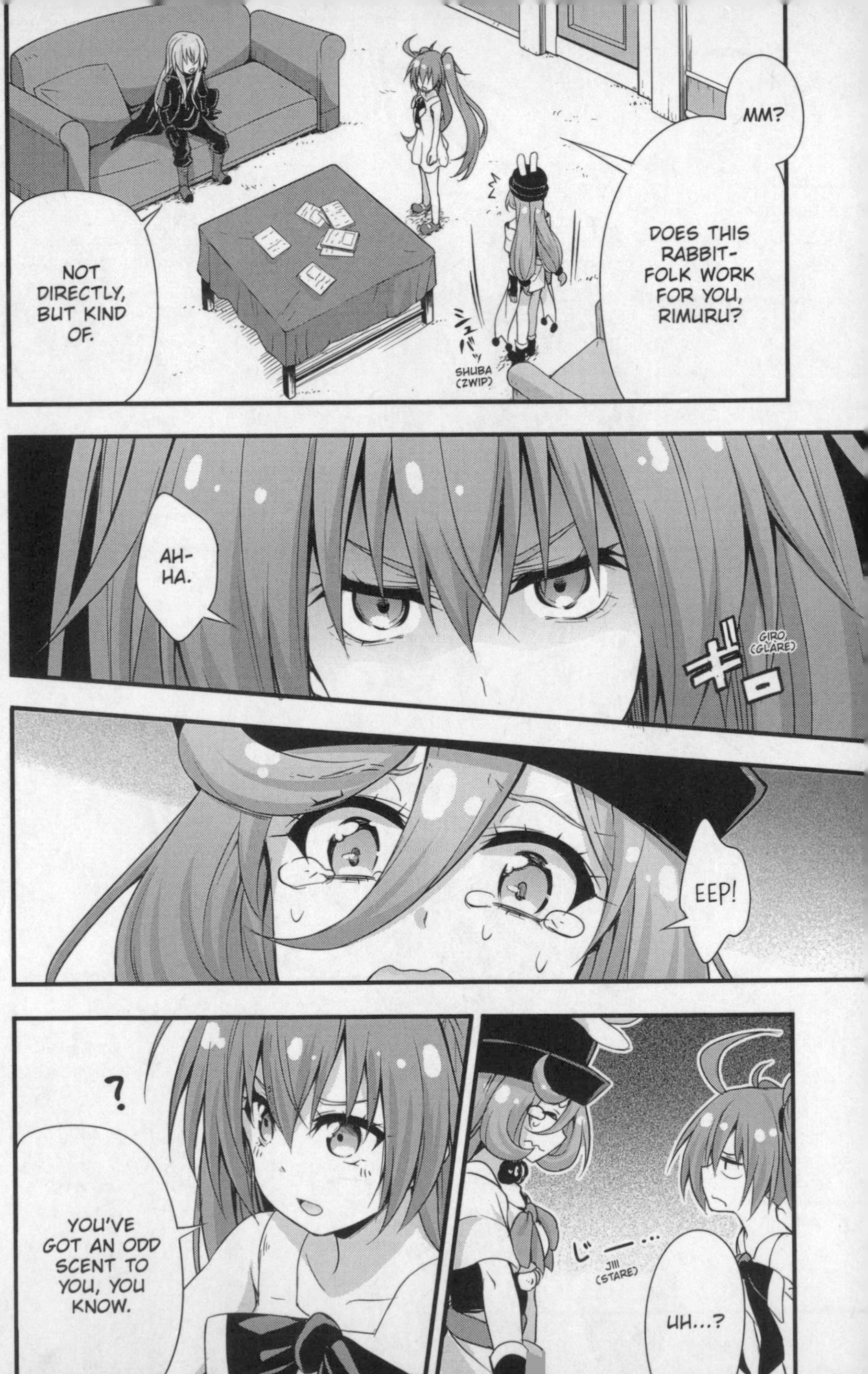
MM?
DOES THIS RABBIT-FOLK WORK FOR YOU, RIMURU?
シュバッ
SHUBA (ZWIP)
NOT DIRECTLY, BUT KIND OF.
ギロ
GIRO (GLARE)
AH-HA.
EEP!
UH...?
じー…
JIII (STARE)
?
YOU'VE GOT AN ODD SCENT TO YOU, YOU KNOW.

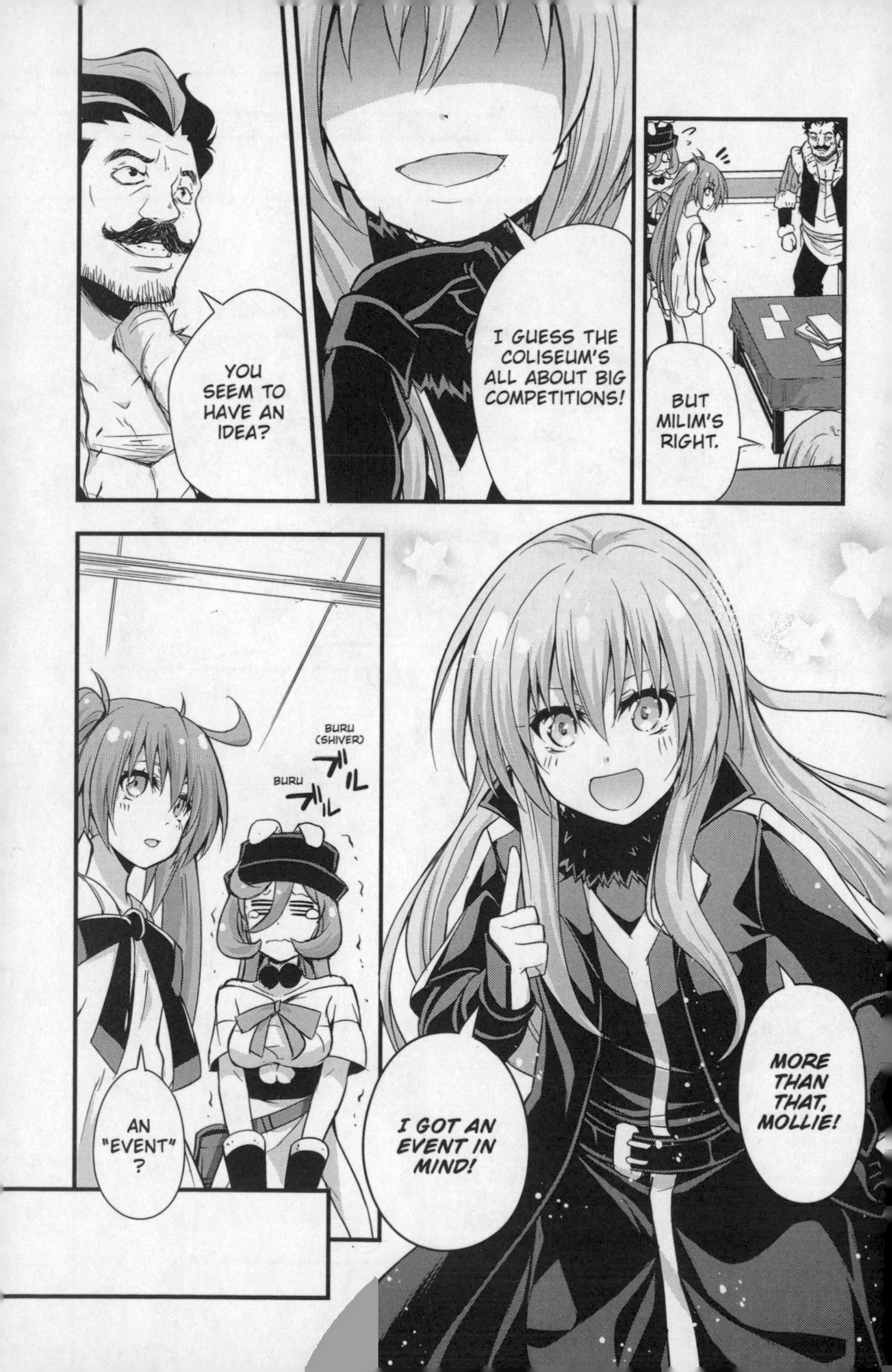
BUT MILIM'S RIGHT.
I GUESS THE COLISEUM'S ALL ABOUT BIG COMPETITIONS!
YOU SEEM TO HAVE AN IDEA?
MORE THAN THAT, MOLLIE!
I GOT AN EVENT IN MIND!
BURU (SHIVER)
BURU
AN "EVENT"?

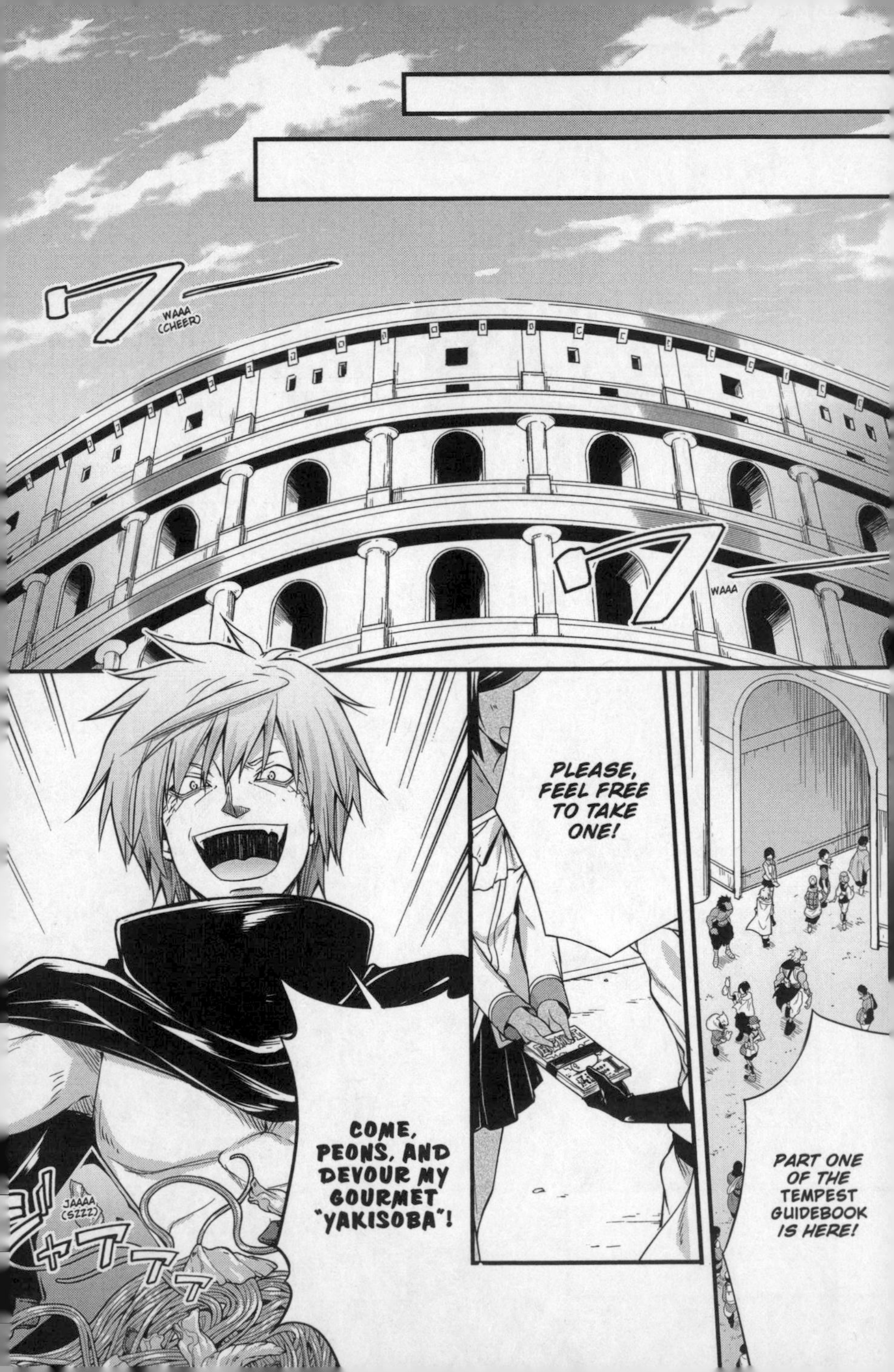
WAAA (CHEER)
WAAA
PART ONE OF THE TEMPEST GUIDEBOOK IS HERE!
PLEASE, FEEL FREE TO TAKE ONE!
COME, PEONS, AND DEVOUR MY GOURMET "YAKISOBA"!
JAAAA (SZZZ)

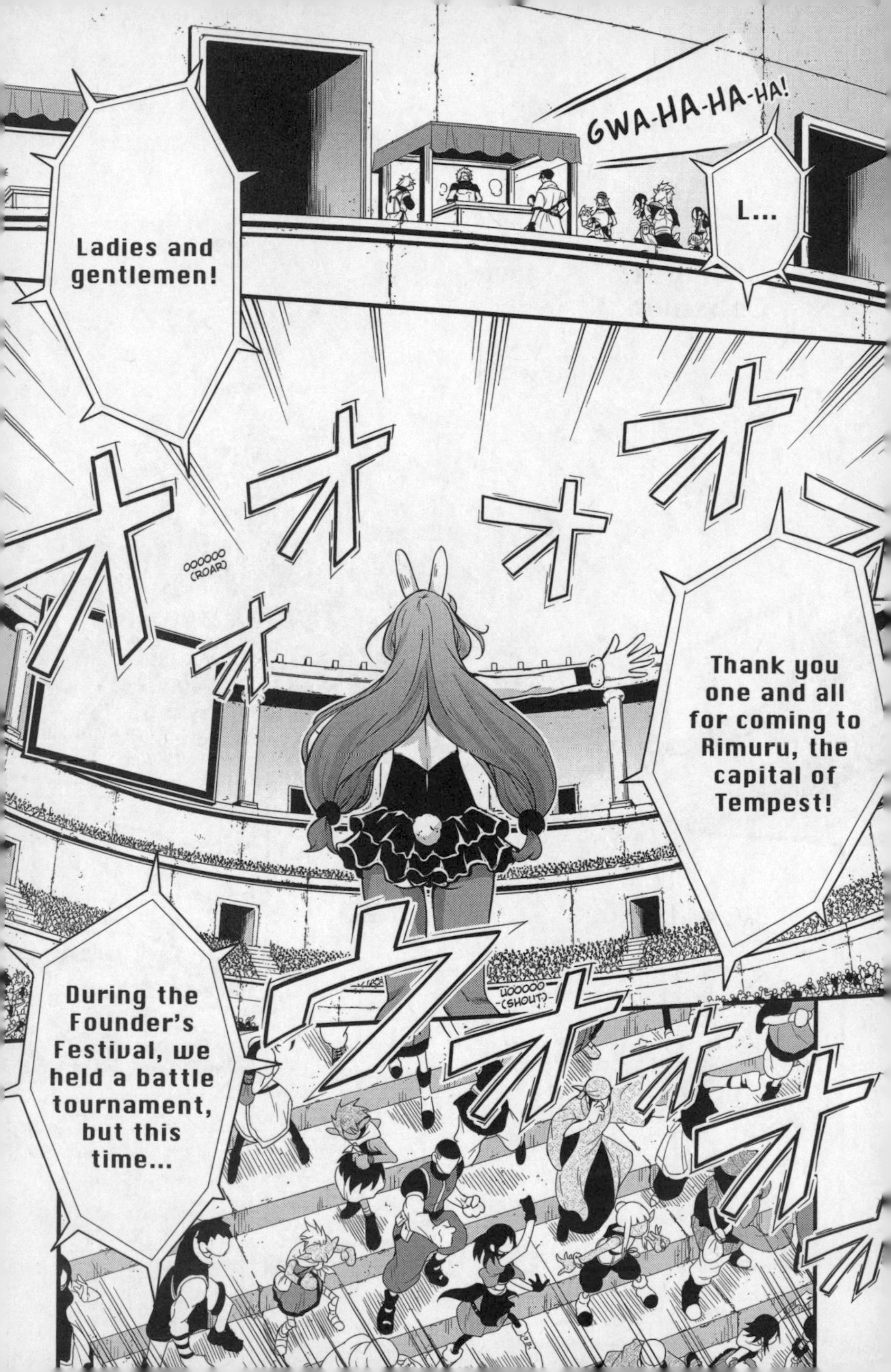
GWA-HA-HA-HA!
L...
Ladies and gentlemen!
Thank you one and all for coming to Rimuru, the capital of Tempest!
OOOOOO (ROAR)
UOOOOO (SHOUT)
During the Founder's Festival, we held a battle tournament, but this time...

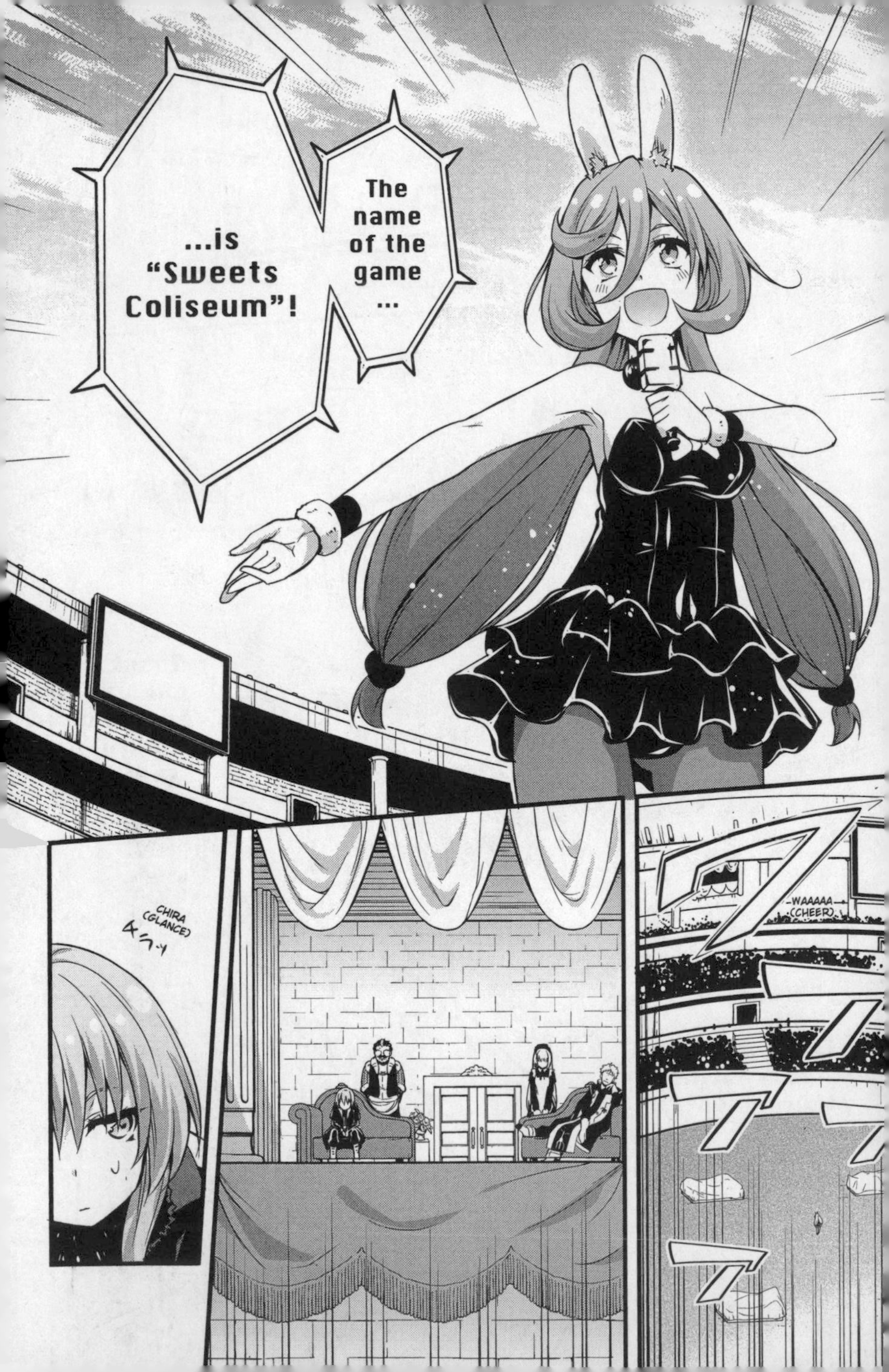
The name of the game ...
...is "Sweets Coliseum"!
WAAAAA (CHEER)
CHIRA (GLANCE)
チラッ

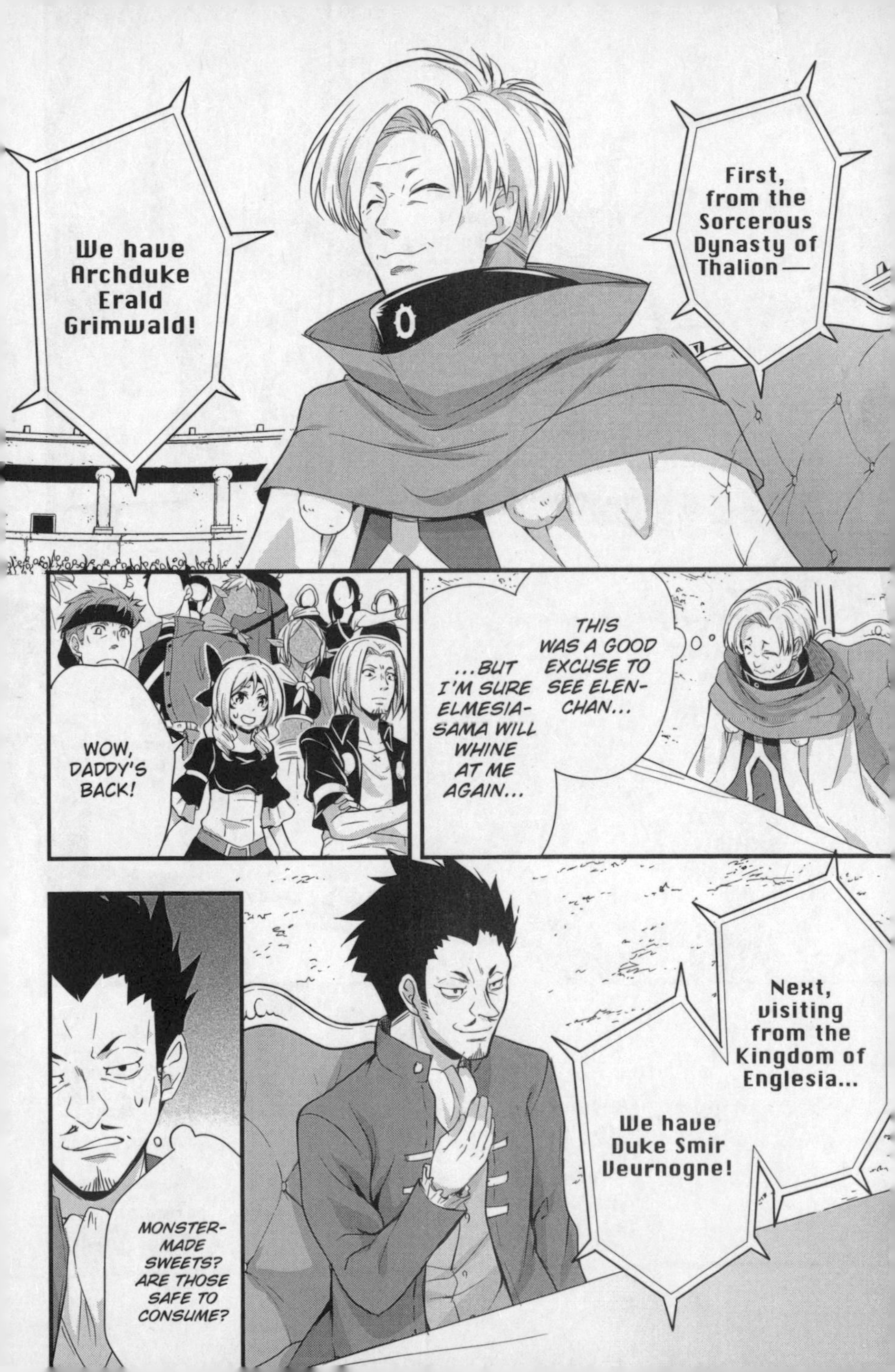
First, from the Sorcerous Dynasty of Thalion—
We have Archduke Erald Grimwald!
THIS WAS A GOOD EXCUSE TO SEE ELEN-CHAN...
...BUT I'M SURE ELMESIA-SAMA WILL WHINE AT ME AGAIN...
WOW, DADDY'S BACK!
Next, visiting from the Kingdom of Englesia...
We have Duke Smir Veurnogne!
MONSTER-MADE SWEETS? ARE THOSE SAFE TO CONSUME?

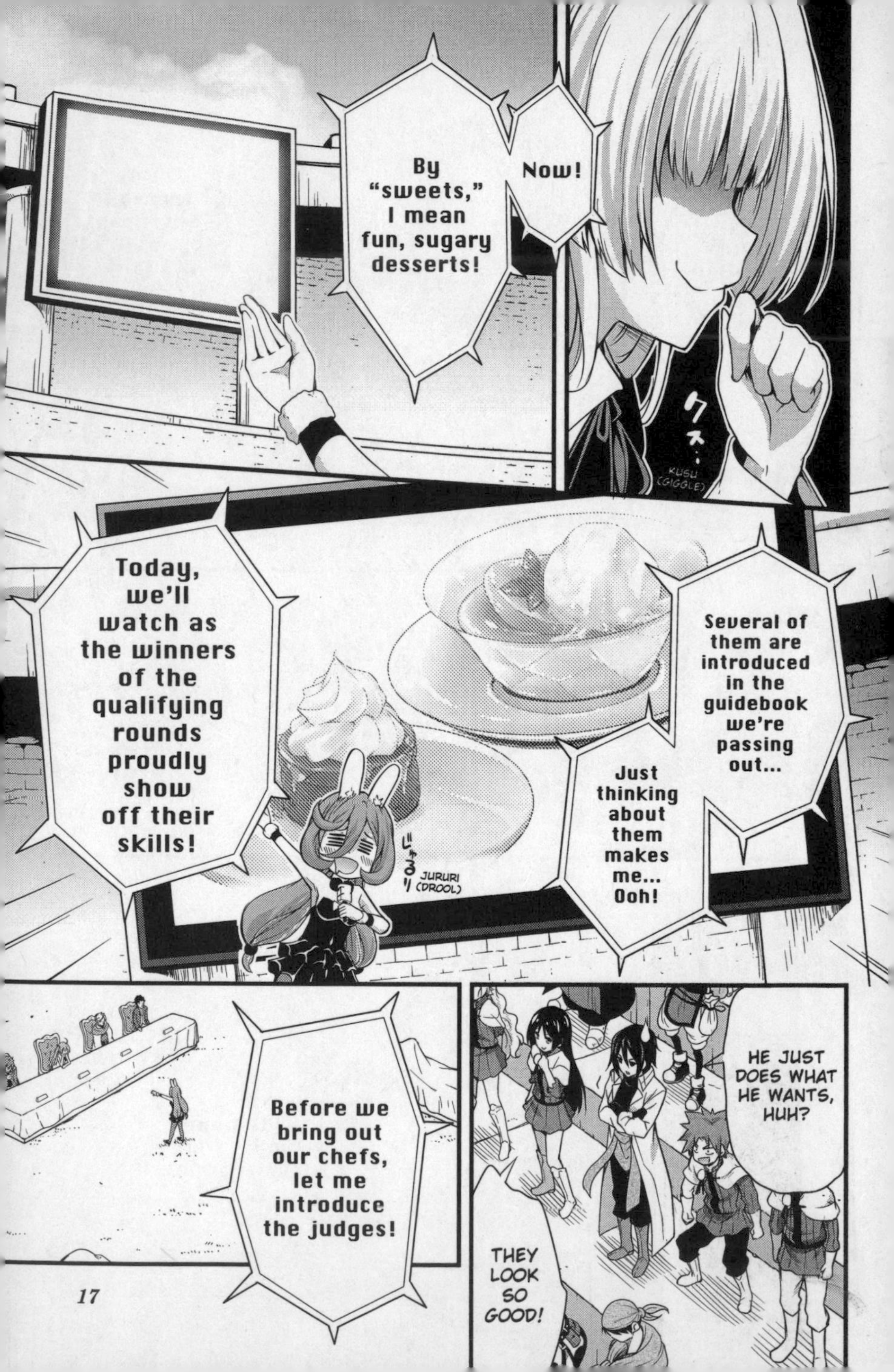
Now!
クス…
KUSU (GIGGLE)
By "sweets," I mean fun, sugary desserts!
Several of them are introduced in the guidebook we're passing out...
Just thinking about them makes me... Ooh!
じゅるり
JURURI (DROOL)
Today, we'll watch as the winners of the qualifying rounds proudly show off their skills!
HE JUST DOES WHAT HE WANTS, HUH?
THEY LOOK SO GOOD!
Before we bring out our chefs, let me introduce the judges!

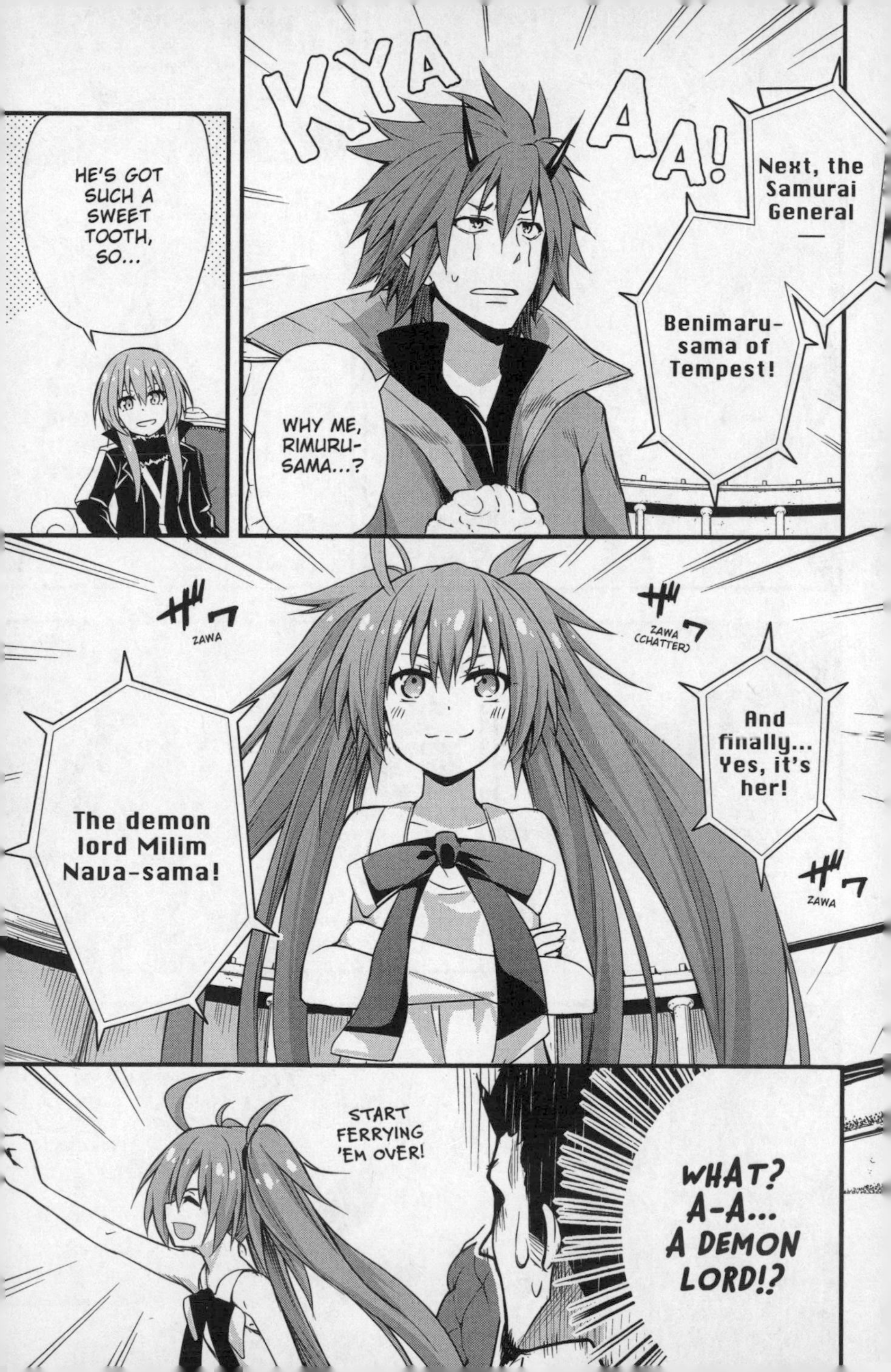
KYAAA!
Next, the Samurai General — Benimaru-sama of Tempest!
WHY ME, RIMURU-SAMA...?
HE'S GOT SUCH A SWEET TOOTH, SO...
ザワ ZAWA (CHATTER)
ザワ ZAWA
And finally... Yes, it's her!
The demon lord Milim Nava-sama!
ザワ ZAWA
WHAT? A-A... A DEMON LORD!?
START FERRYING 'EM OVER!

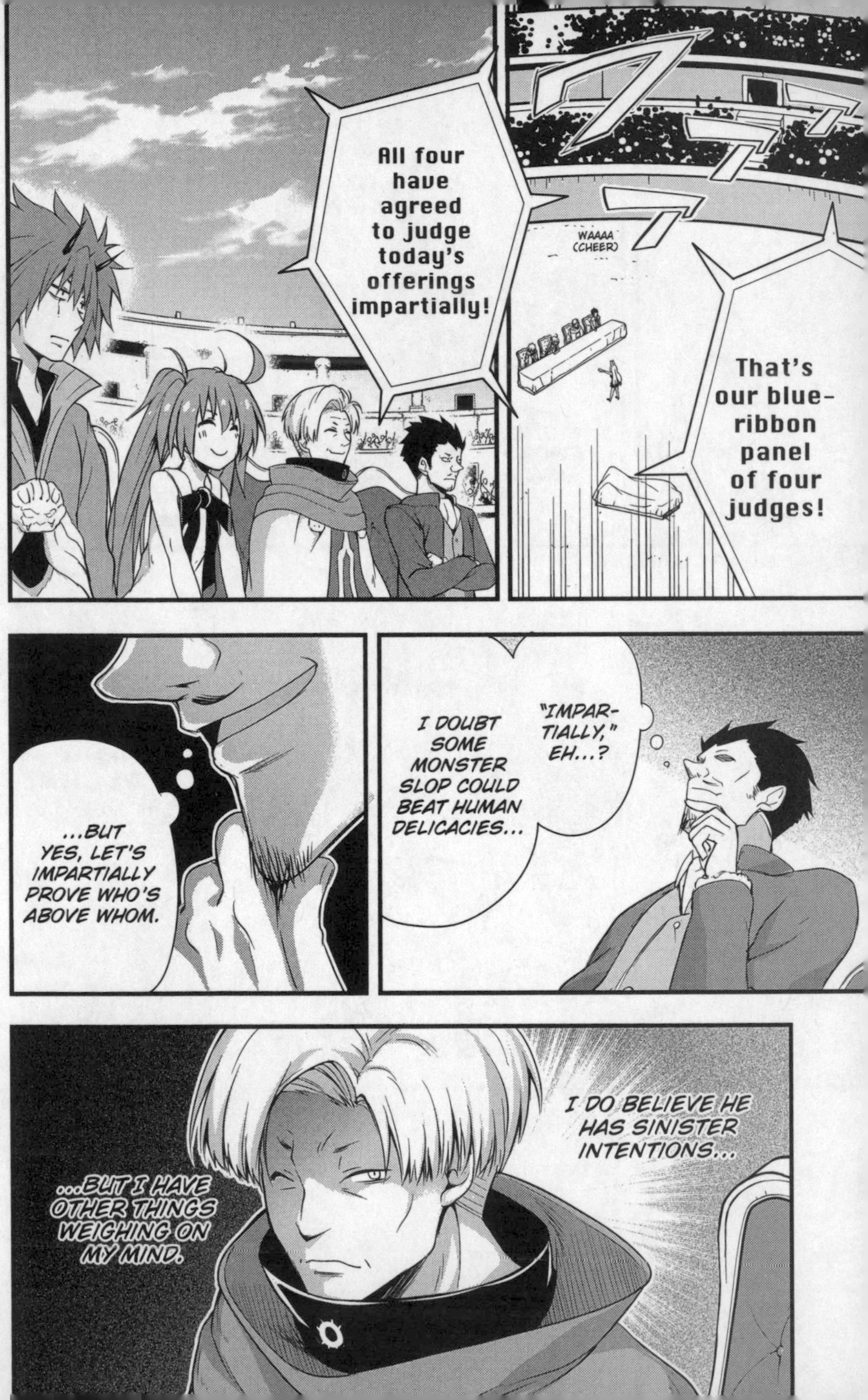
WAAAA (CHEER)
That's our blue-ribbon panel of four judges!
All four have agreed to judge today's offerings impartially!
"IMPAR-TIALLY," EH...?
I DOUBT SOME MONSTER SLOP COULD BEAT HUMAN DELICACIES...
...BUT YES, LET'S IMPARTIALLY PROVE WHO'S ABOVE WHOM.
I DO BELIEVE HE HAS SINISTER INTENTIONS...
...BUT I HAVE OTHER THINGS WEIGHING ON MY MIND.

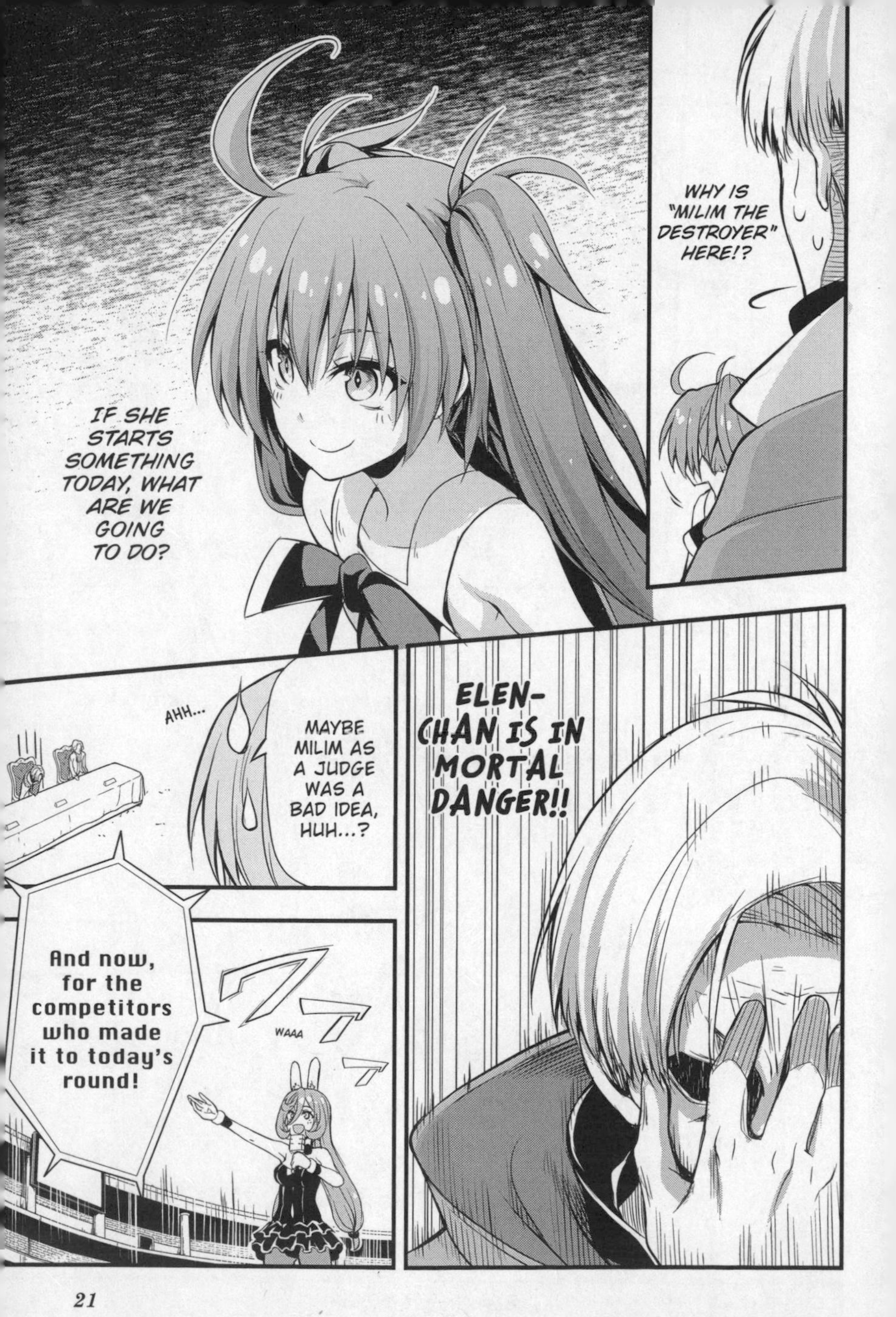
WHY IS "MILIM THE DESTROYER" HERE!?
IF SHE STARTS SOMETHING TODAY, WHAT ARE WE GOING TO DO?
ELEN-CHAN IS IN MORTAL DANGER!!
AHH...
MAYBE MILIM AS A JUDGE WAS A BAD IDEA, HUH...?
And now, for the competitors who made it to today's round!
WAAA

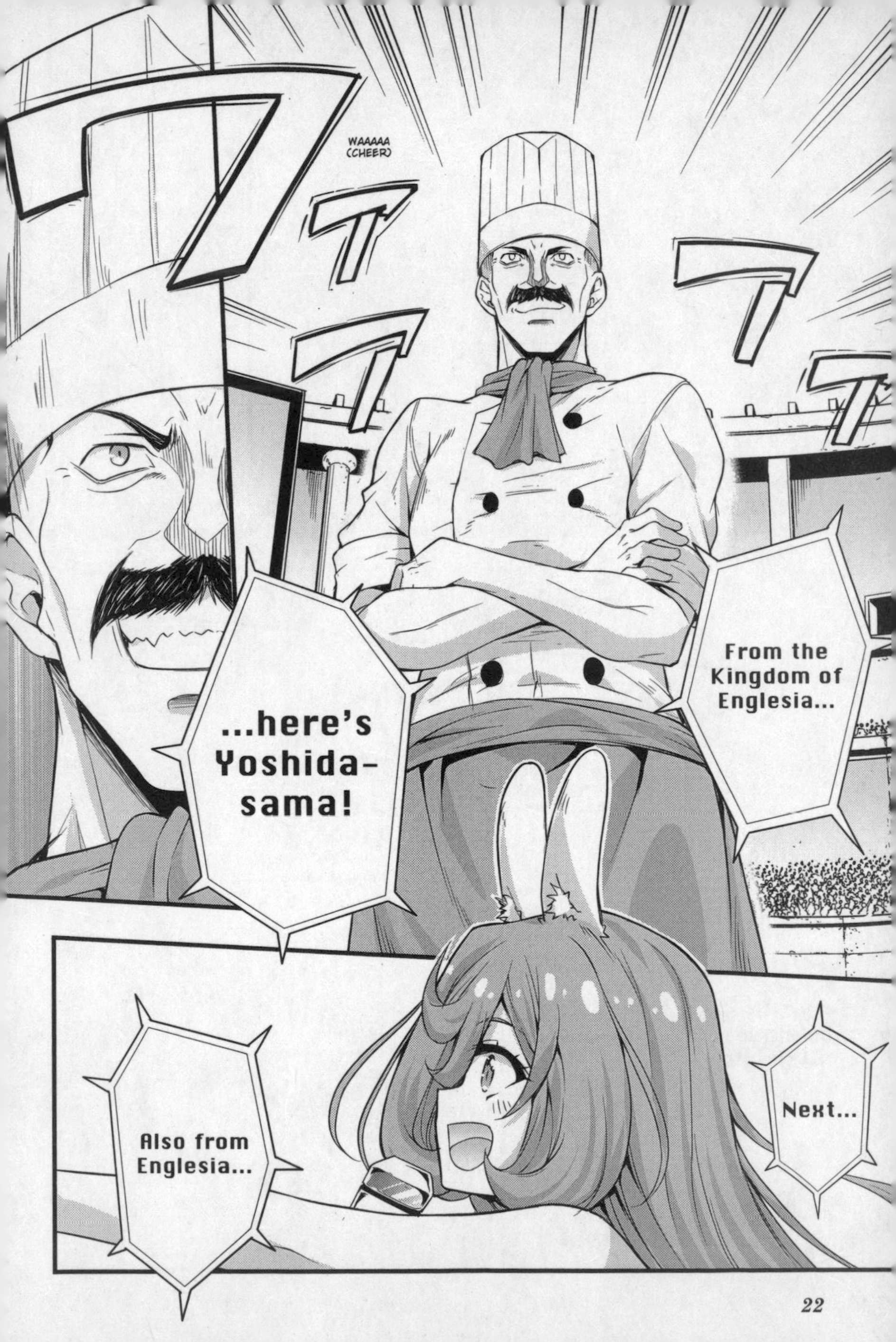
WAAAAA (CHEER)
From the Kingdom of Englesia...
...here's Yoshida-sama!
Next...
Also from Englesia...

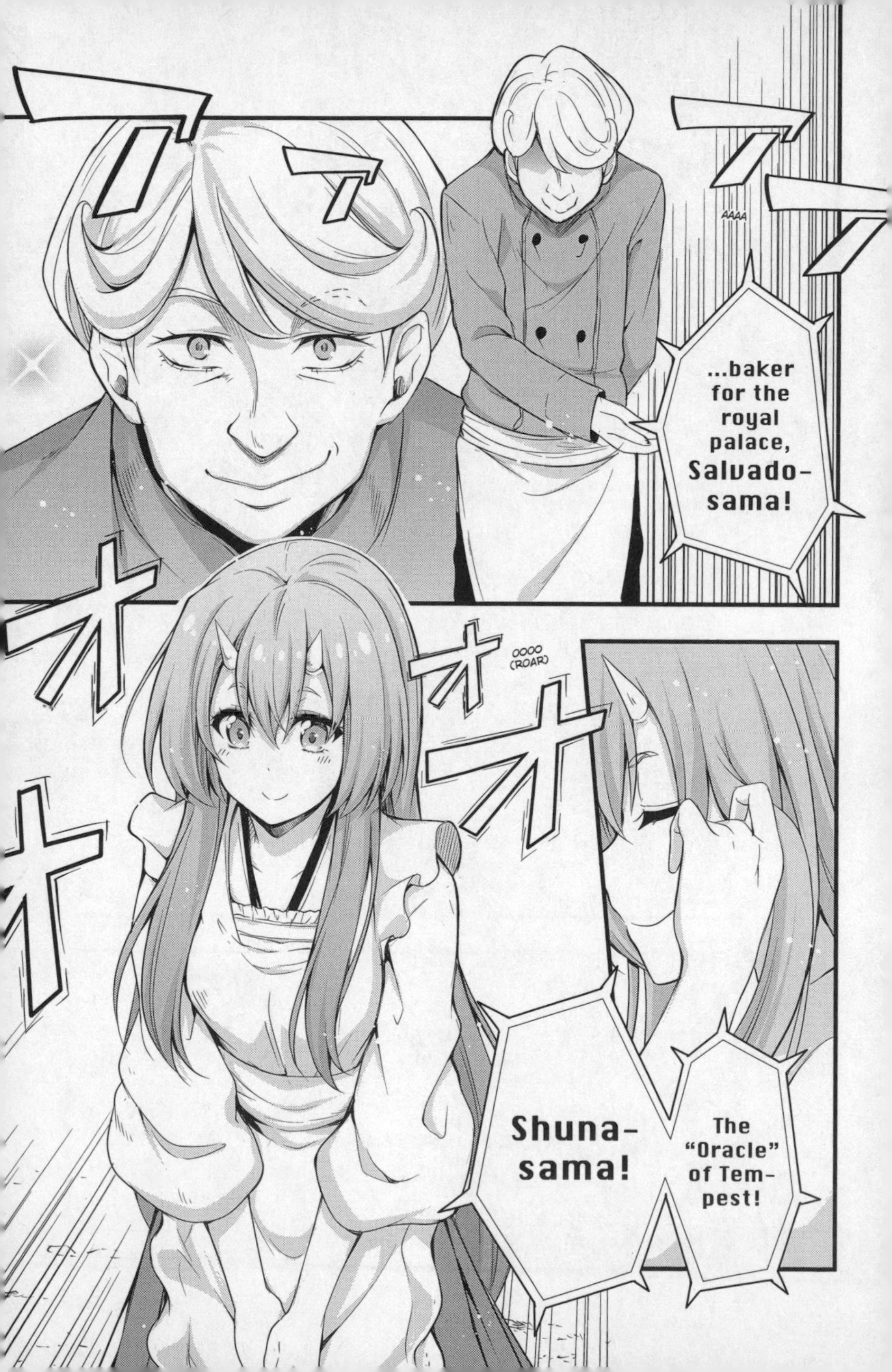
AAAA
...baker for the royal palace, Salvado-sama!
OOOO (ROAR)
The "Oracle" of Tempest!
Shuna-sama!

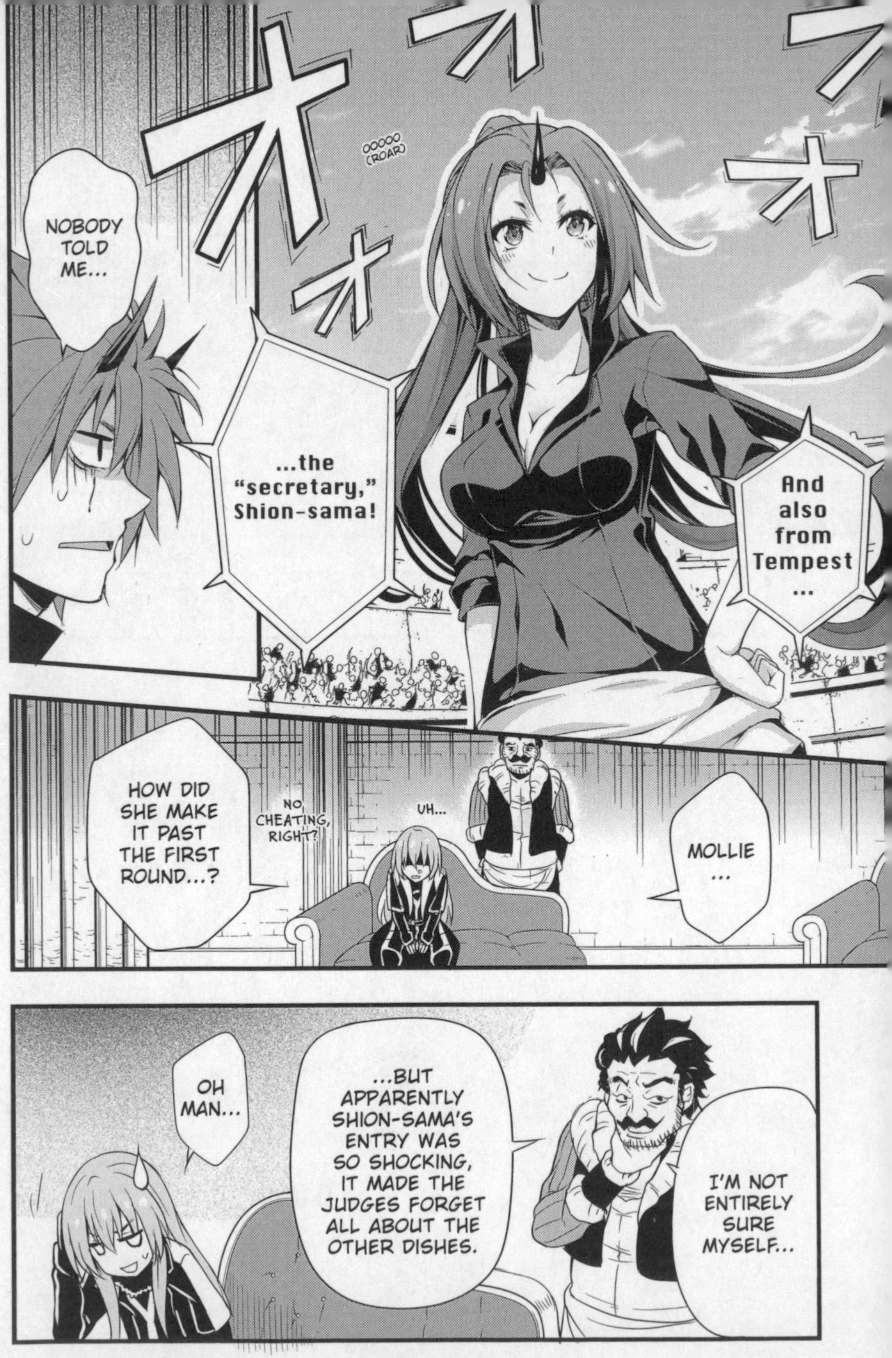
And also from Tempest ...
...the "secretary," Shion-sama!
OOOOO (ROAR)
NOBODY TOLD ME...
MOLLIE ...
UH...
NO CHEATING, RIGHT?
HOW DID SHE MAKE IT PAST THE FIRST ROUND...?
I'M NOT ENTIRELY SURE MYSELF...
...BUT APPARENTLY SHION-SAMA'S ENTRY WAS SO SHOCKING, IT MADE THE JUDGES FORGET ALL ABOUT THE OTHER DISHES.
OH MAN...

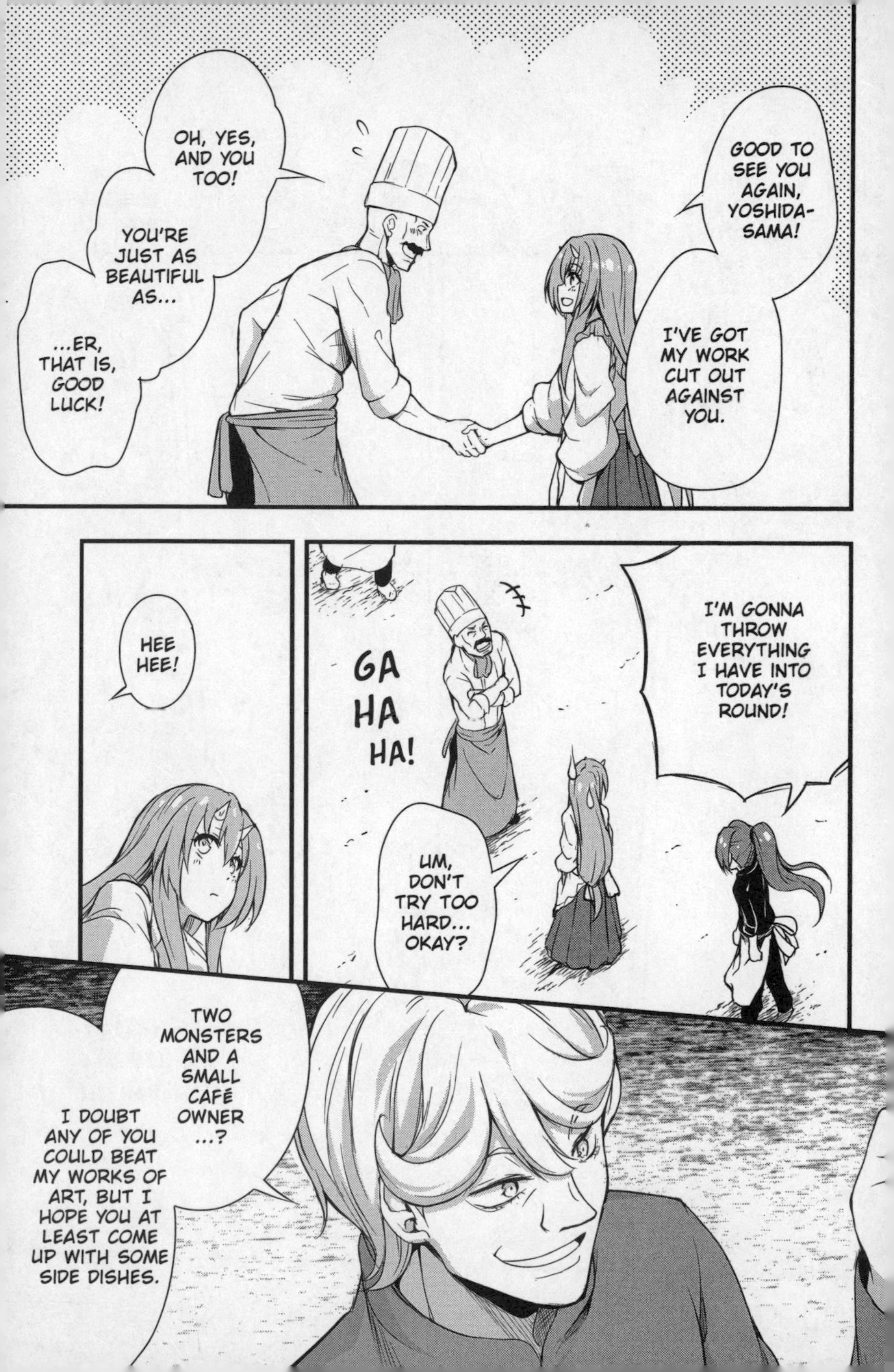
GOOD TO SEE YOU AGAIN, YOSHIDA-SAMA!
I'VE GOT MY WORK CUT OUT AGAINST YOU.
OH, YES, AND YOU TOO!
YOU'RE JUST AS BEAUTIFUL AS...
...ER, THAT IS, GOOD LUCK!
I'M GONNA THROW EVERYTHING I HAVE INTO TODAY'S ROUND!
GA HA HA!
UM, DON'T TRY TOO HARD... OKAY?
HEE HEE!
TWO MONSTERS AND A SMALL CAFÉ OWNER ...?
I DOUBT ANY OF YOU COULD BEAT MY WORKS OF ART, BUT I HOPE YOU AT LEAST COME UP WITH SOME SIDE DISHES.

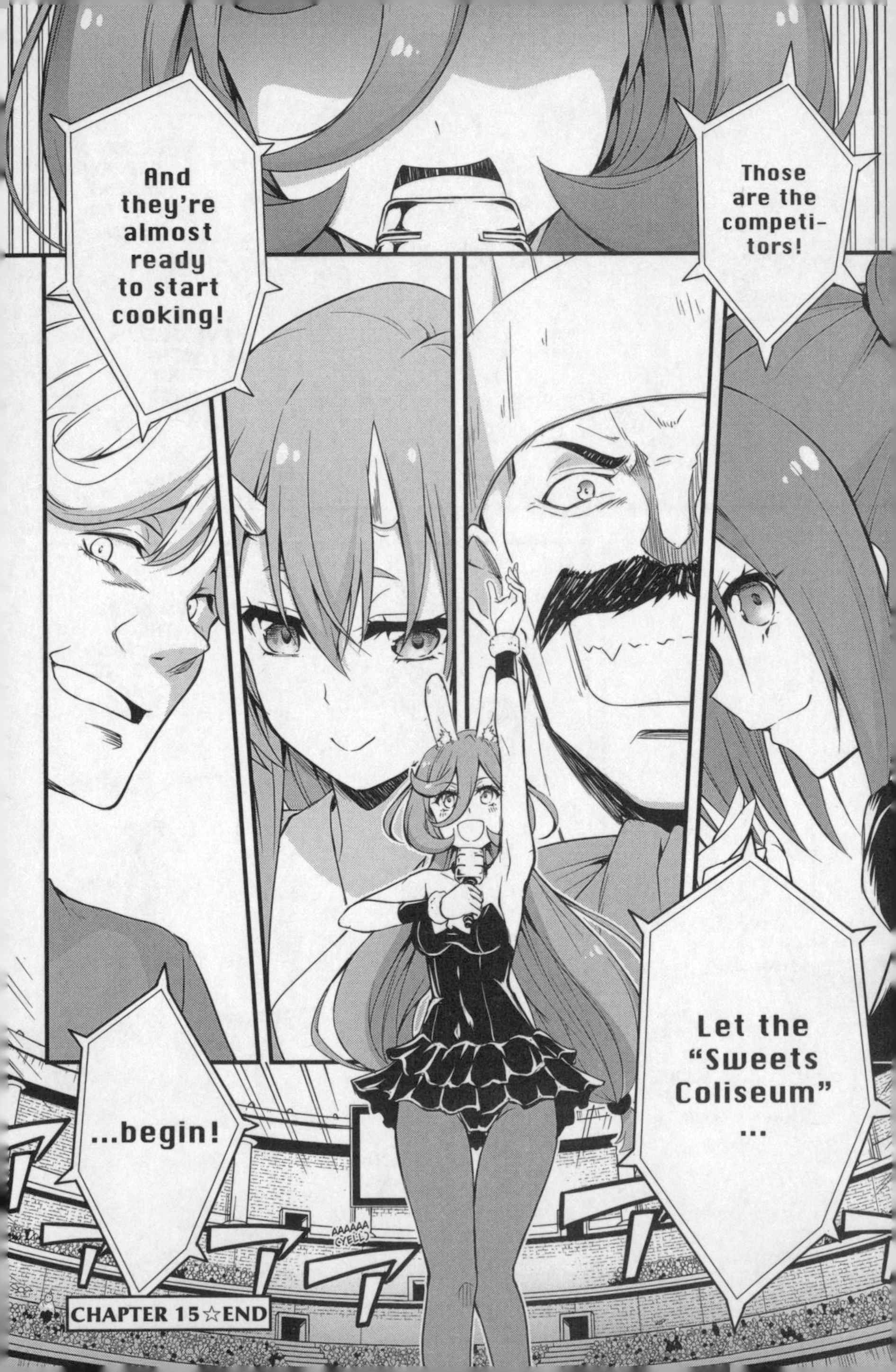
Those are the competitors!
And they're almost ready to start cooking!
Let the "Sweets Coliseum"...
...begin!
AAAAAA (YELL)
CHAPTER 15☆END

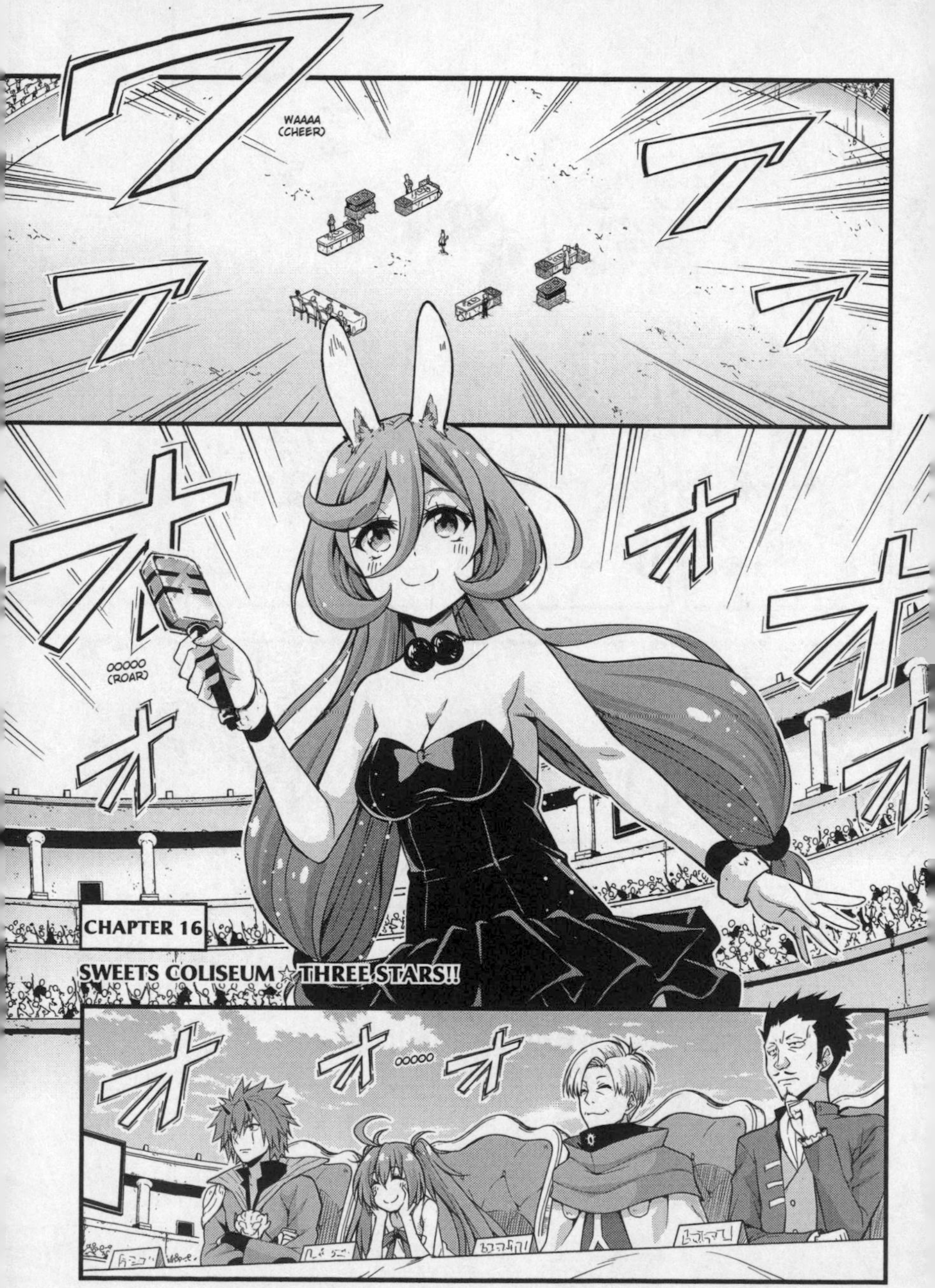
ワァァァ
WAAAA
(CHEER)
オオオオオオ
OOOOO
(ROAR)
CHAPTER 16
SWEETS COLISEUM☆THREE STARS!!
オ オ…オ

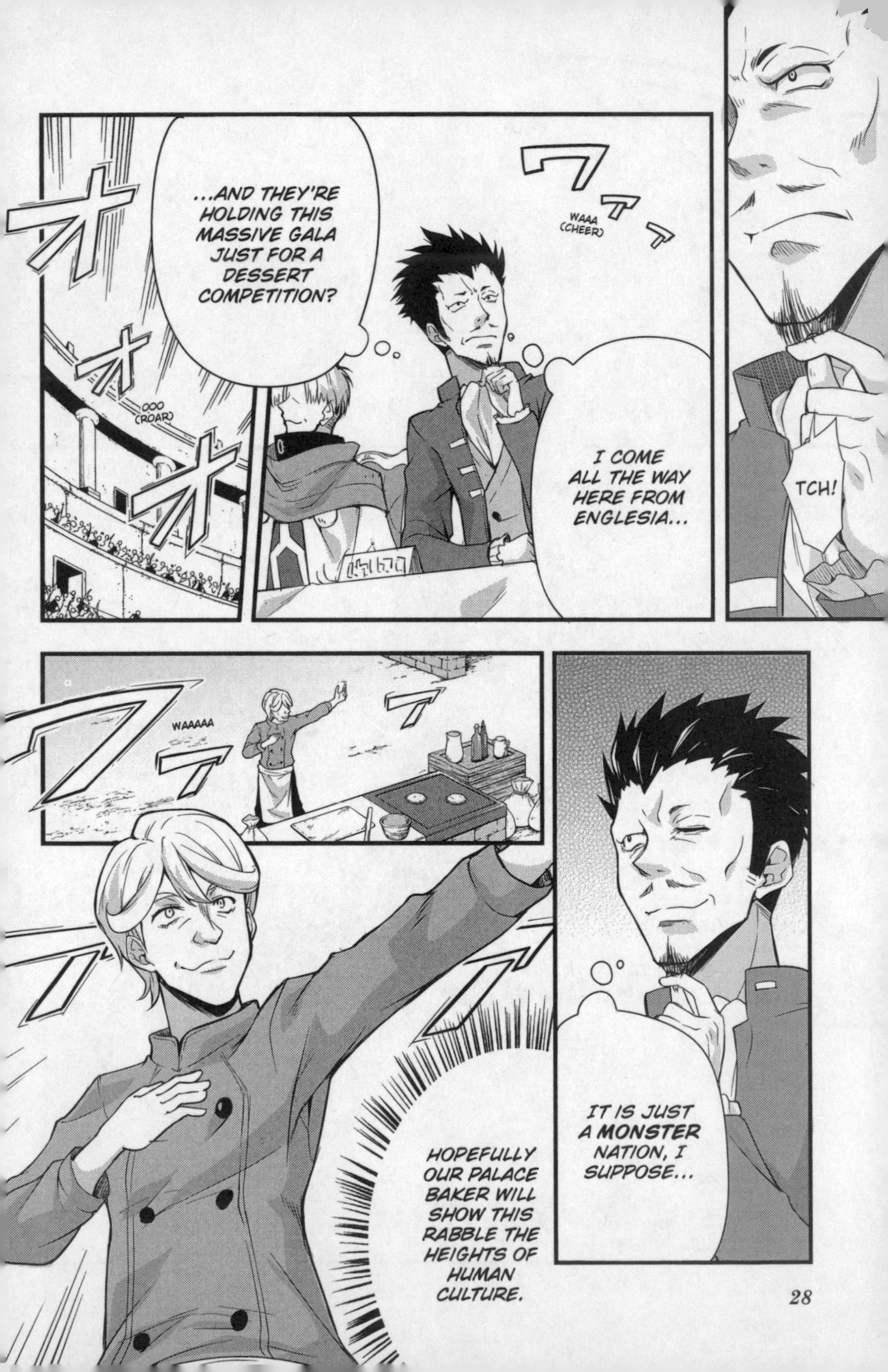
TCH!
WAAA (CHEER)
I COME ALL THE WAY HERE FROM ENGLESIA...
...AND THEY'RE HOLDING THIS MASSIVE GALA JUST FOR A DESSERT COMPETITION?
OOO (ROAR)
IT IS JUST A MONSTER NATION, I SUPPOSE...
WAAAAA
HOPEFULLY OUR PALACE BAKER WILL SHOW THIS RABBLE THE HEIGHTS OF HUMAN CULTURE.

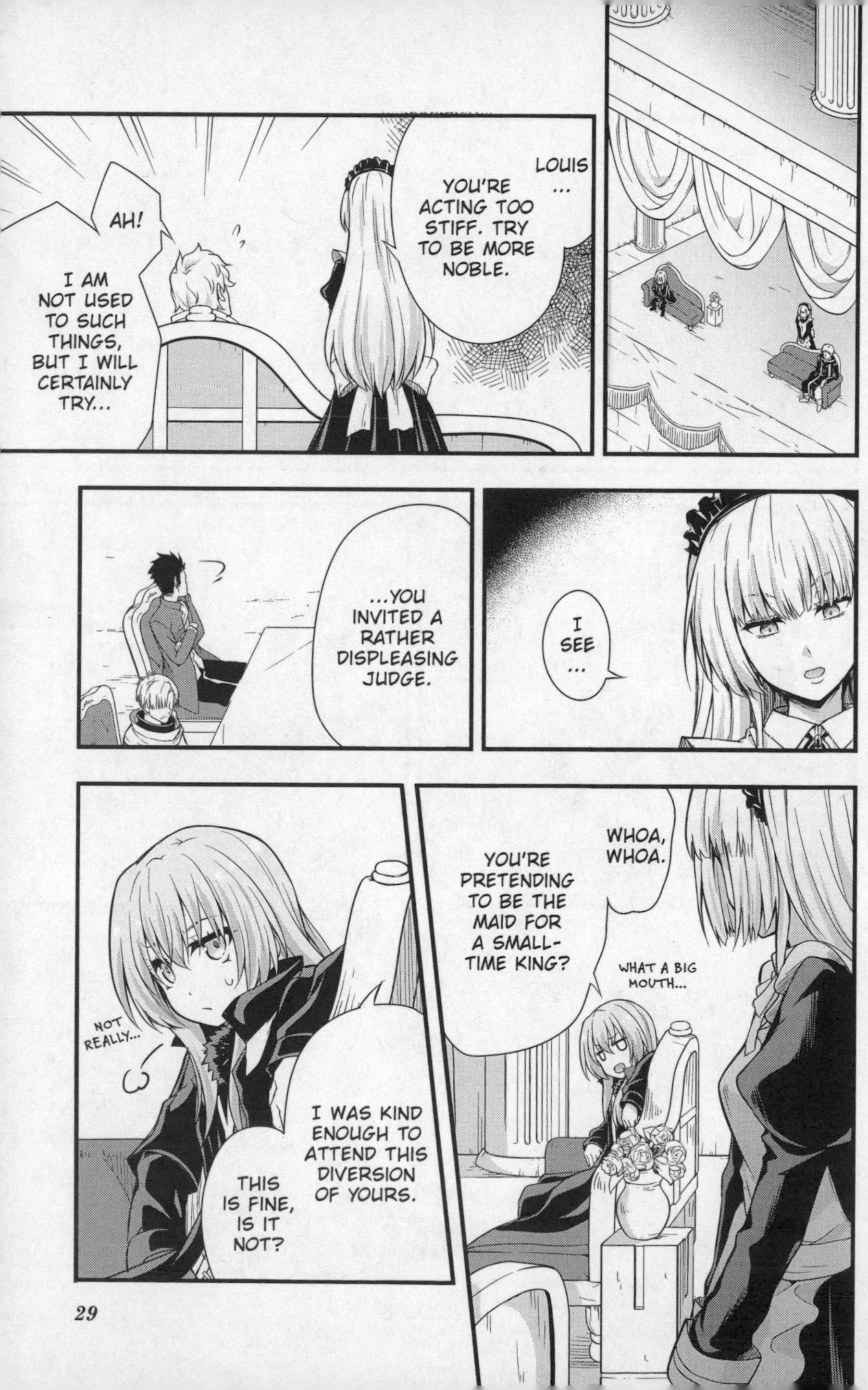
LOUIS ...
YOU'RE ACTING TOO STIFF. TRY TO BE MORE NOBLE.
AH!
I AM NOT USED TO SUCH THINGS, BUT I WILL CERTAINLY TRY...
I SEE ...
...YOU INVITED A RATHER DISPLEASING JUDGE.
WHOA, WHOA.
YOU'RE PRETENDING TO BE THE MAID FOR A SMALL-TIME KING?
WHAT A BIG MOUTH...
I WAS KIND ENOUGH TO ATTEND THIS DIVERSION OF YOURS.
THIS IS FINE, IS IT NOT?
NOT REALLY...

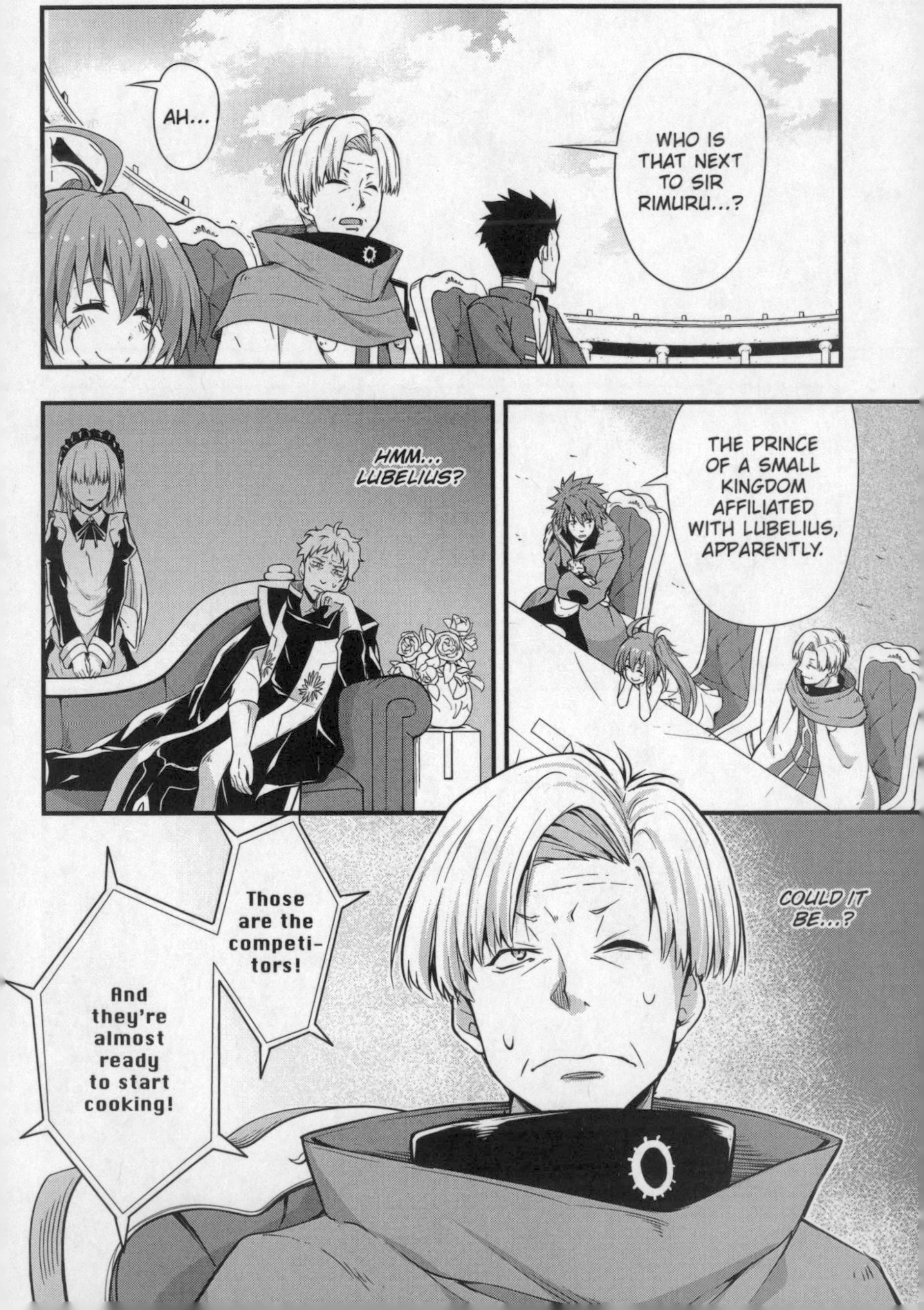
WHO IS THAT NEXT TO SIR RIMURU...?
AH...
THE PRINCE OF A SMALL KINGDOM AFFILIATED WITH LUBELIUS, APPARENTLY.
HMM... LUBELIUS?
COULD IT BE...?
Those are the competitors!
And they're almost ready to start cooking!

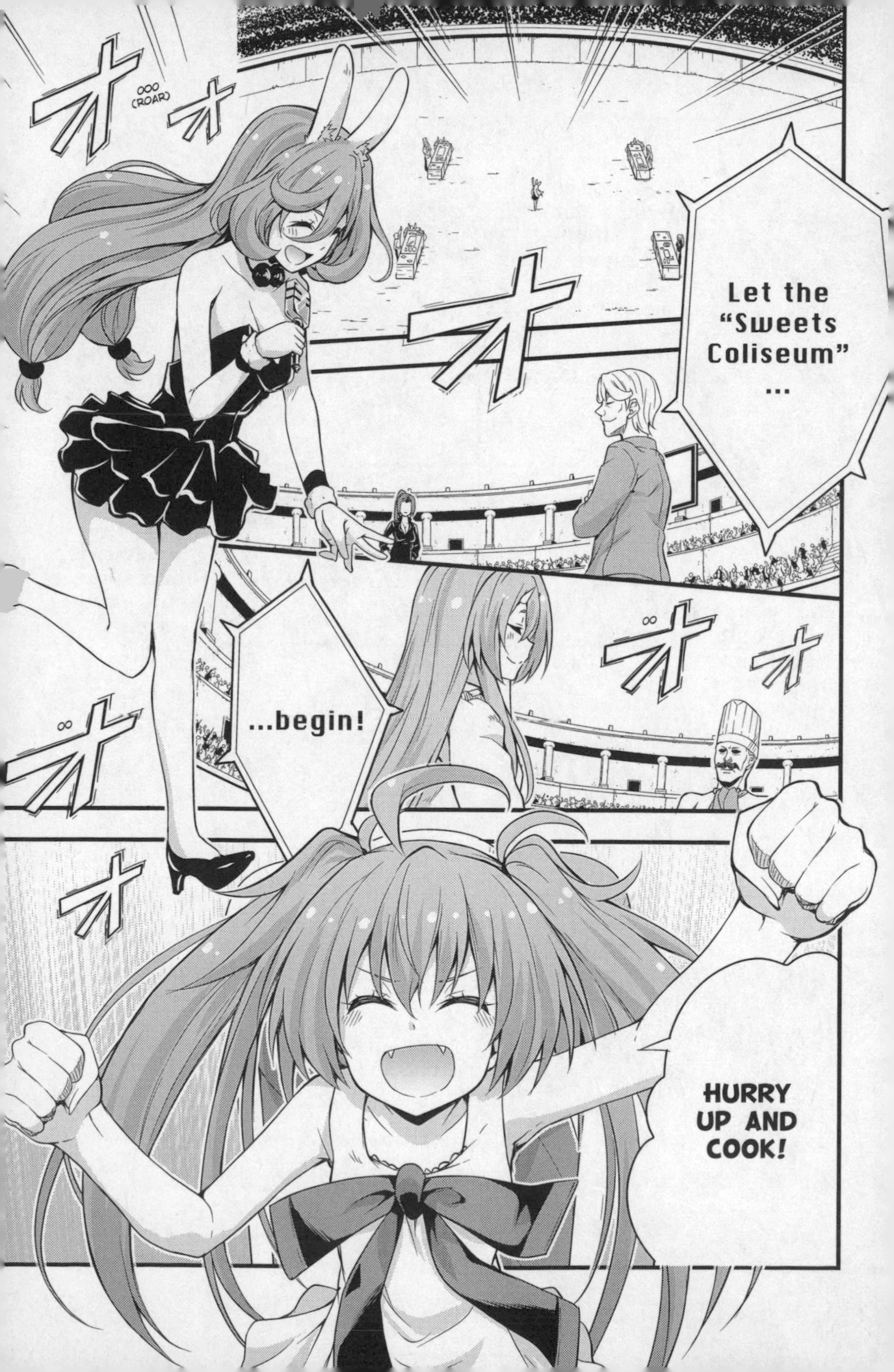
Let the "Sweets Coliseum" ...
OOO (ROAR)
...begin!
HURRY UP AND COOK!

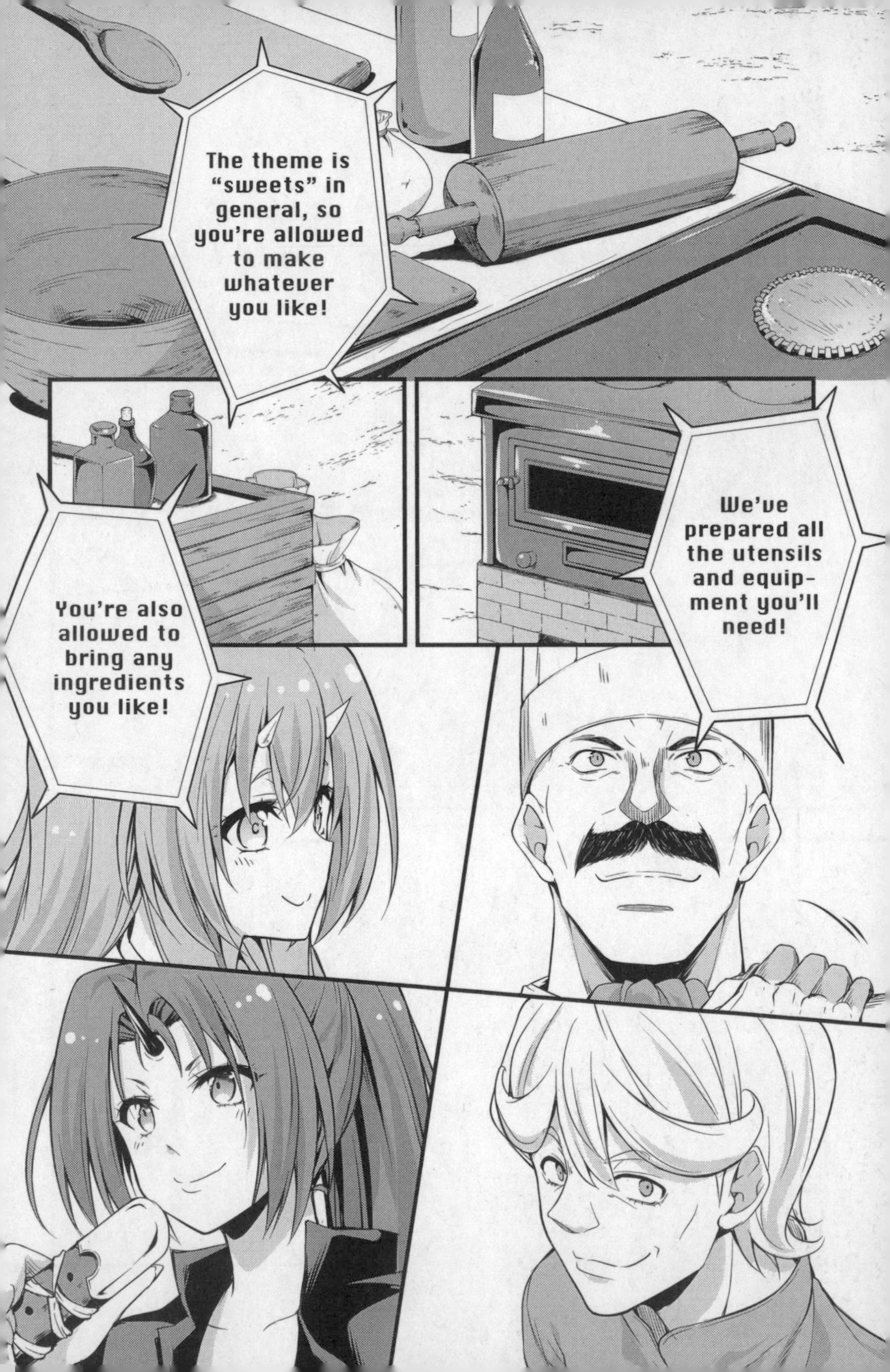
The theme is "sweets" in general, so you're allowed to make whatever you like!
We've prepared all the utensils and equip-ment you'll need!
You're also allowed to bring any ingredients you like!

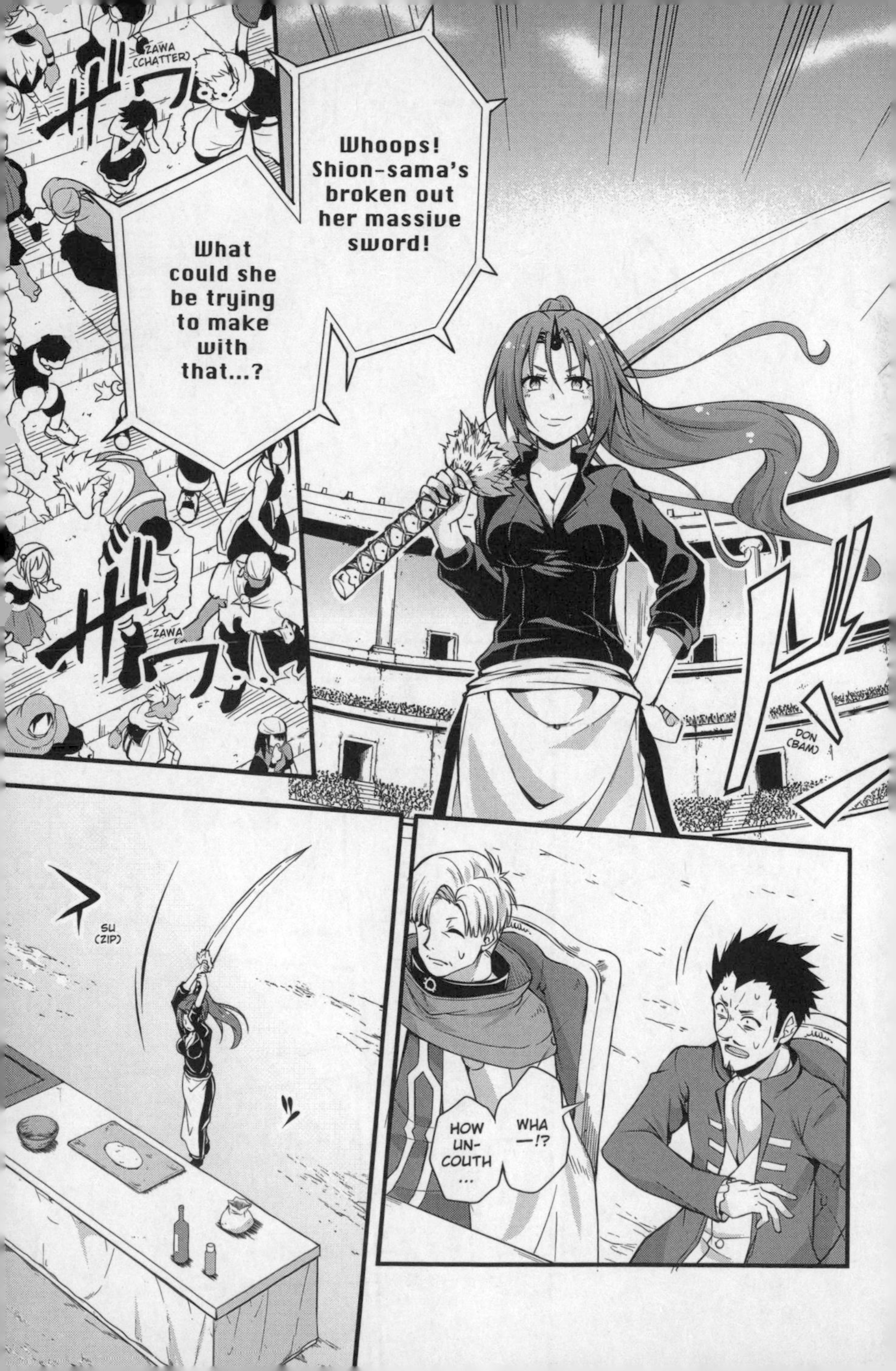
Whoops! Shion-sama's broken out her massive sword!
What could she be trying to make with that...?
ZAWA (CHATTER)
ZAWA
DON (BAM)
WHA—!?
HOW UN-COUTH...
SU (ZIP)

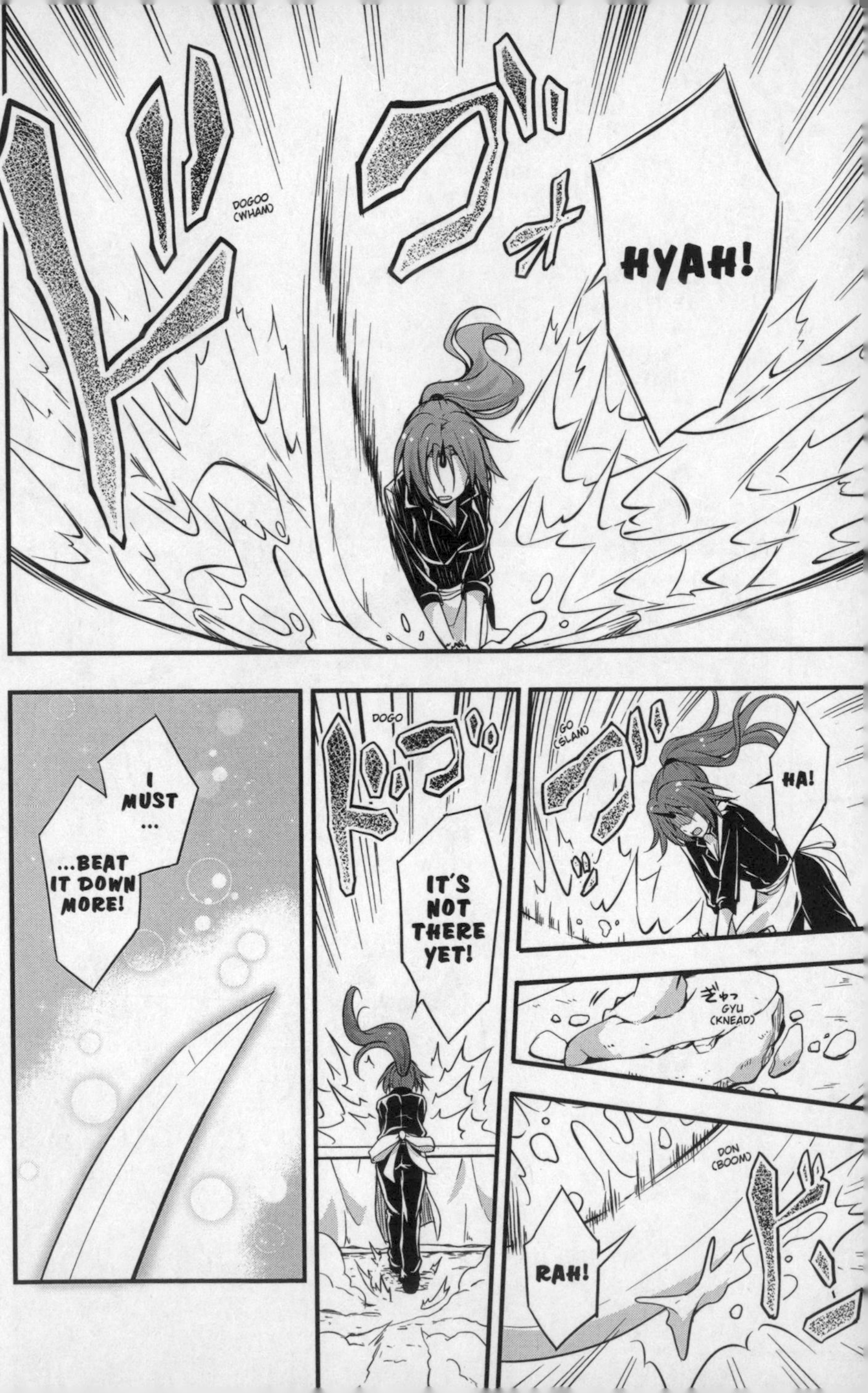
HYAH!
DOGOO (WHAM)
GO (SLAM)
HA!
GYU (KNEAD)
DON (BOOM)
RAH!
DOGO
IT'S NOT THERE YET!
I MUST ...
...BEAT IT DOWN MORE!

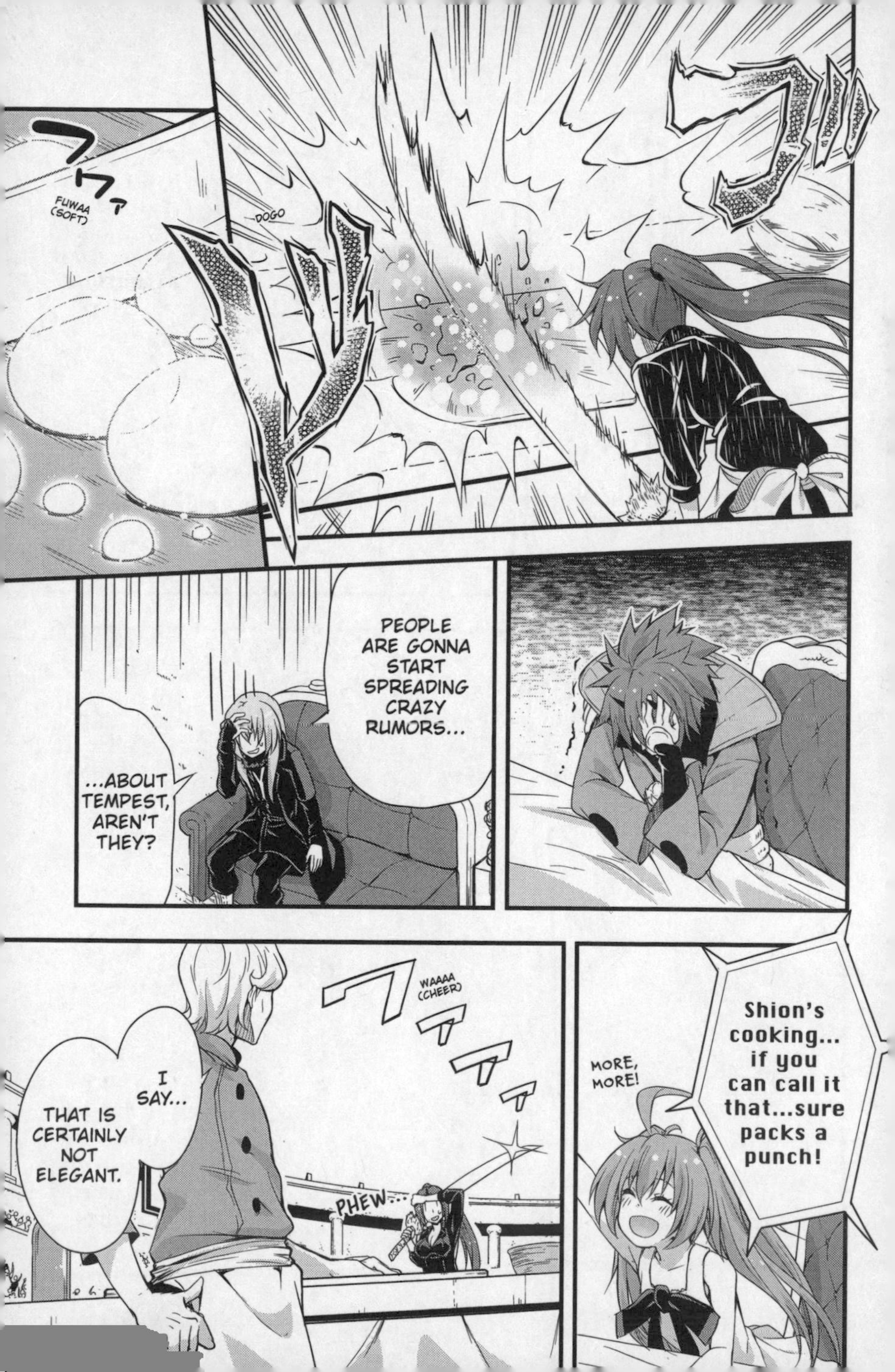
DOGO
FUWAA (SOFT)
PEOPLE ARE GONNA START SPREADING CRAZY RUMORS...
...ABOUT TEMPEST, AREN'T THEY?
Shion's cooking... if you can call it that...sure packs a punch!
MORE, MORE!
WAAAA (CHEER)
I SAY...
THAT IS CERTAINLY NOT ELEGANT.
PHEW...

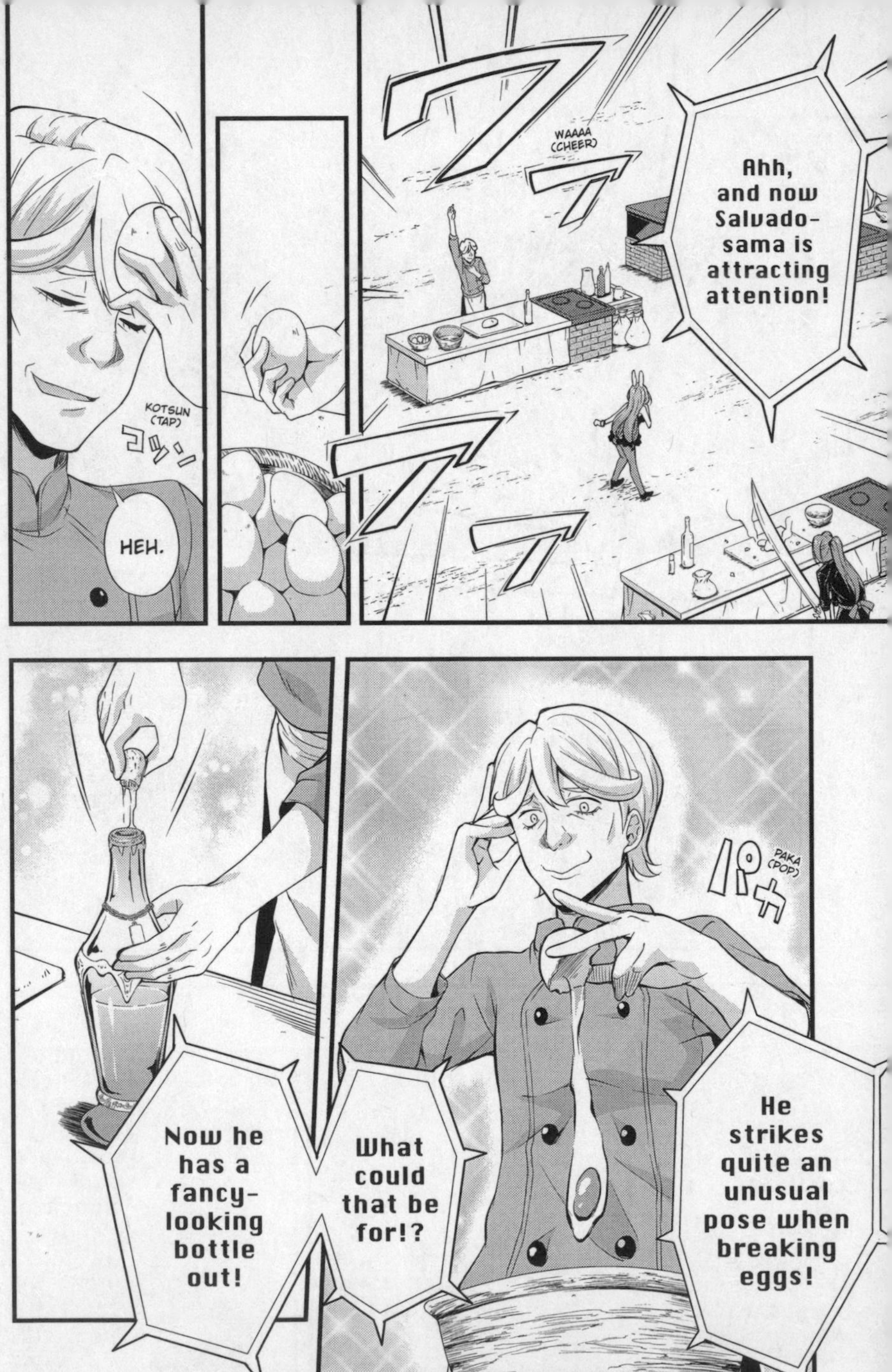
WAAAA (CHEER)
Ahh, and now Salvado-sama is attracting attention!
KOTSUN (TAP)
HEH.
PAKA (POP)
He strikes quite an unusual pose when breaking eggs!
Now he has a fancy-looking bottle out!
What could that be for!?

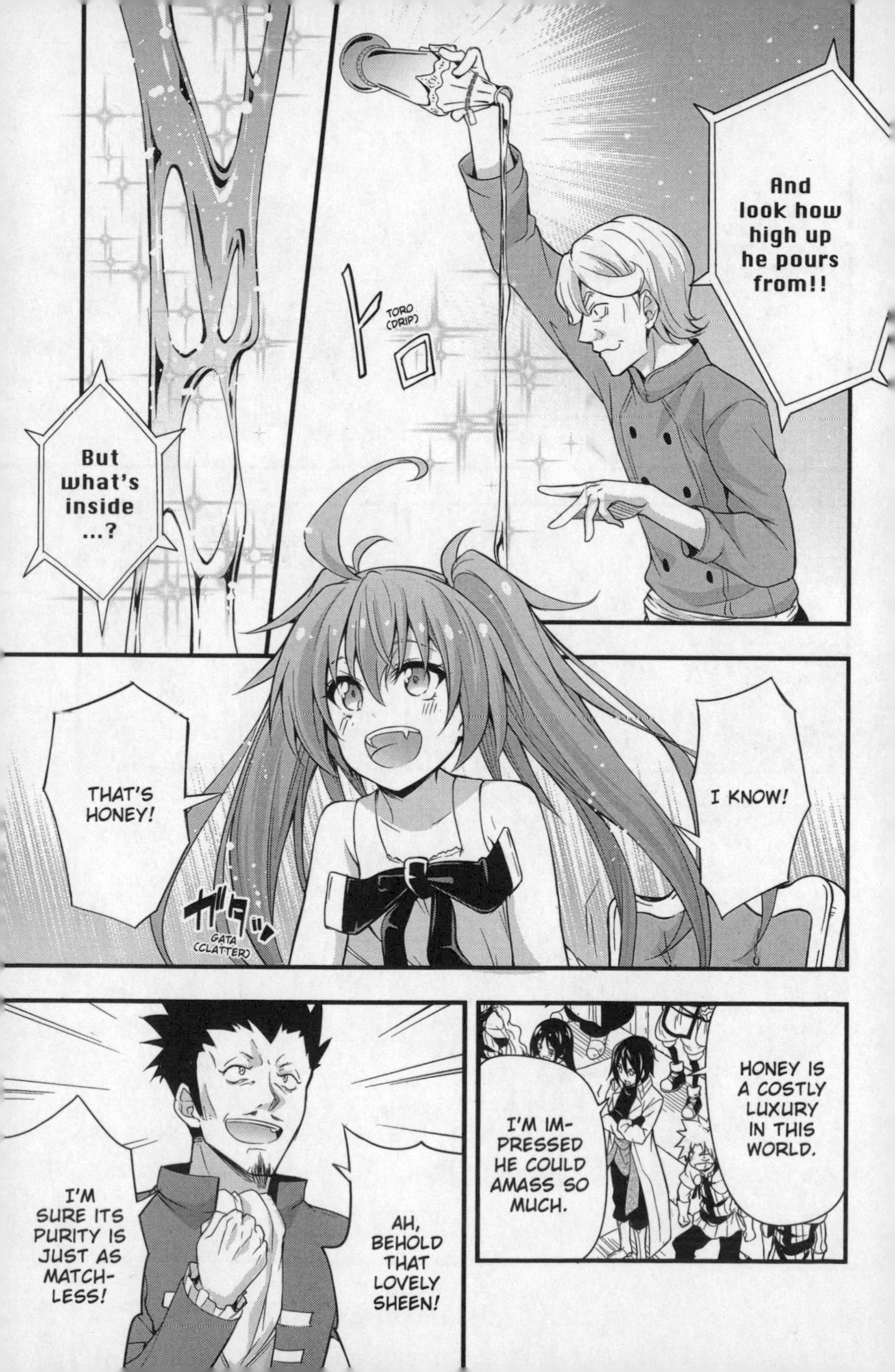
And look how high up he pours from!!
TORO (DRIP)
But what's inside ...?
I KNOW!
THAT'S HONEY!
GATA (CLATTER)
HONEY IS A COSTLY LUXURY IN THIS WORLD.
I'M IMPRESSED HE COULD AMASS SO MUCH.
AH, BEHOLD THAT LOVELY SHEEN!
I'M SURE ITS PURITY IS JUST AS MATCHLESS!

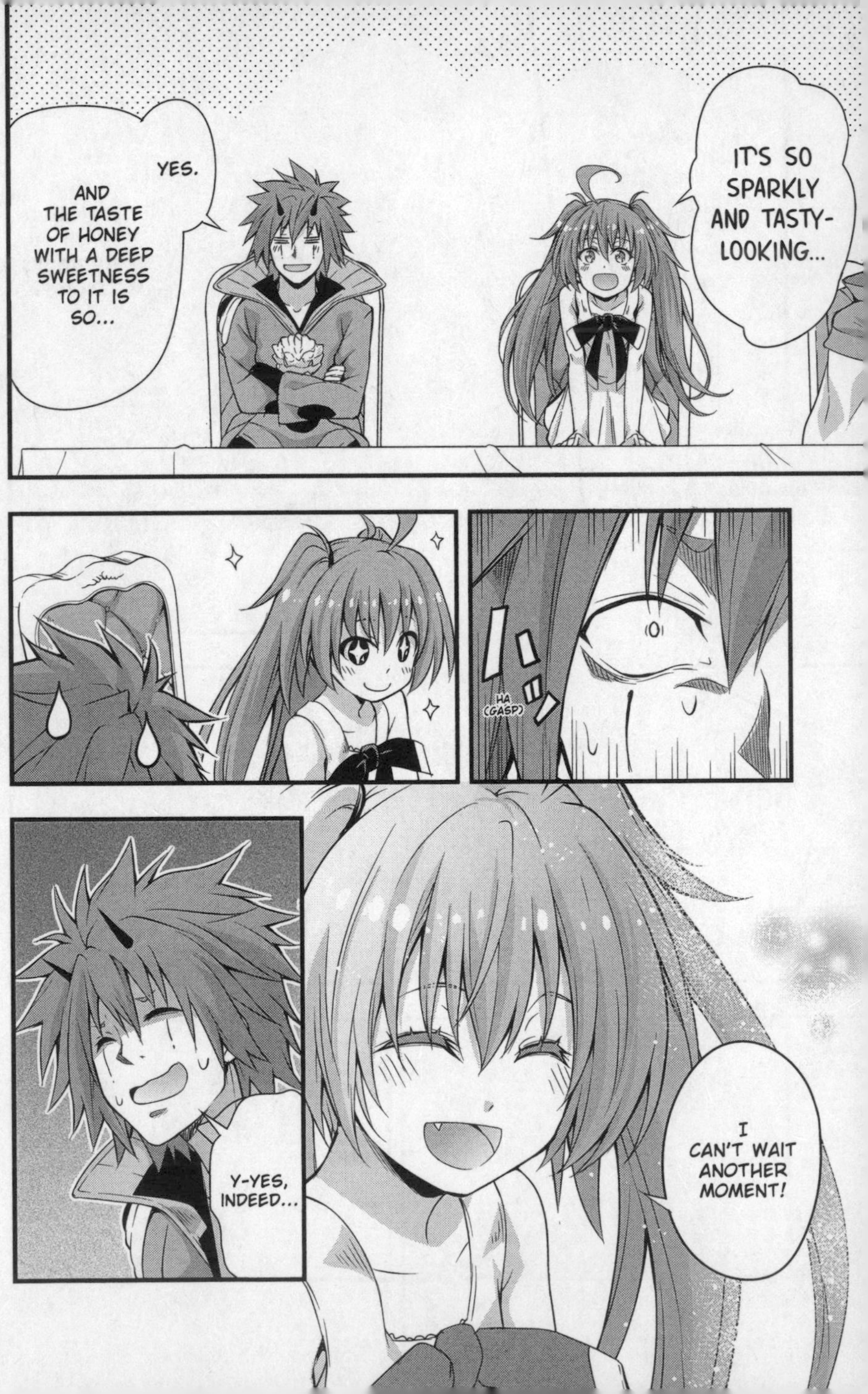
IT'S SO SPARKLY AND TASTY-LOOKING...
YES.
AND THE TASTE OF HONEY WITH A DEEP SWEETNESS TO IT IS SO...
HA (GASP)
I CAN'T WAIT ANOTHER MOMENT!
Y-YES, INDEED...

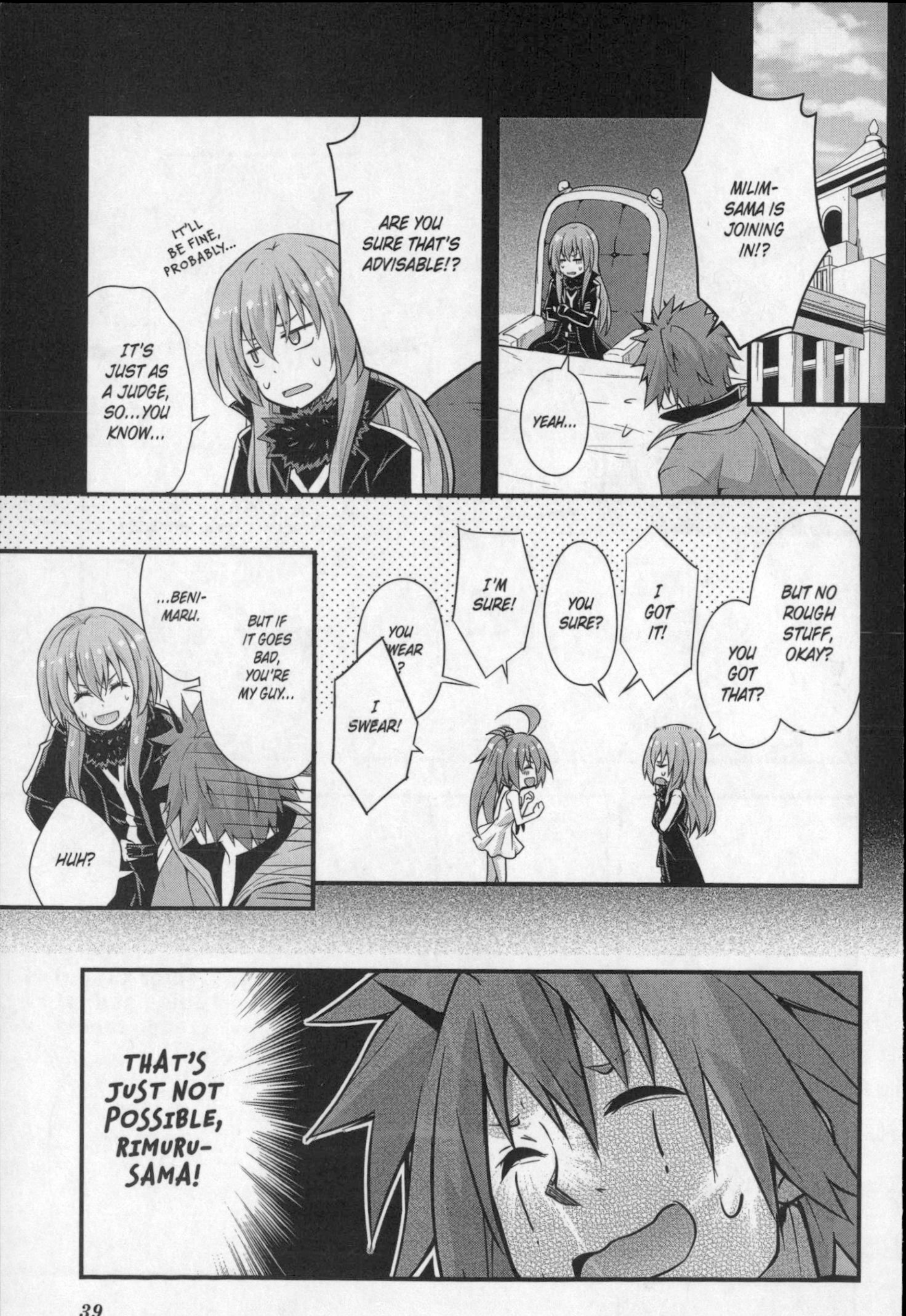
MILIM-SAMA IS JOINING IN!?
YEAH...
ARE YOU SURE THAT'S ADVISABLE!?
IT'LL BE FINE, PROBABLY...
IT'S JUST AS A JUDGE, SO...YOU KNOW...
BUT NO ROUGH STUFF, OKAY?
YOU GOT THAT?
I GOT IT!
YOU SURE?
I'M SURE!
YOU WEAR ?
I SWEAR!
...BENI-MARU.
BUT IF IT GOES BAD, YOU'RE MY GUY...
HUH?
THAT'S JUST NOT POSSIBLE, RIMURU-SAMA!

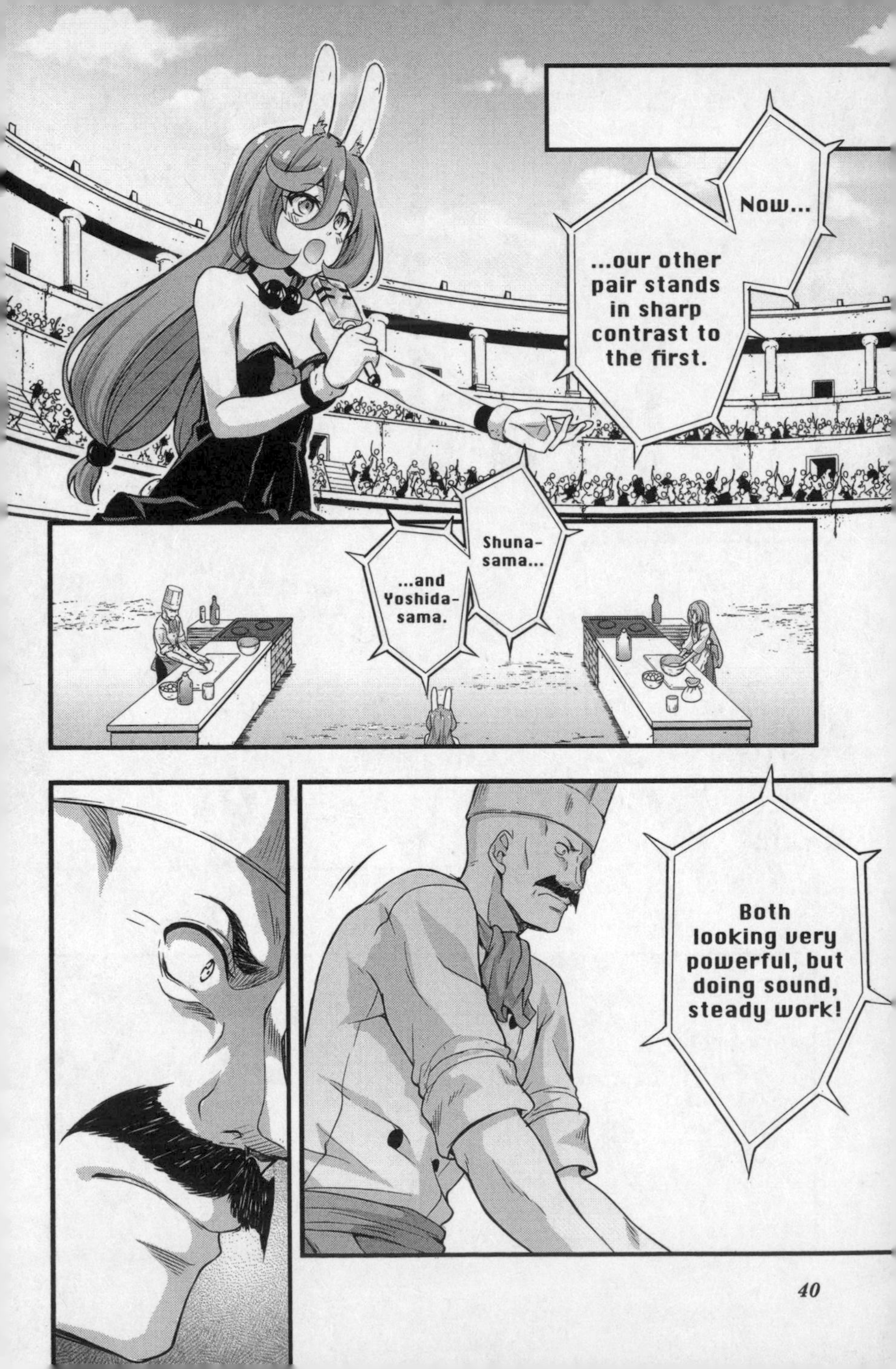

Now...
...our other pair stands in sharp contrast to the first.
Shuna-sama...
...and Yoshida-sama.
Both looking very powerful, but doing sound, steady work!

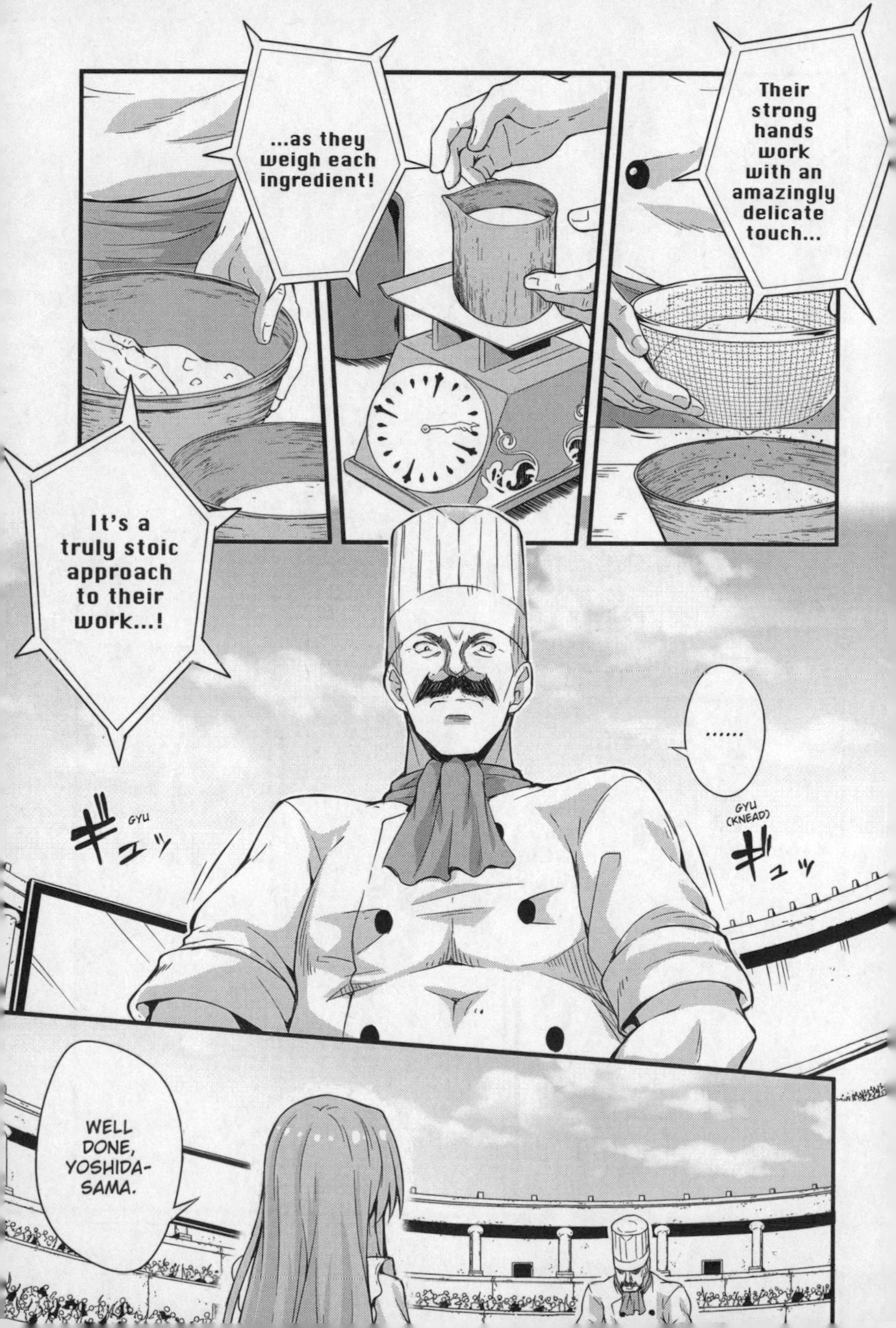
Their strong hands work with an amazingly delicate touch...
...as they weigh each ingredient!
It's a truly stoic approach to their work...!
......
GYU (KNEAD)
GYU
WELL DONE, YOSHIDA-SAMA.

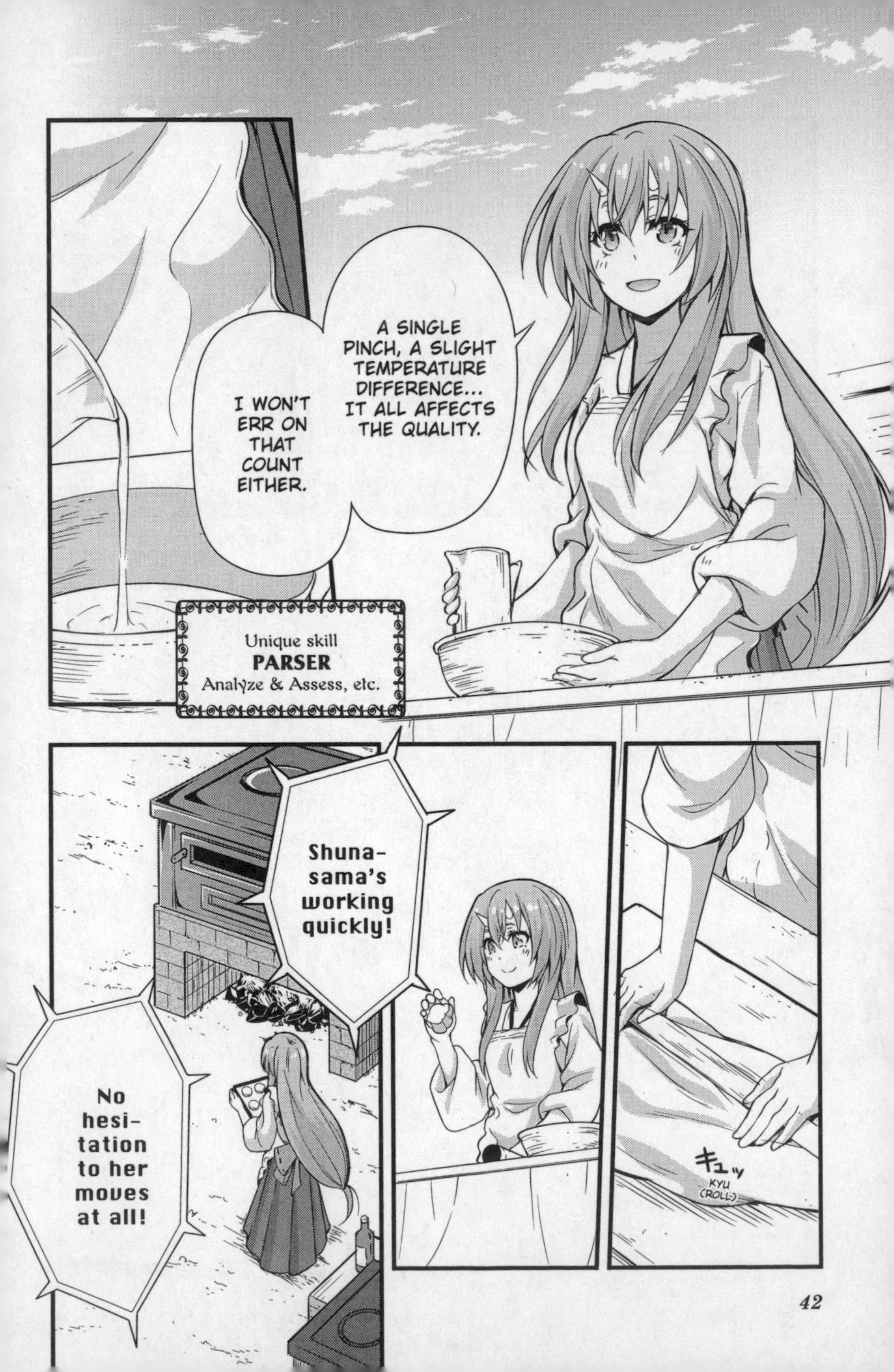
A SINGLE PINCH, A SLIGHT TEMPERATURE DIFFERENCE... IT ALL AFFECTS THE QUALITY.
I WON'T ERR ON THAT COUNT EITHER.
Unique skill
PARSER
Analyze & Assess, etc.
キュッ
KYU (ROLL-)
Shuna-sama's working quickly!
No hesi-tation to her moves at all!

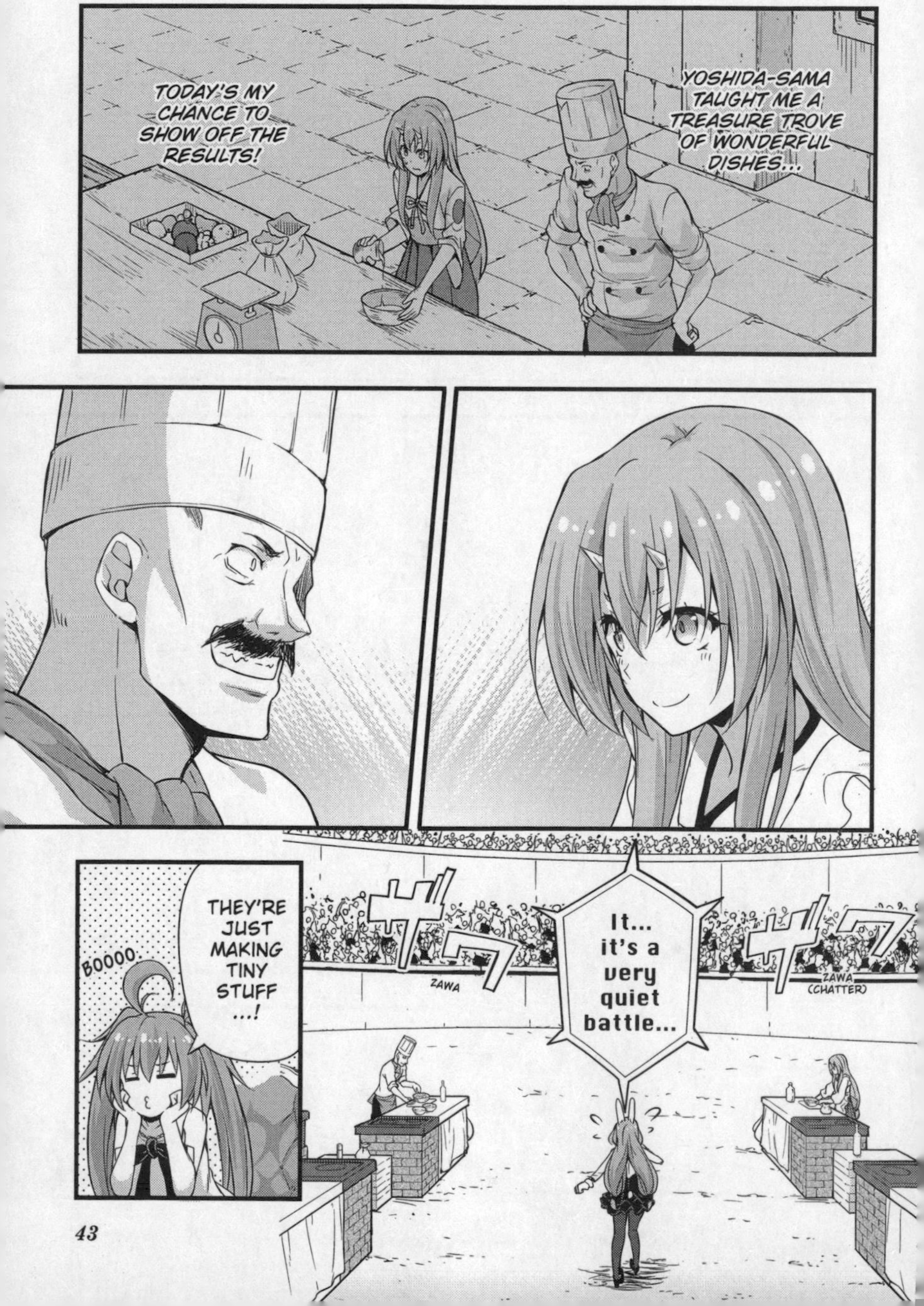
YOSHIDA-SAMA TAUGHT ME A TREASURE TROVE OF WONDERFUL DISHES...
TODAY'S MY CHANCE TO SHOW OFF THE RESULTS!
ZAWA (CHATTER)
It... it's a very quiet battle...
ZAWA
THEY'RE JUST MAKING TINY STUFF...!
BOOOO

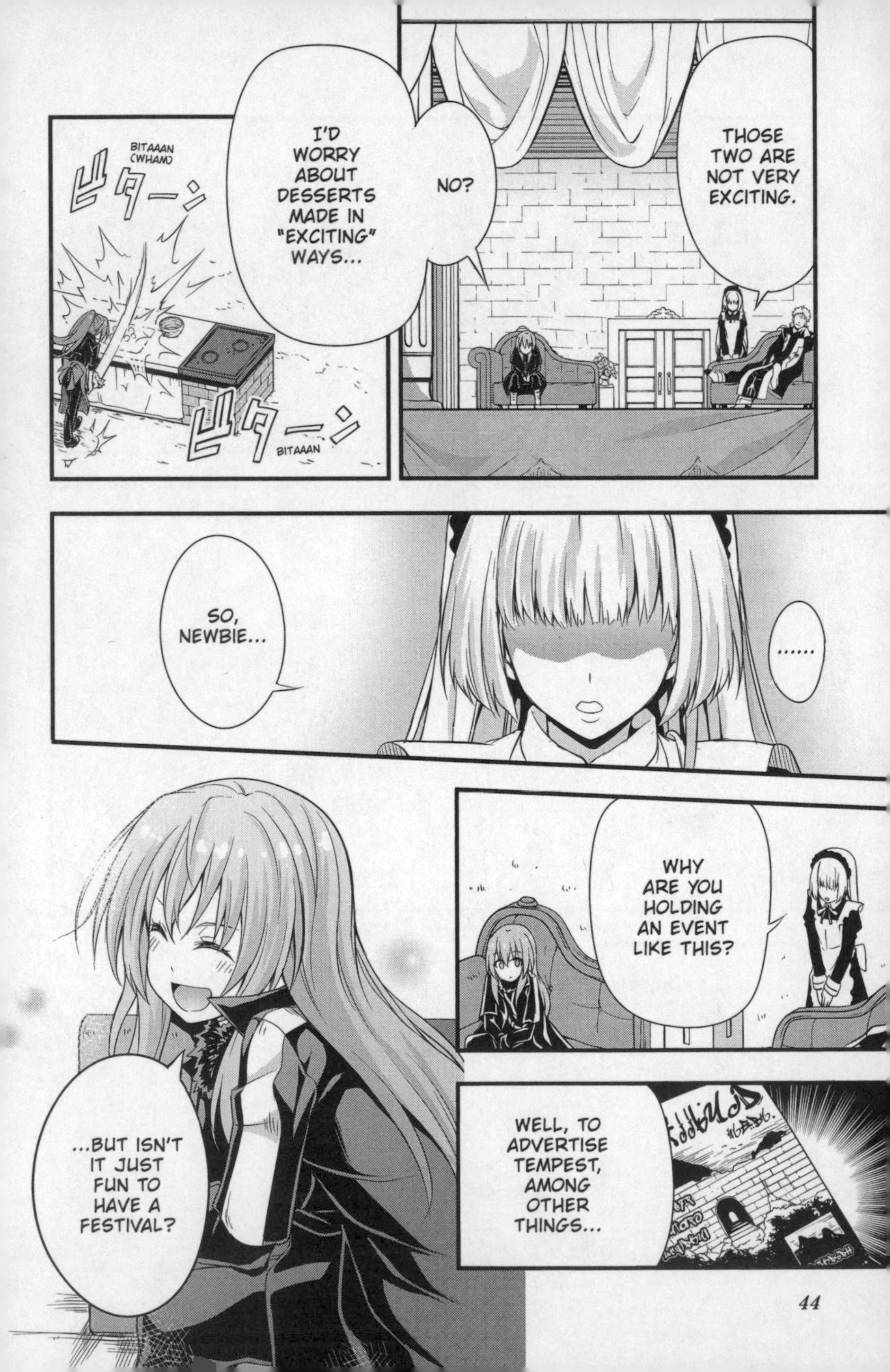
THOSE TWO ARE NOT VERY EXCITING.
NO?
I'D WORRY ABOUT DESSERTS MADE IN "EXCITING" WAYS...
BITAAAN (WHAM)
ビターン
ビターン
BITAAAN
......
SO, NEWBIE...
WHY ARE YOU HOLDING AN EVENT LIKE THIS?
WELL, TO ADVERTISE TEMPEST, AMONG OTHER THINGS...
...BUT ISN'T IT JUST FUN TO HAVE A FESTIVAL?

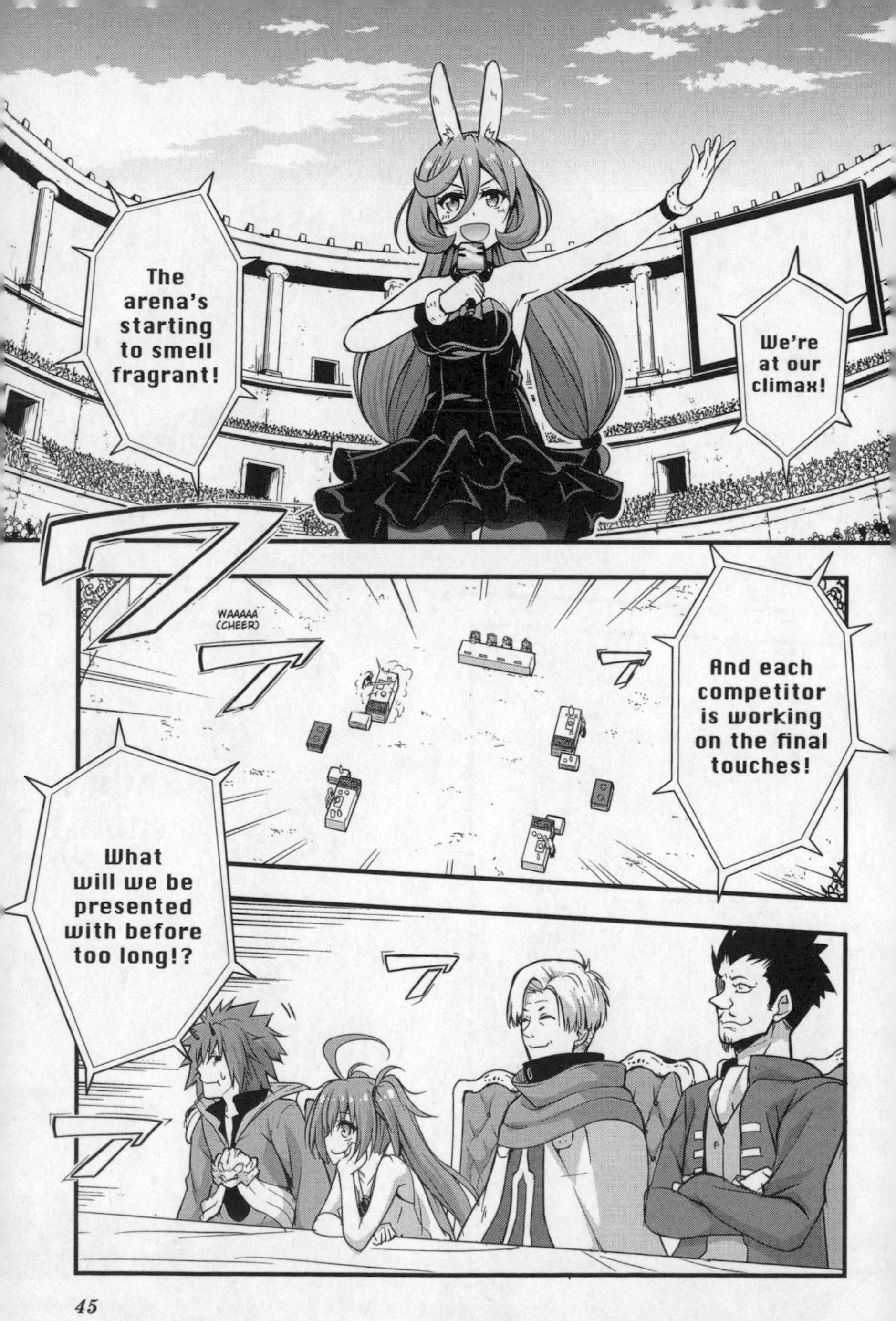

We're at our climax!
The arena's starting to smell fragrant!
And each competitor is working on the final touches!
WAAAAA (CHEER)
What will we be presented with before too long!?

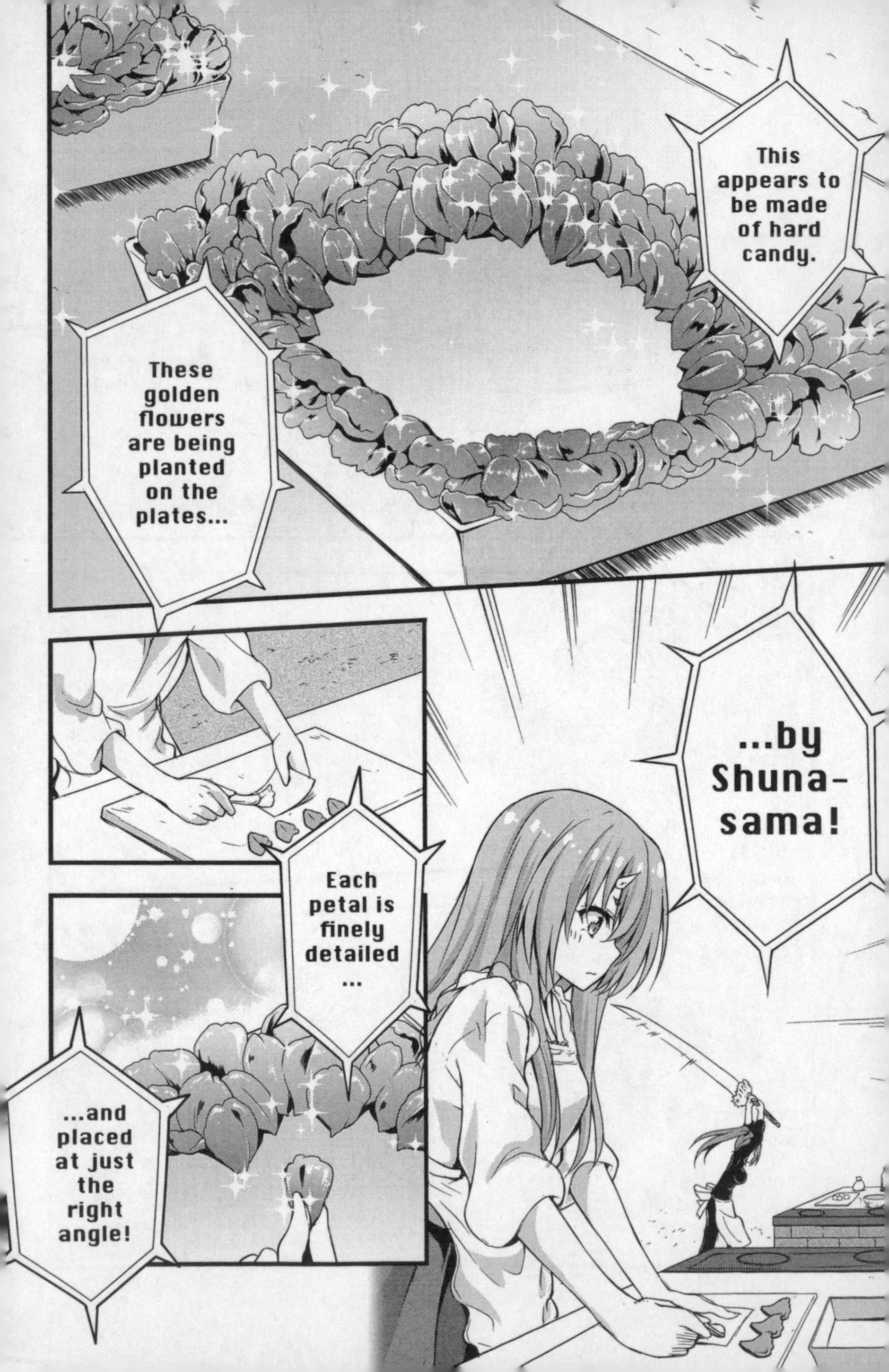
This appears to be made of hard candy.
These golden flowers are being planted on the plates...
...by Shuna-sama!
Each petal is finely detailed...
...and placed at just the right angle!

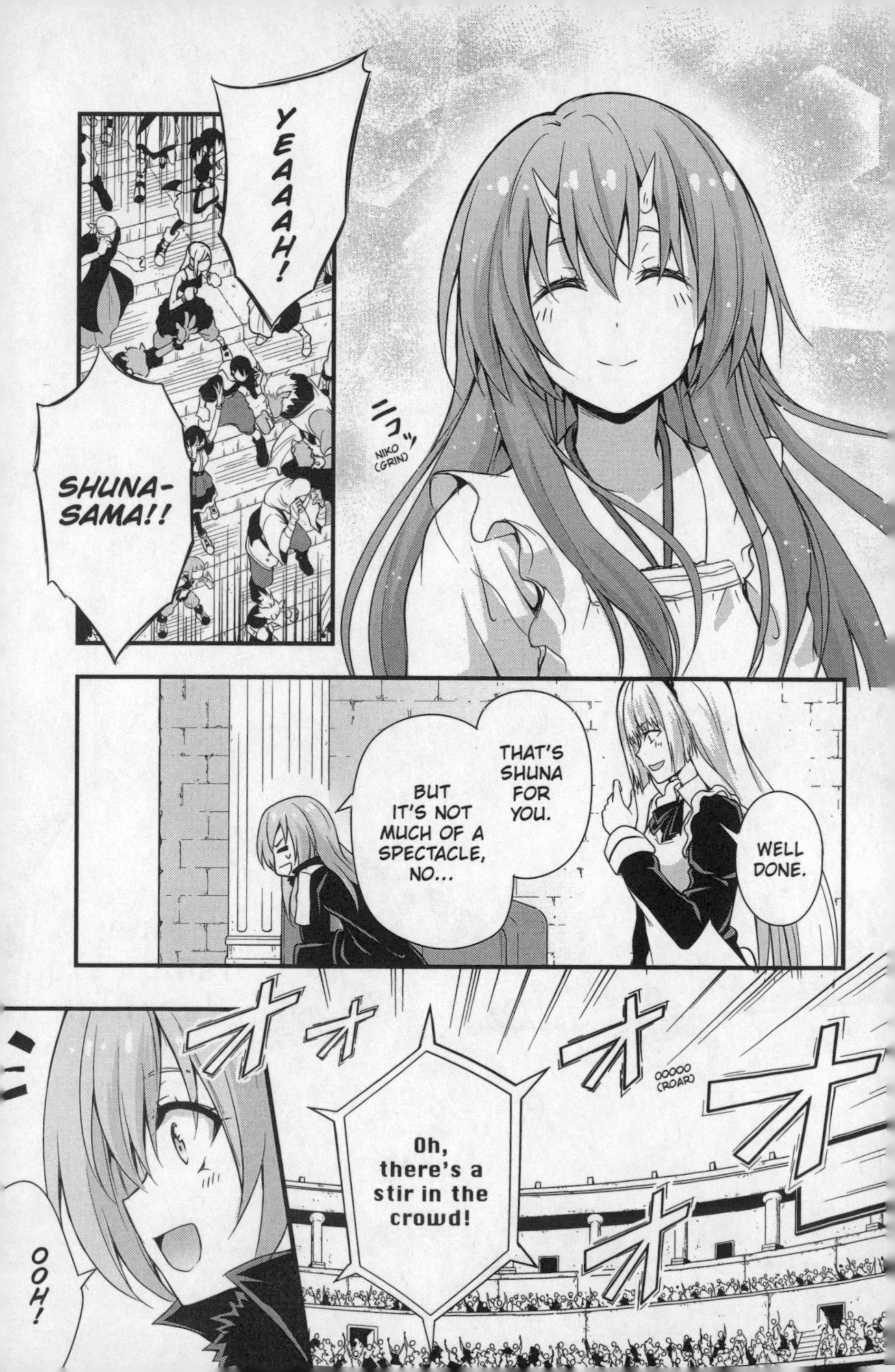
ニコッ
NIKO (GRIN)
YEAAAAH!
SHUNA-SAMA!!
WELL DONE.
THAT'S SHUNA FOR YOU.
BUT IT'S NOT MUCH OF A SPECTACLE, NO...
オォォオオ
OOOOO (ROAR)
Oh, there's a stir in the crowd!
OOH!

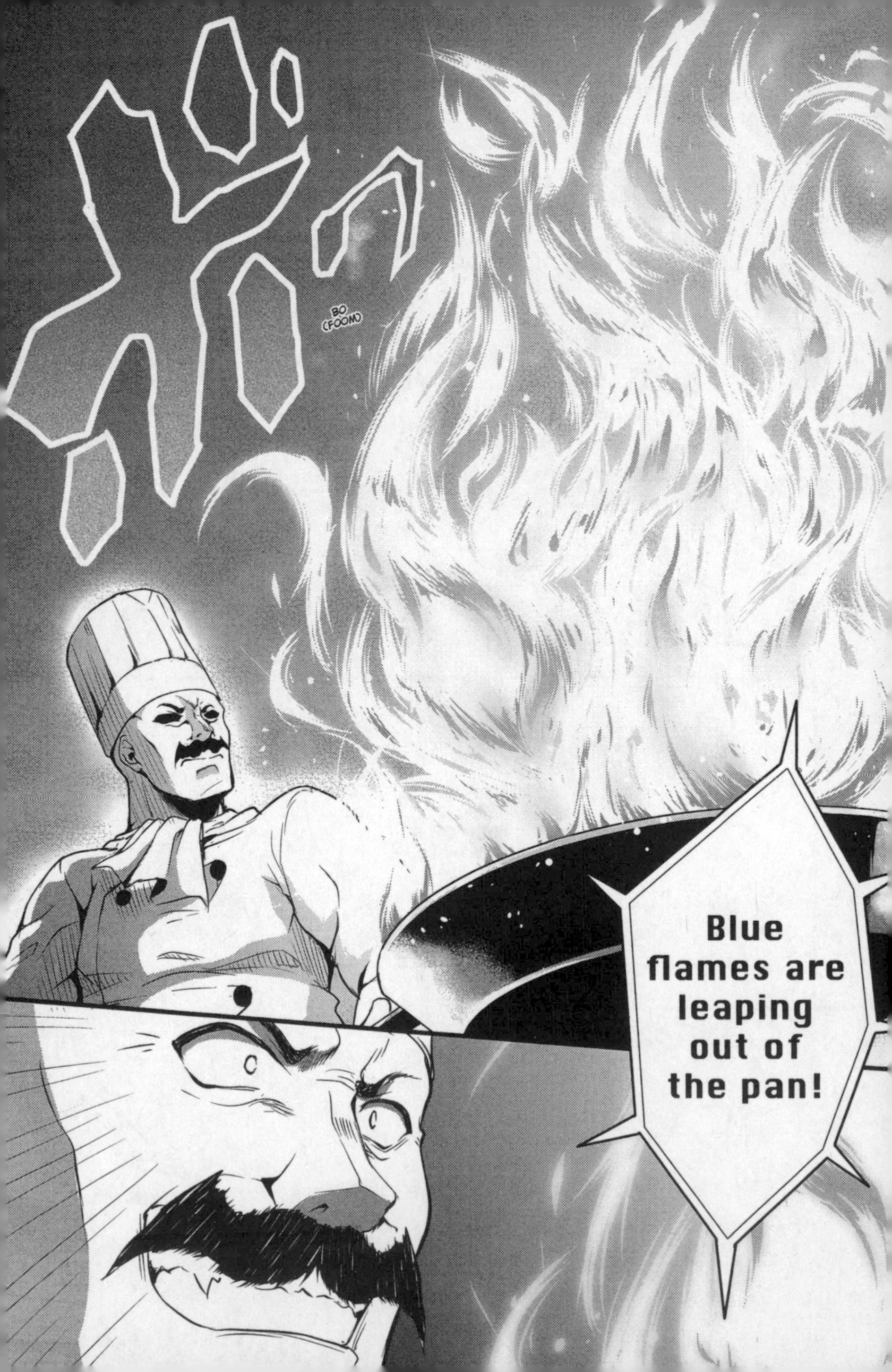
BO
(FOOM)
Blue flames are leaping out of the pan!

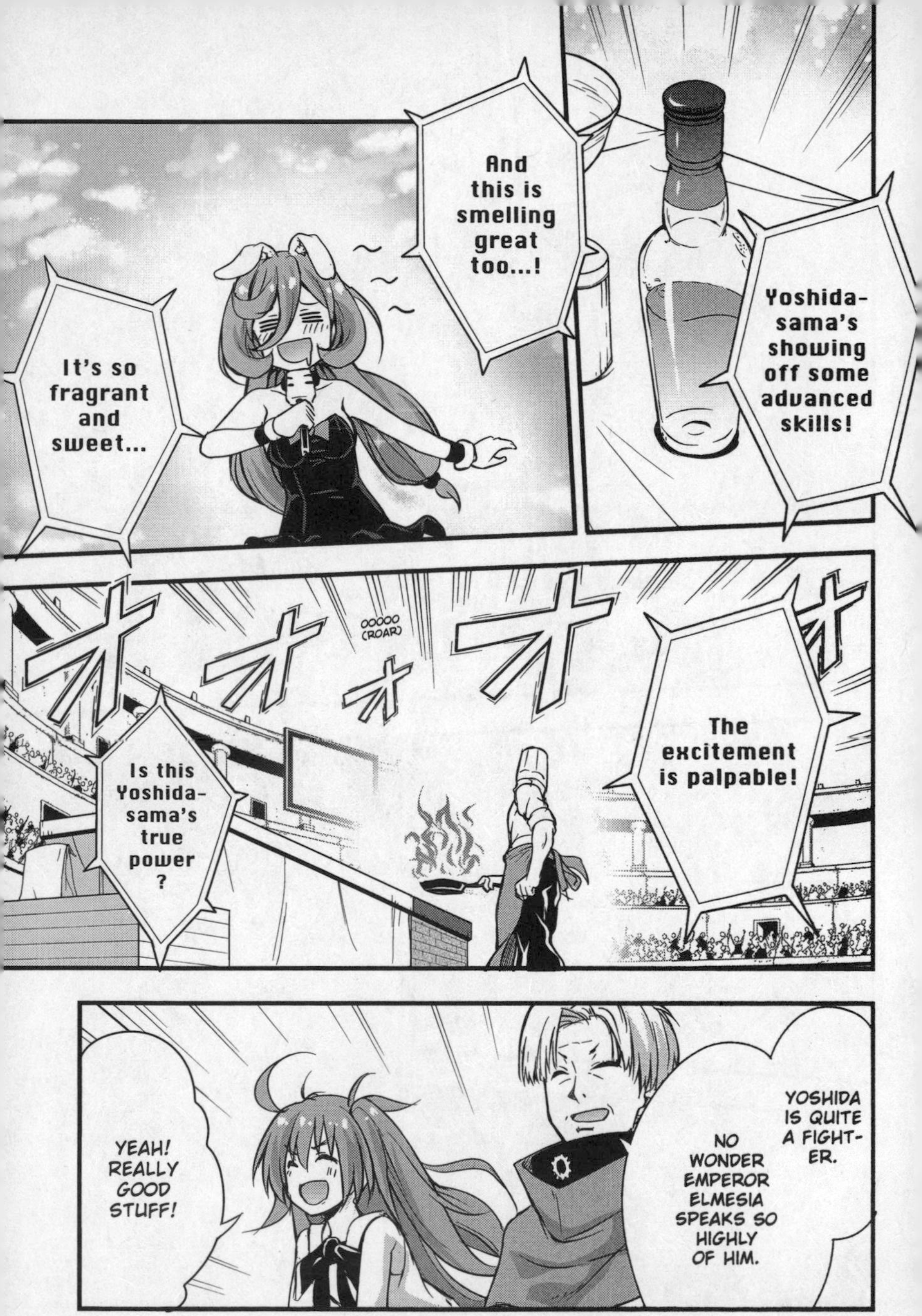
Yoshida-sama's showing off some advanced skills!
And this is smelling great too...!
It's so fragrant and sweet...
The excitement is palpable!
OOOOO (ROAR)
Is this Yoshida-sama's true power?
YOSHIDA IS QUITE A FIGHTER.
NO WONDER EMPEROR ELMESIA SPEAKS SO HIGHLY OF HIM.
YEAH! REALLY GOOD STUFF!

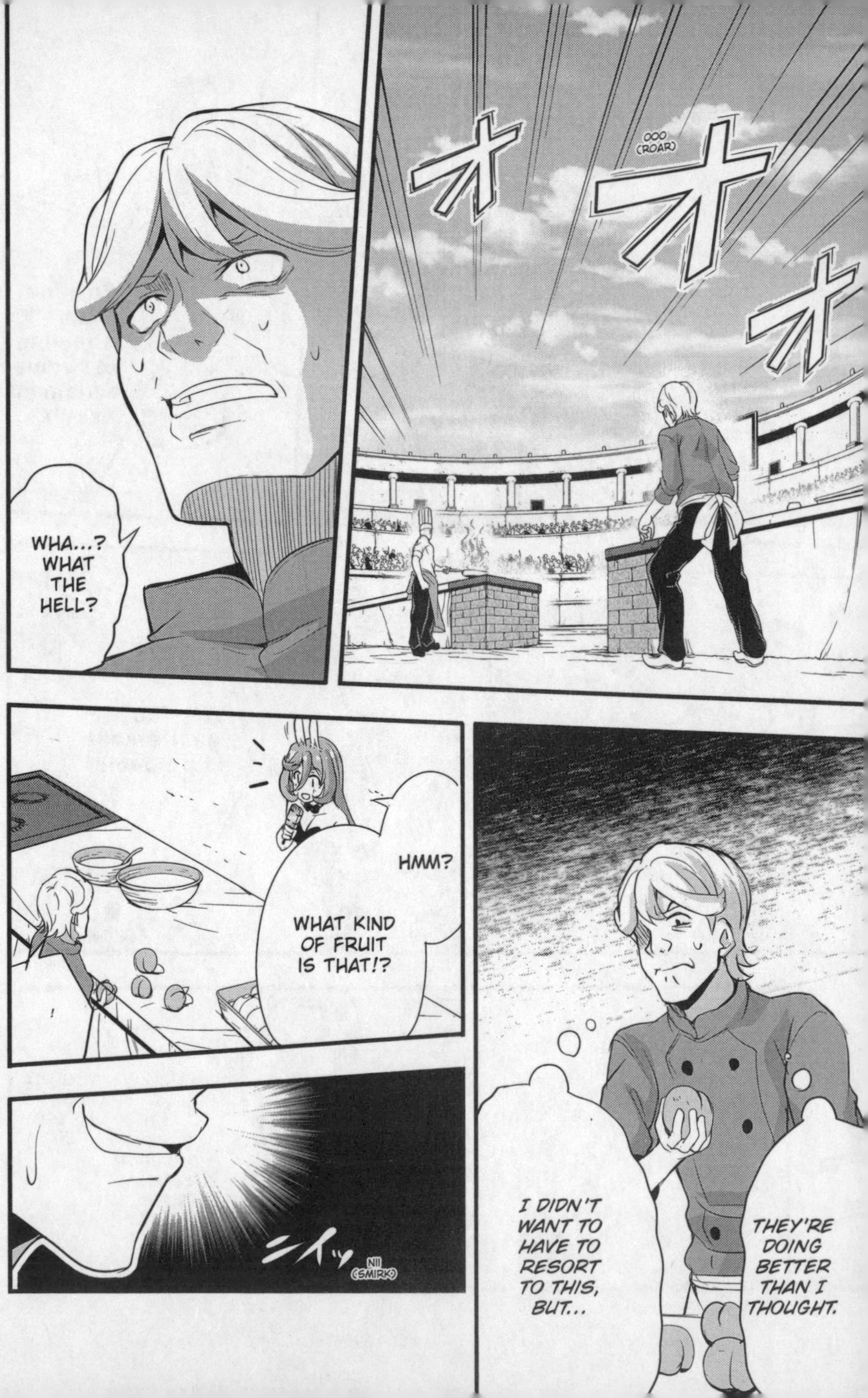

オオオ
OOO (ROAR)
WHA...? WHAT THE HELL?
HMM?
WHAT KIND OF FRUIT IS THAT!?
THEY'RE DOING BETTER THAN I THOUGHT.
I DIDN'T WANT TO HAVE TO RESORT TO THIS, BUT...
ニイッ
NII (SMIRK)

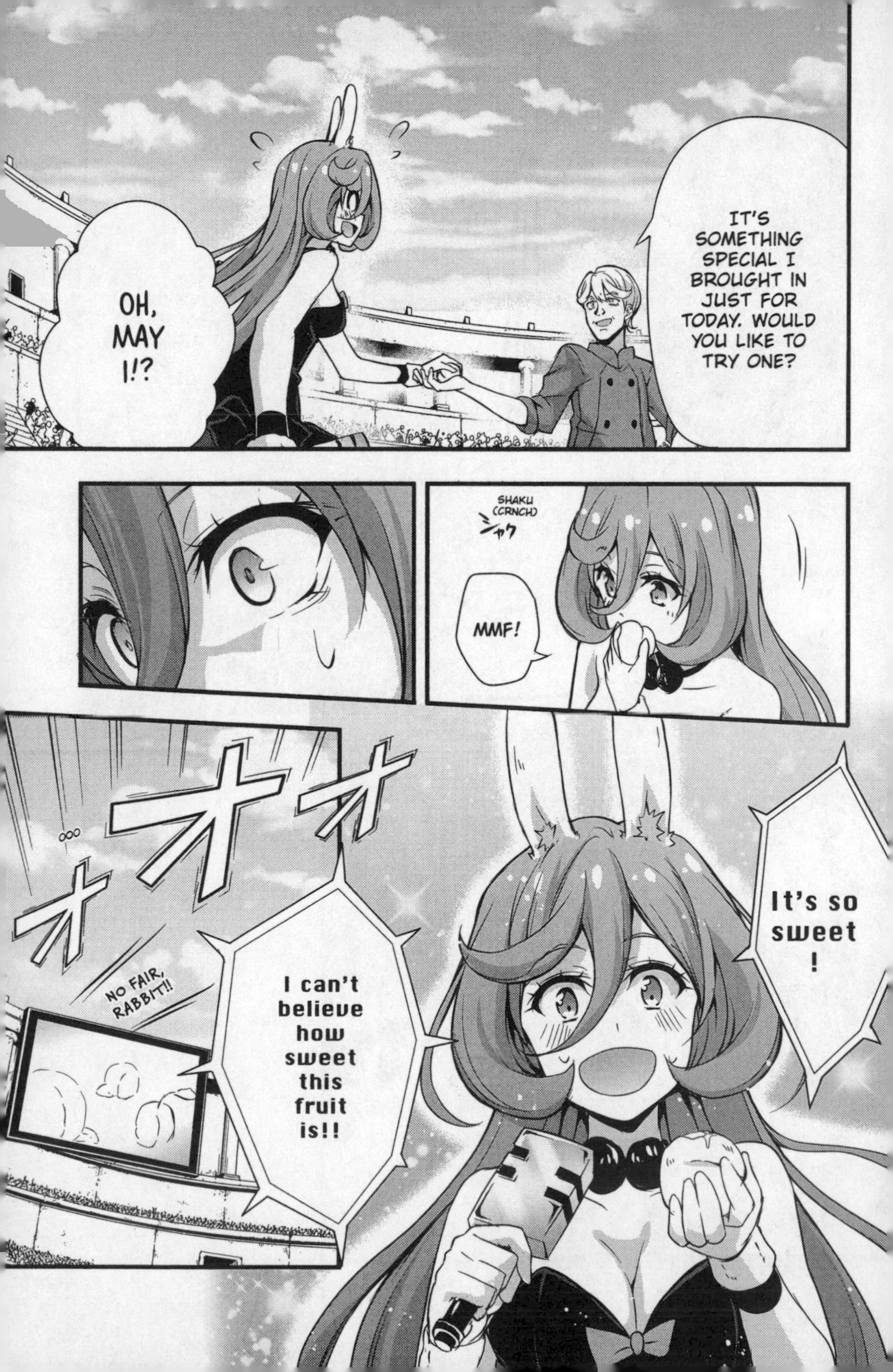
IT'S SOMETHING SPECIAL I BROUGHT IN JUST FOR TODAY. WOULD YOU LIKE TO TRY ONE?
OH, MAY I!?
SHAKU (CRNCH)
MMF!
It's so sweet!
I can't believe how sweet this fruit is!!
NO FAIR, RABBIT!!
ooo

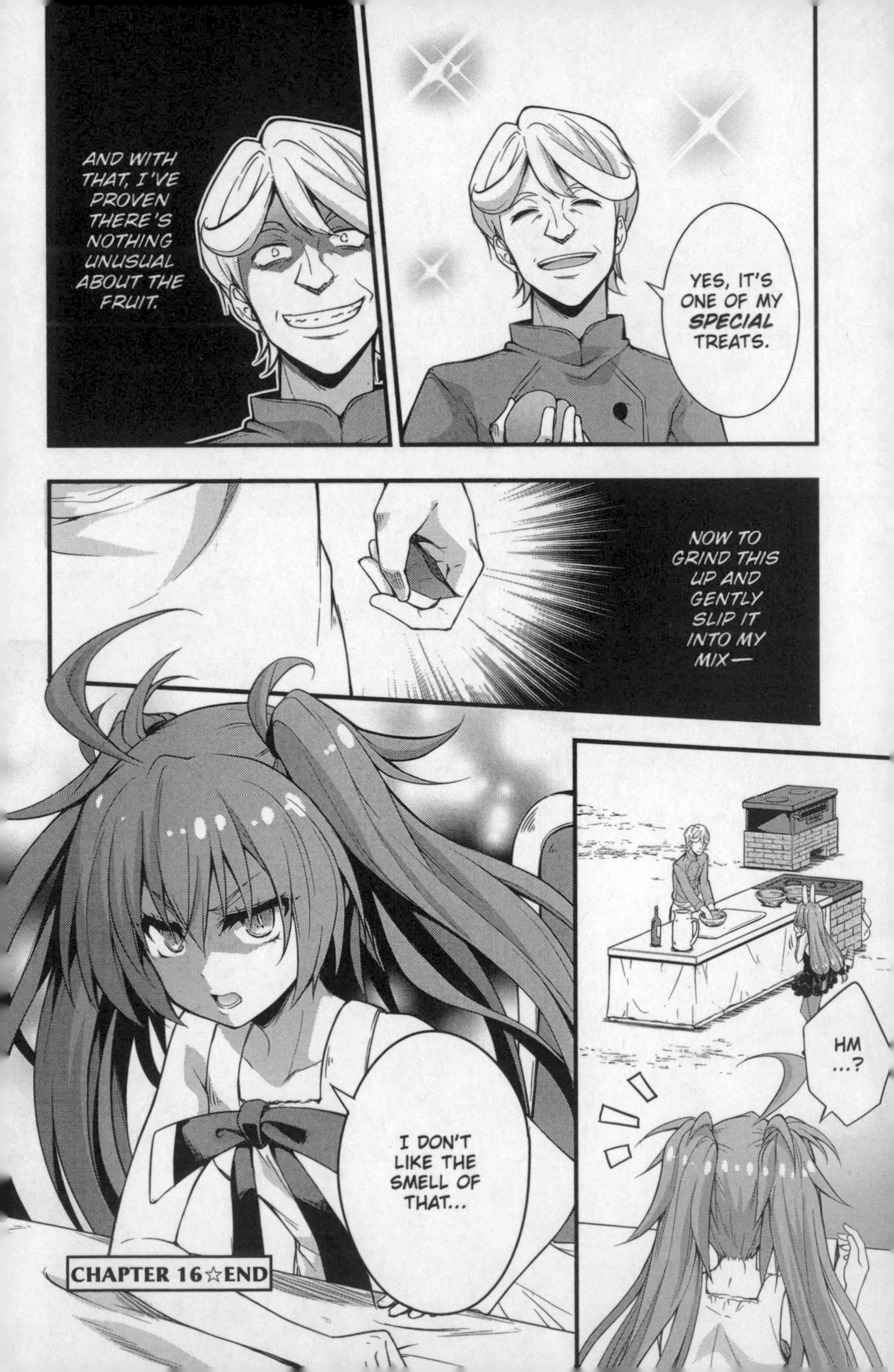
YES, IT'S ONE OF MY **SPECIAL** TREATS.
AND WITH THAT, I'VE PROVEN THERE'S NOTHING UNUSUAL ABOUT THE FRUIT.
NOW TO GRIND THIS UP AND GENTLY SLIP IT INTO MY MIX—
HM ...?
I DON'T LIKE THE SMELL OF THAT...
CHAPTER 16☆END

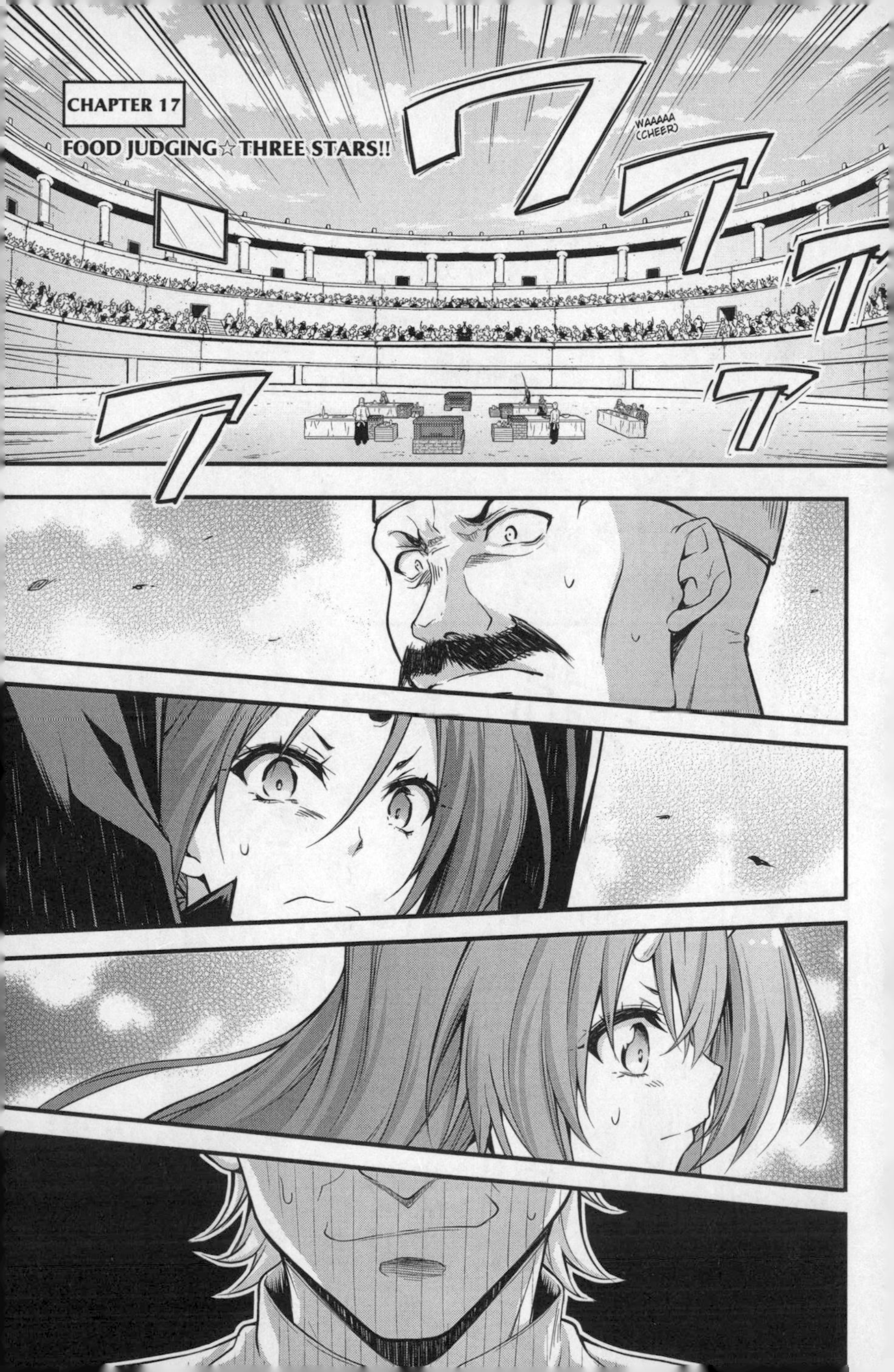
CHAPTER 17
FOOD JUDGING☆THREE STARS!!
WAAAAA (CHEER)

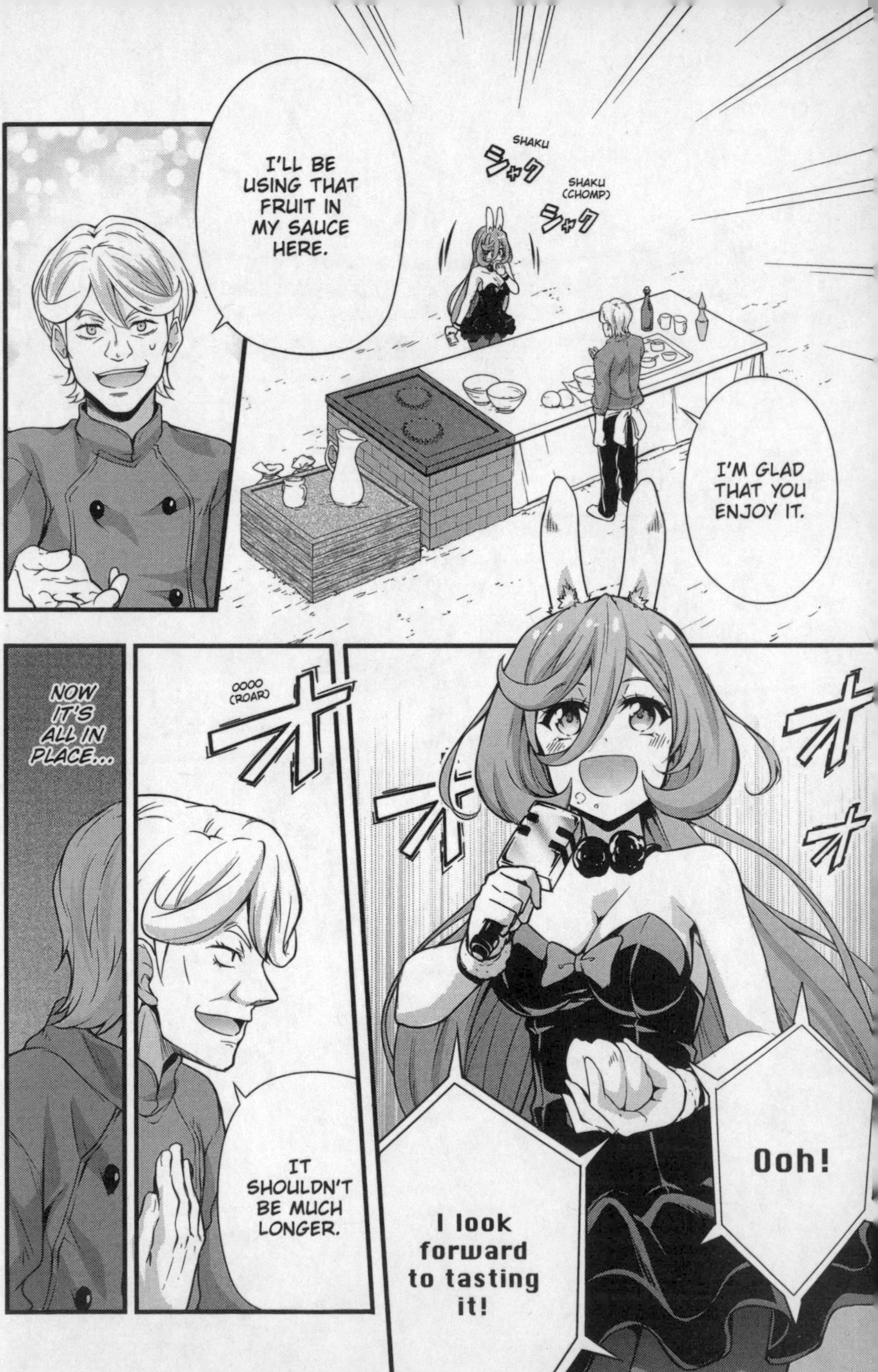
SHAKU
SHAKU (CHOMP)
I'M GLAD THAT YOU ENJOY IT.
I'LL BE USING THAT FRUIT IN MY SAUCE HERE.
OOOO (ROAR)
Ooh!
I look forward to tasting it!
IT SHOULDN'T BE MUCH LONGER.
NOW IT'S ALL IN PLACE...

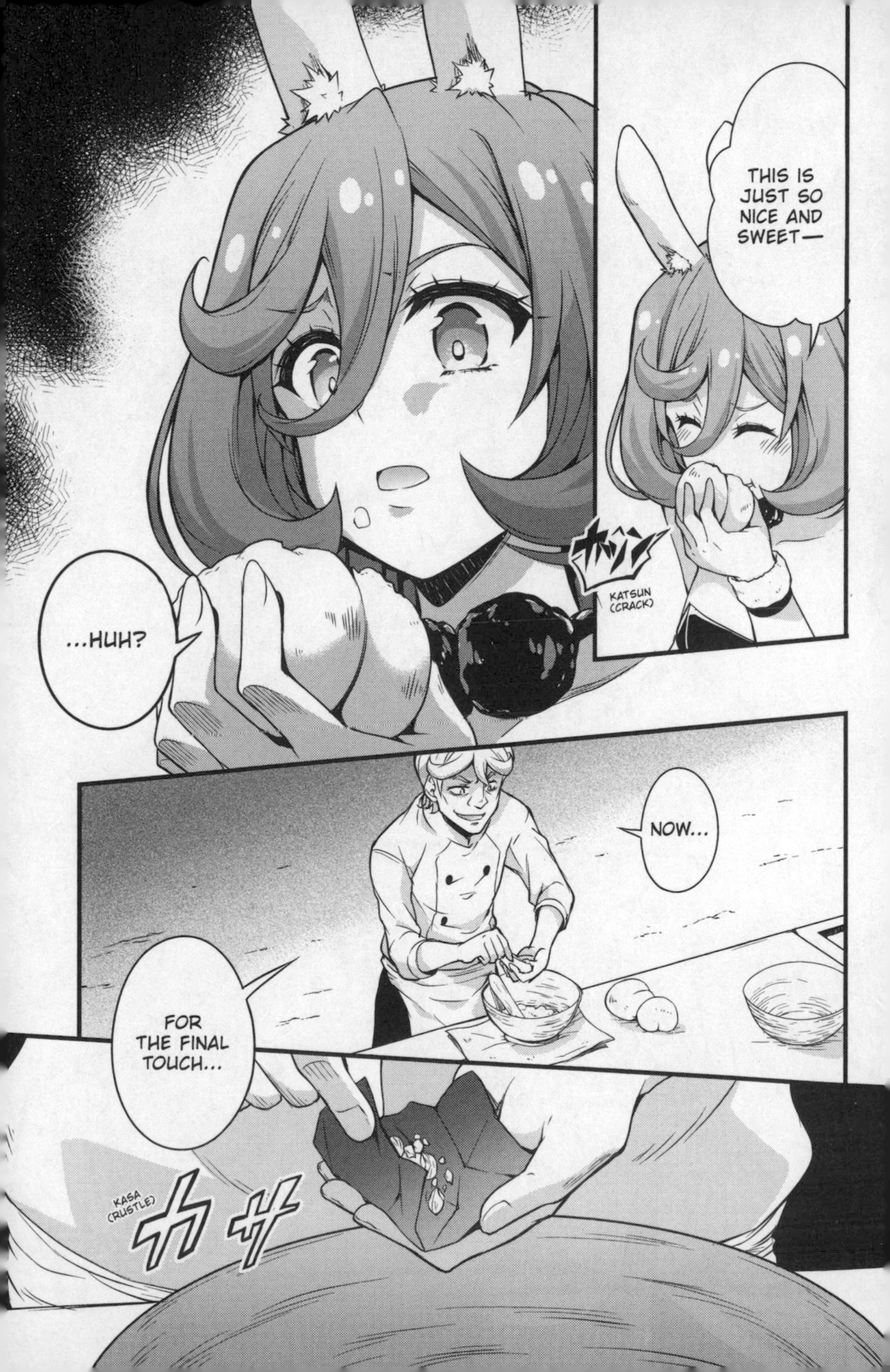
THIS IS JUST SO NICE AND SWEET—
KATSUN (CRACK)
...HUH?
NOW...
FOR THE FINAL TOUCH...
KASA (RUSTLE)

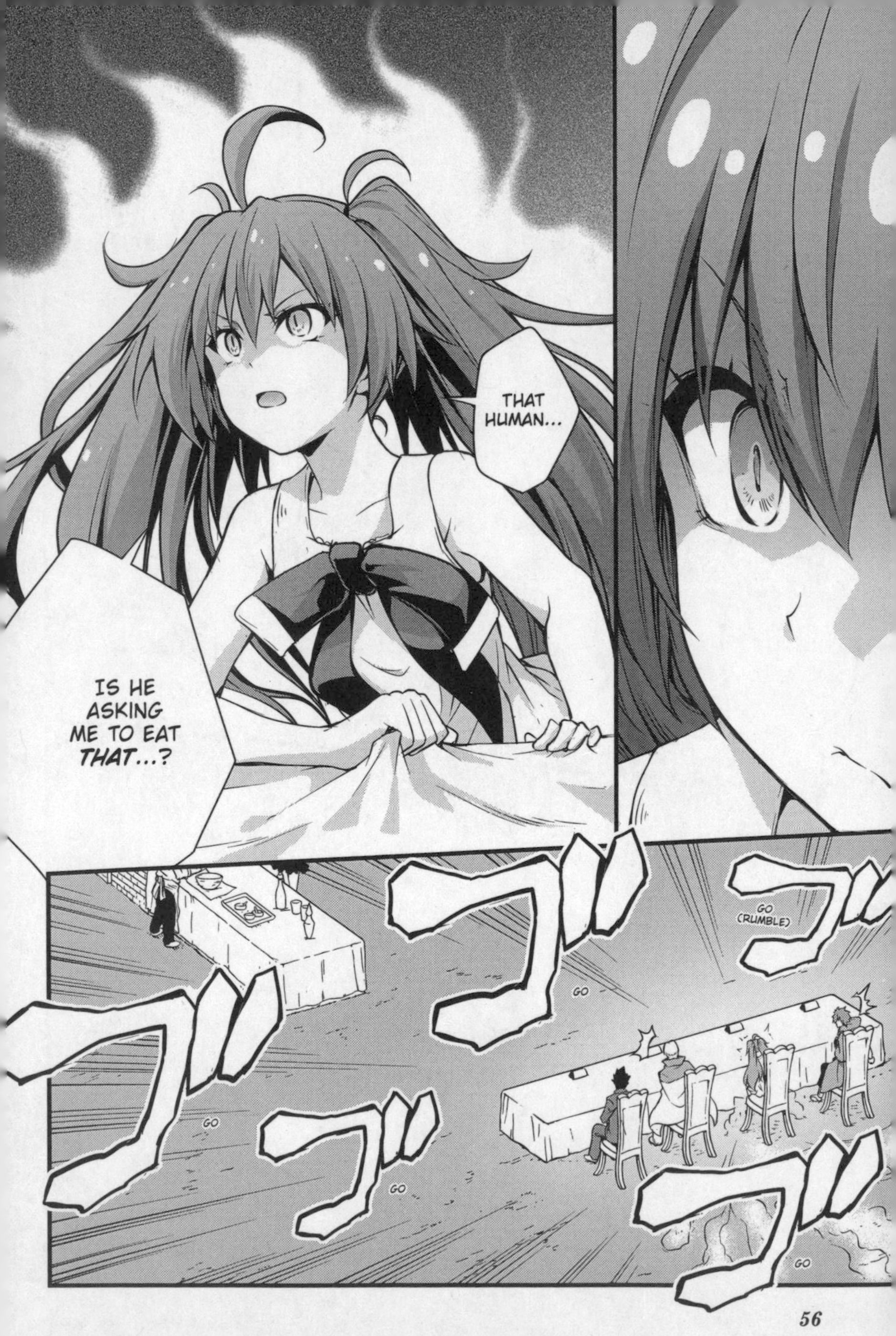
THAT HUMAN...
IS HE ASKING ME TO EAT *THAT*...?
GO (RUMBLE)
GO
GO
GO
GO

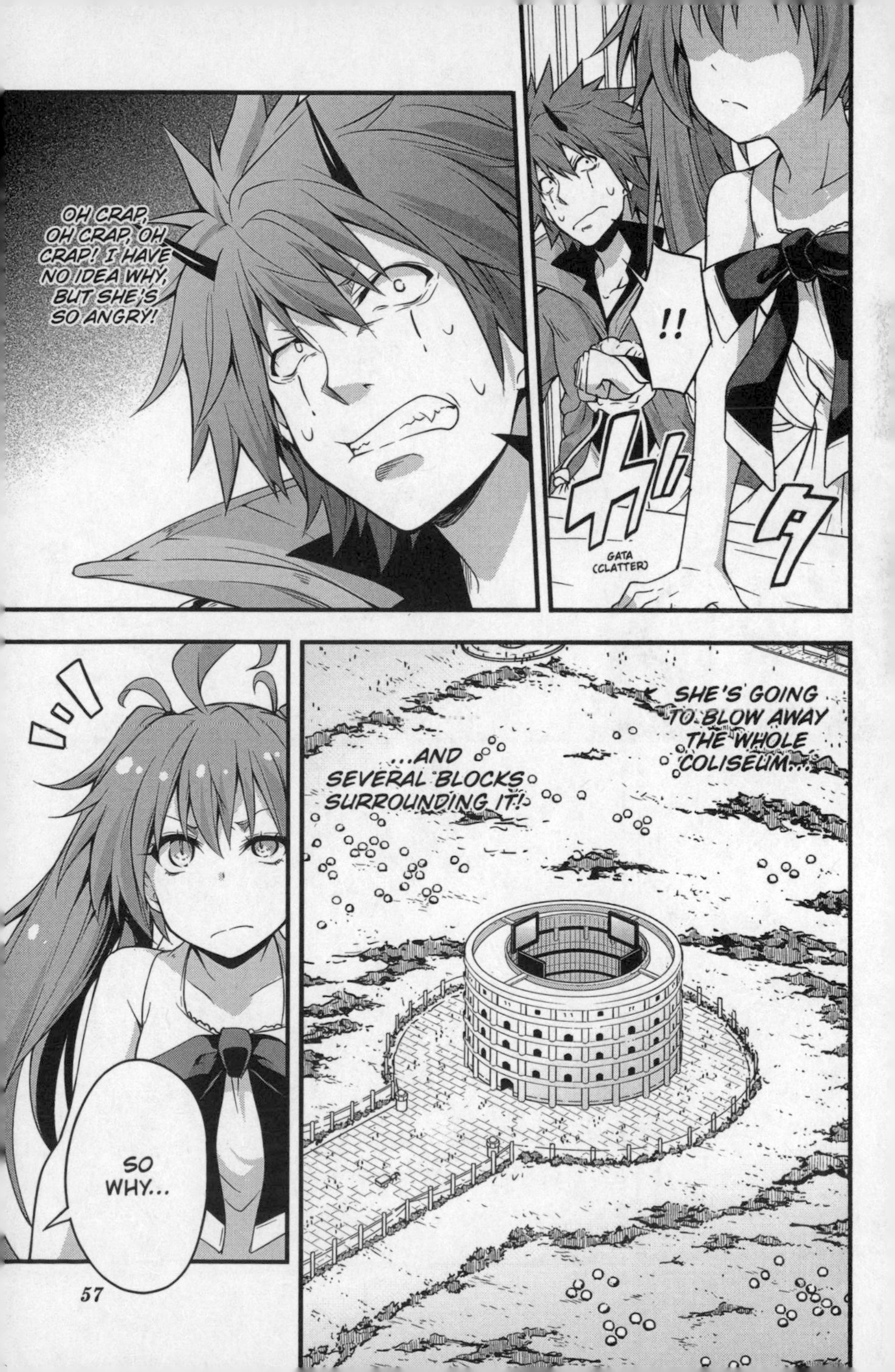
!!
GATA (CLATTER)
OH CRAP, OH CRAP, OH CRAP! I HAVE NO IDEA WHY, BUT SHE'S SO ANGRY!
SHE'S GOING TO BLOW AWAY THE WHOLE COLISEUM...
...AND SEVERAL BLOCKS SURROUNDING IT!
SO WHY...

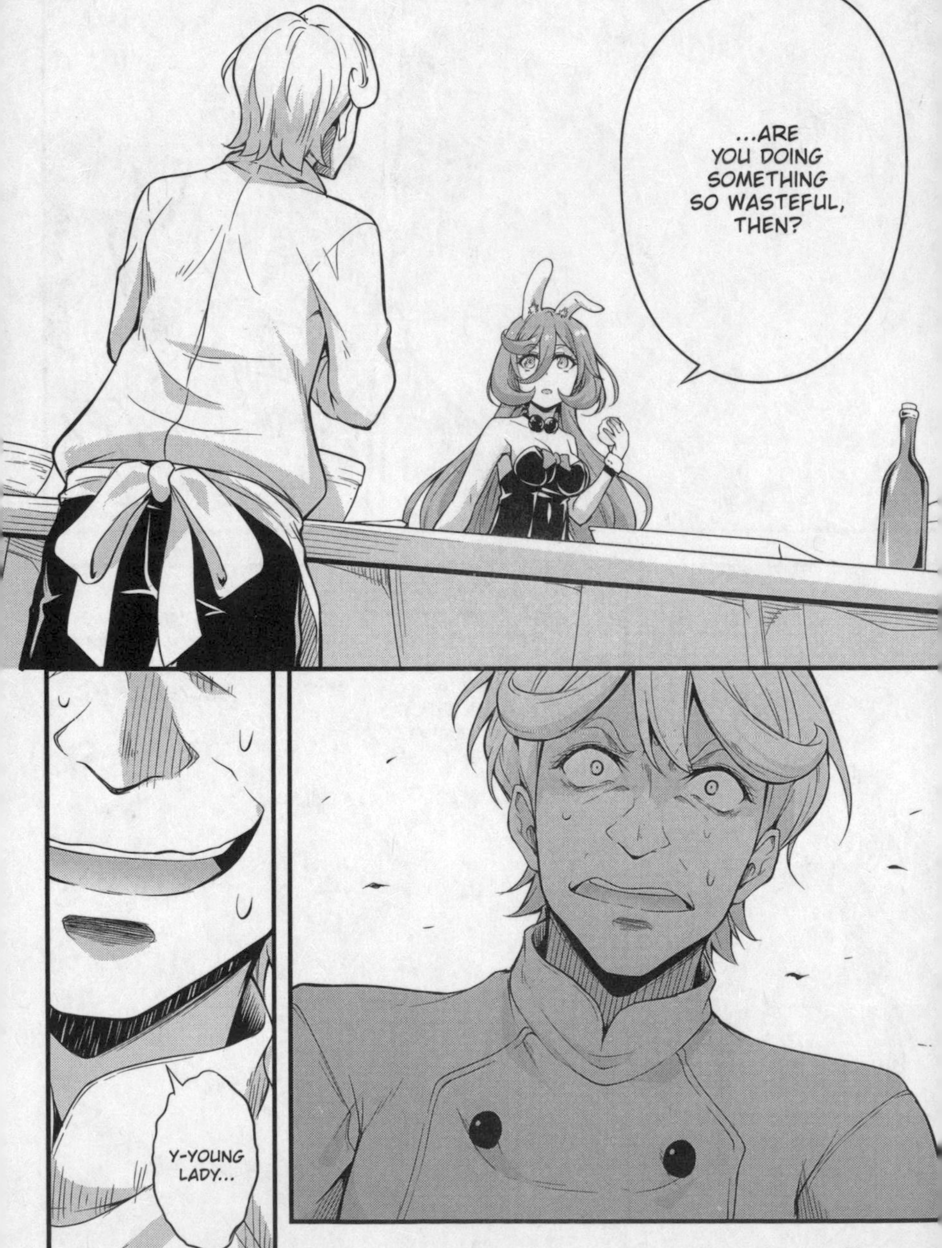

...ARE YOU DOING SOMETHING SO WASTEFUL, THEN?
Y-YOUNG LADY...

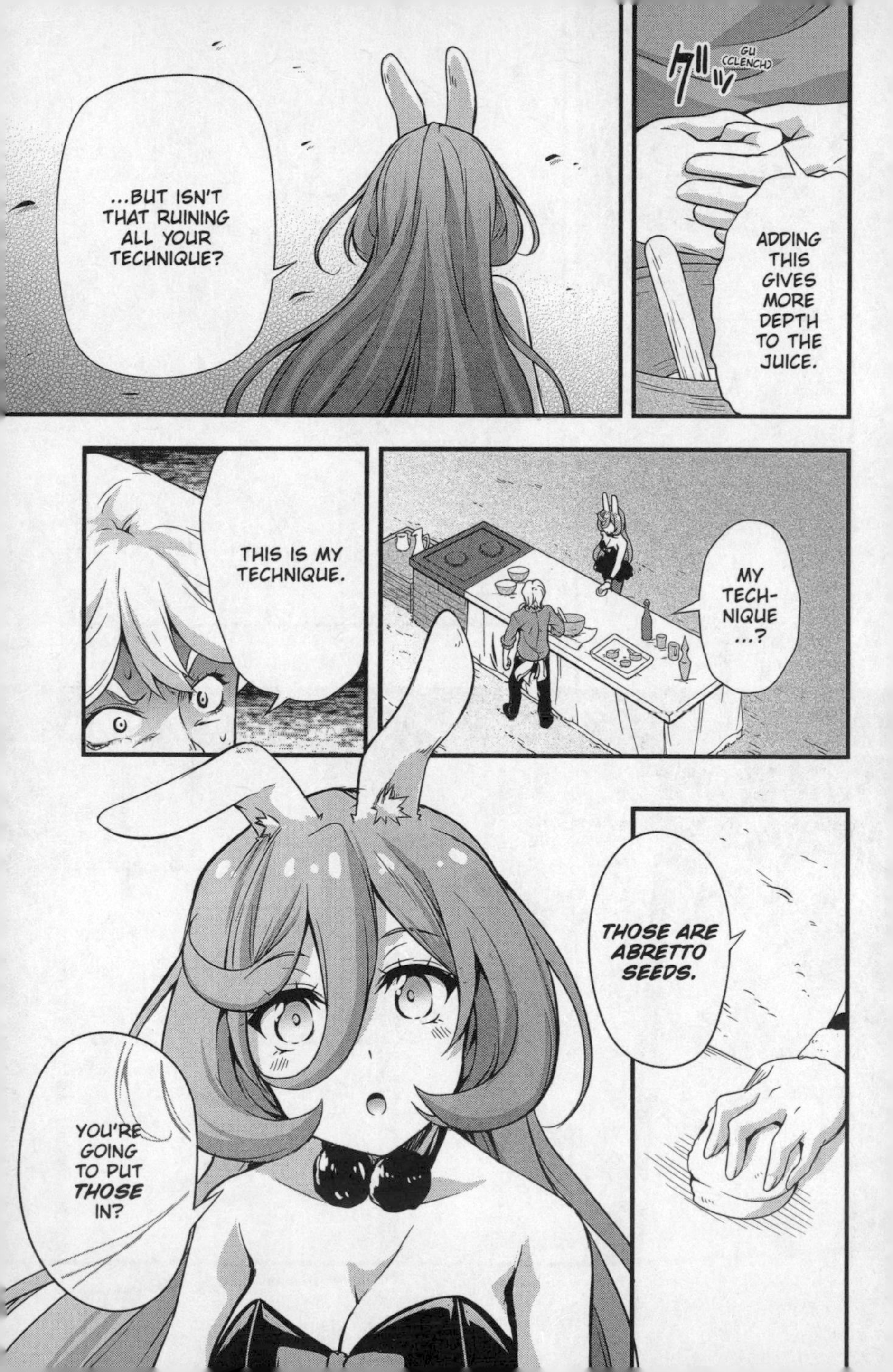
グッ
GU (CLENCH)
ADDING THIS GIVES MORE DEPTH TO THE JUICE.
...BUT ISN'T THAT RUINING ALL YOUR TECHNIQUE?
MY TECH-NIQUE ...?
THIS IS MY TECHNIQUE.
THOSE ARE ABRETTO SEEDS.
YOU'RE GOING TO PUT *THOSE* IN?

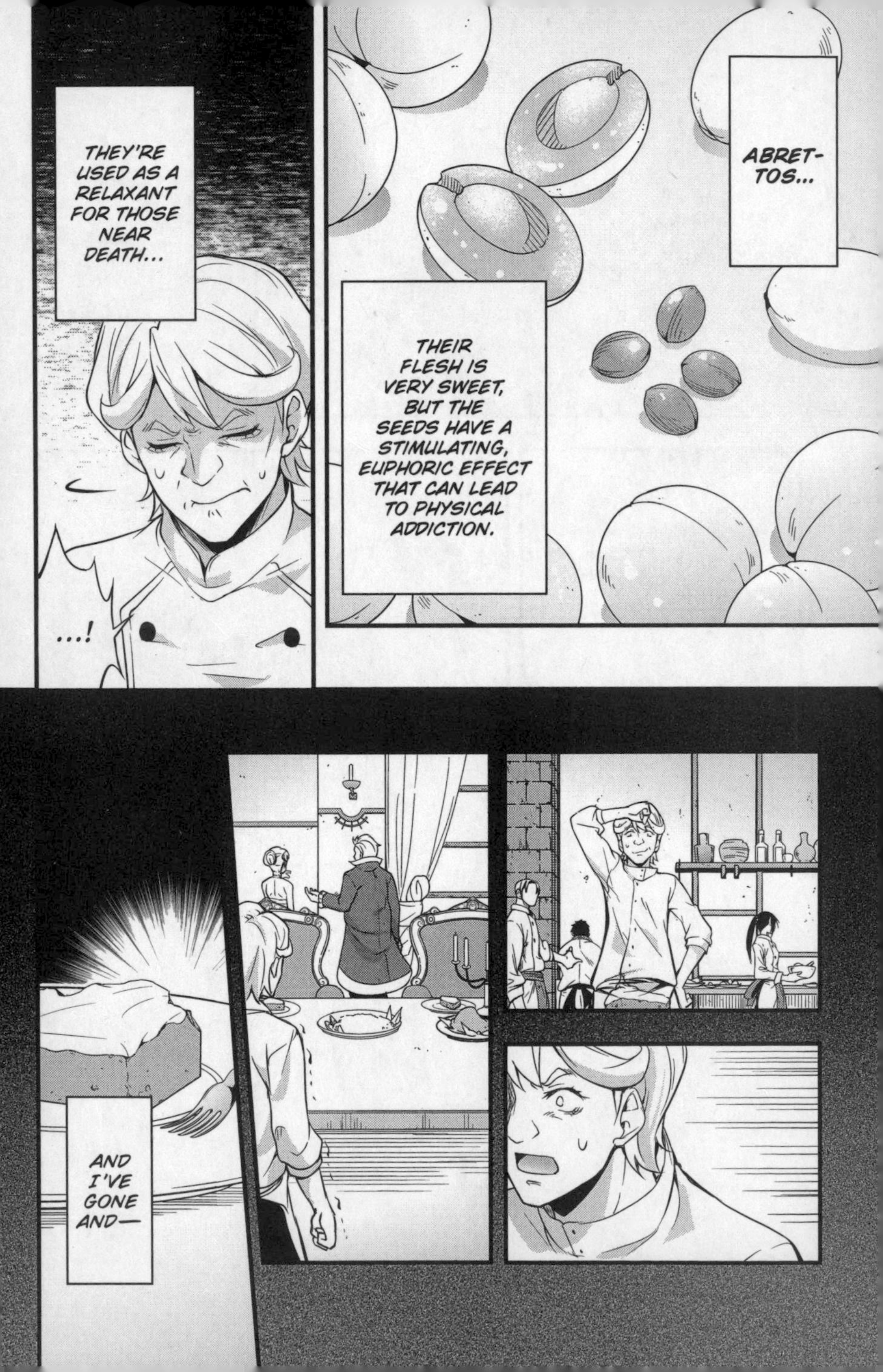
ABRET-TOS...
THEIR FLESH IS VERY SWEET, BUT THE SEEDS HAVE A STIMULATING, EUPHORIC EFFECT THAT CAN LEAD TO PHYSICAL ADDICTION.
THEY'RE USED AS A RELAXANT FOR THOSE NEAR DEATH...
...!
AND I'VE GONE AND—

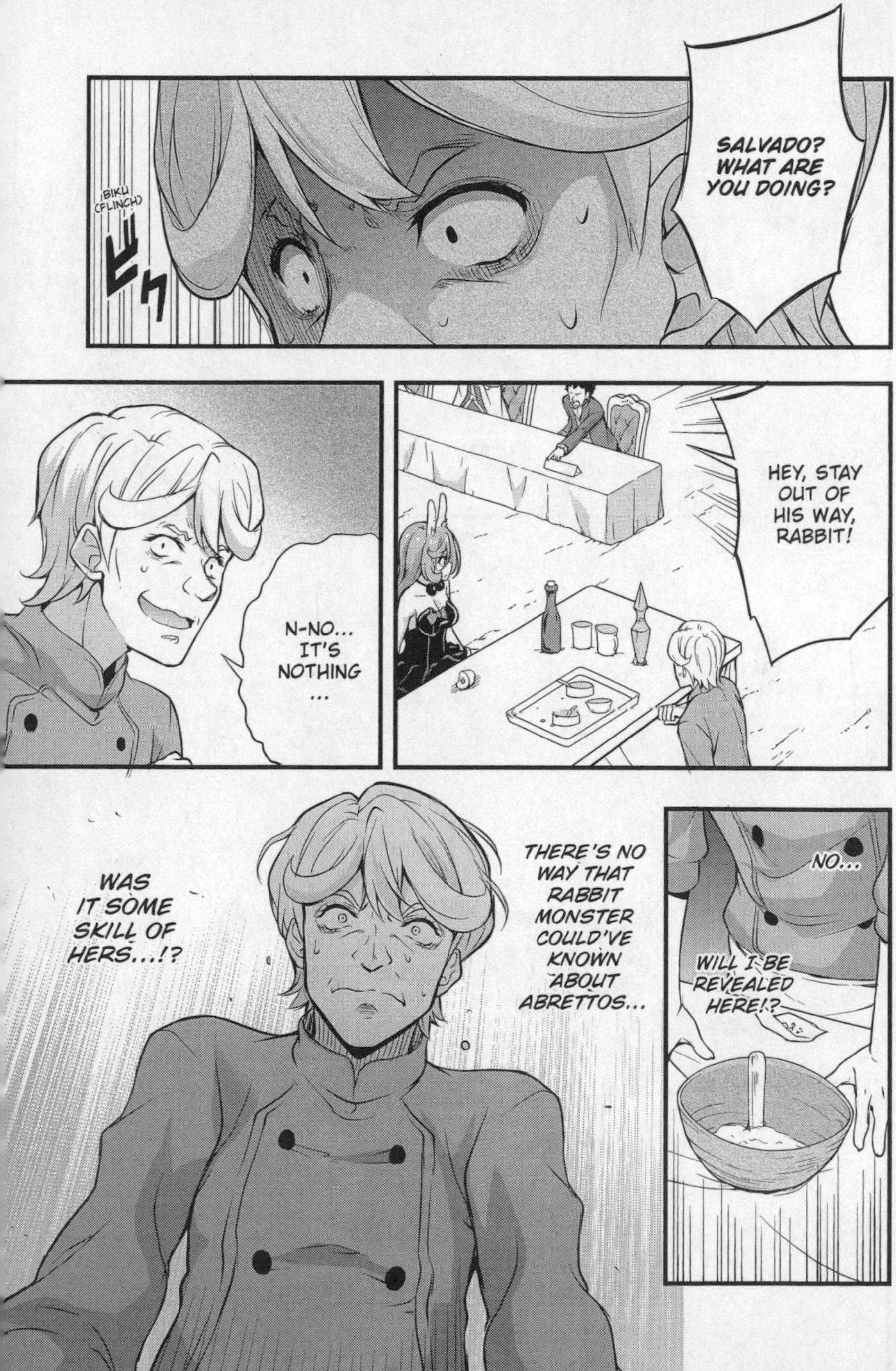
SALVADO? WHAT ARE YOU DOING?
BIKU (FLINCH)
ビク
HEY, STAY OUT OF HIS WAY, RABBIT!
N-NO... IT'S NOTHING ...
NO...
WILL I BE REVEALED HERE!?
THERE'S NO WAY THAT RABBIT MONSTER COULD'VE KNOWN ABOUT ABRETTOS...
WAS IT SOME SKILL OF HERS...!?

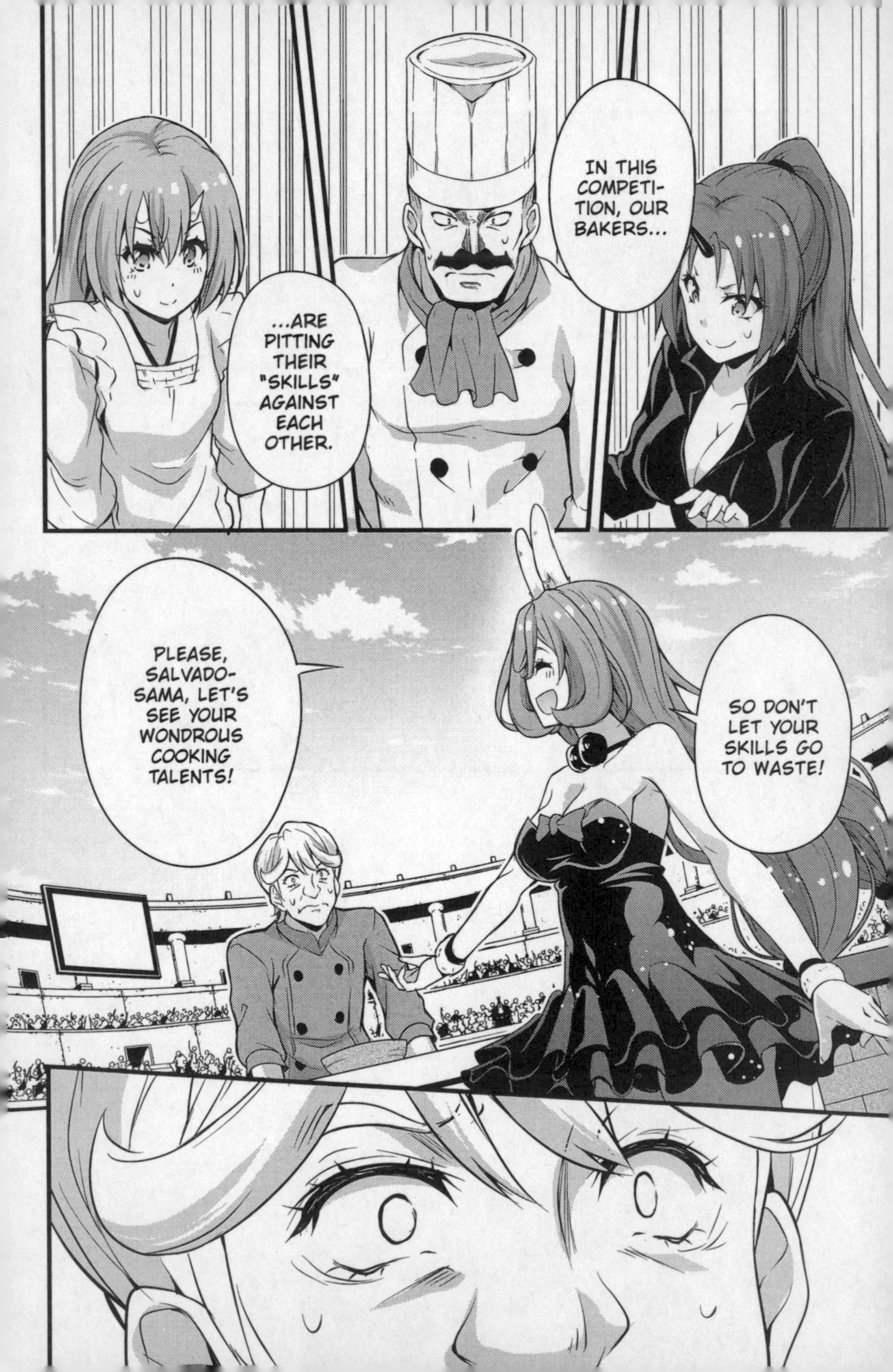
IN THIS COMPETITION, OUR BAKERS...
...ARE PITTING THEIR "SKILLS" AGAINST EACH OTHER.
SO DON'T LET YOUR SKILLS GO TO WASTE!
PLEASE, SALVADO-SAMA, LET'S SEE YOUR WONDROUS COOKING TALENTS!

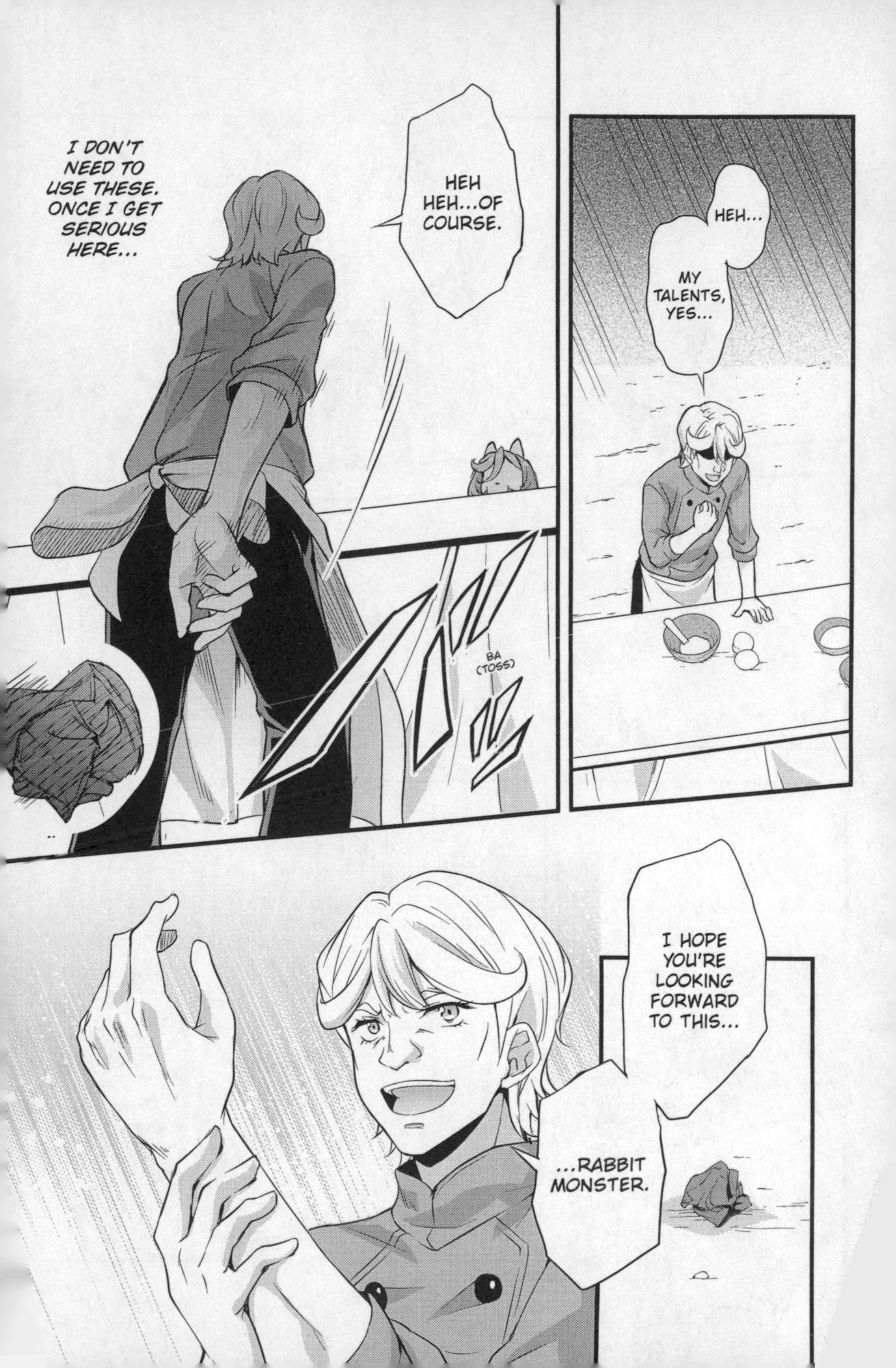
HEH...
MY TALENTS, YES...
HEH HEH...OF COURSE.
I DON'T NEED TO USE THESE. ONCE I GET SERIOUS HERE...
BA (TOSS)
I HOPE YOU'RE LOOKING FORWARD TO THIS...
...RABBIT MONSTER.

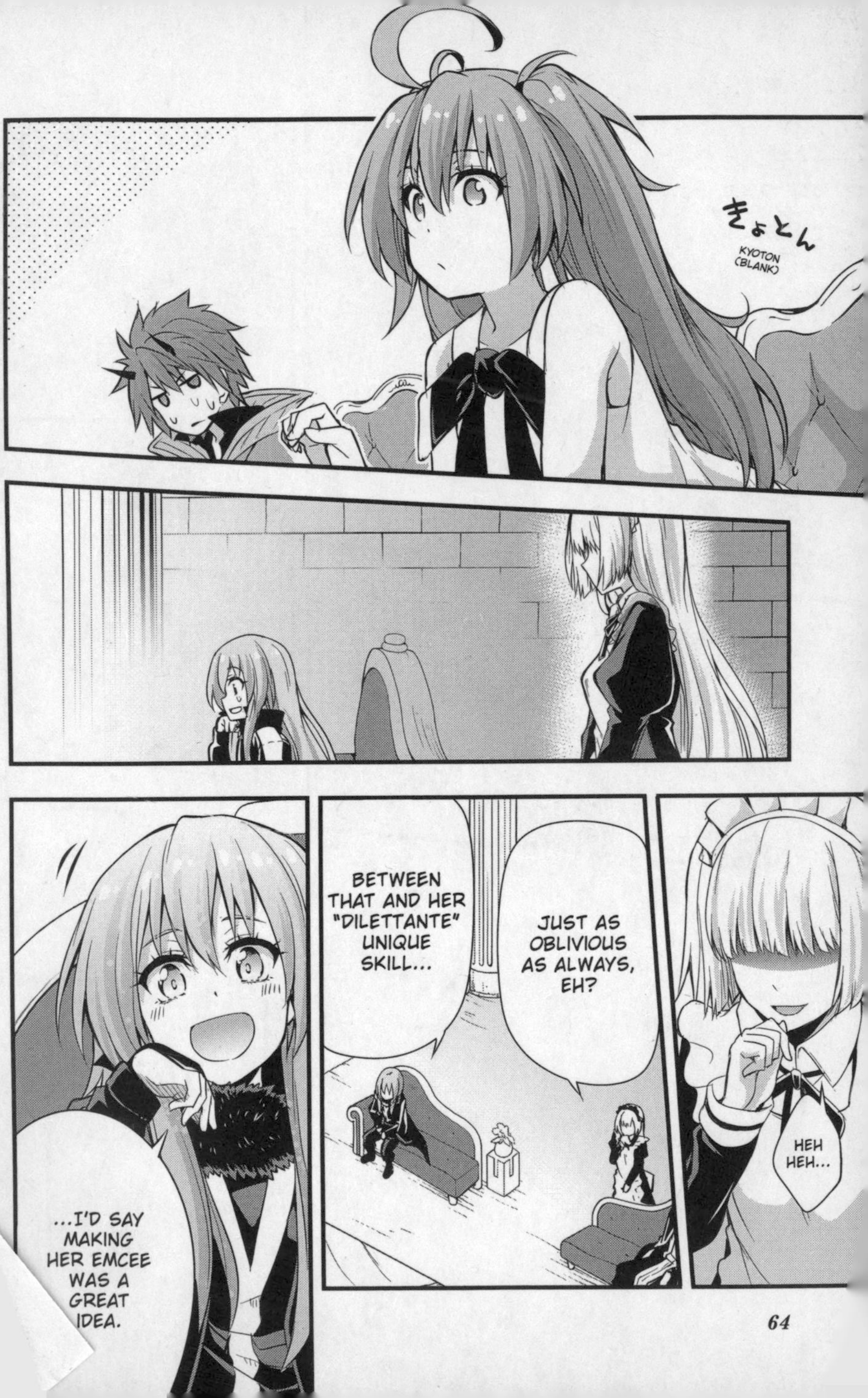
きょとん
KYOTON (BLANK)
HEH HEH...
JUST AS OBLIVIOUS AS ALWAYS, EH?
BETWEEN THAT AND HER "DILETTANTE" UNIQUE SKILL...
...I'D SAY MAKING HER EMCEE WAS A GREAT IDEA.

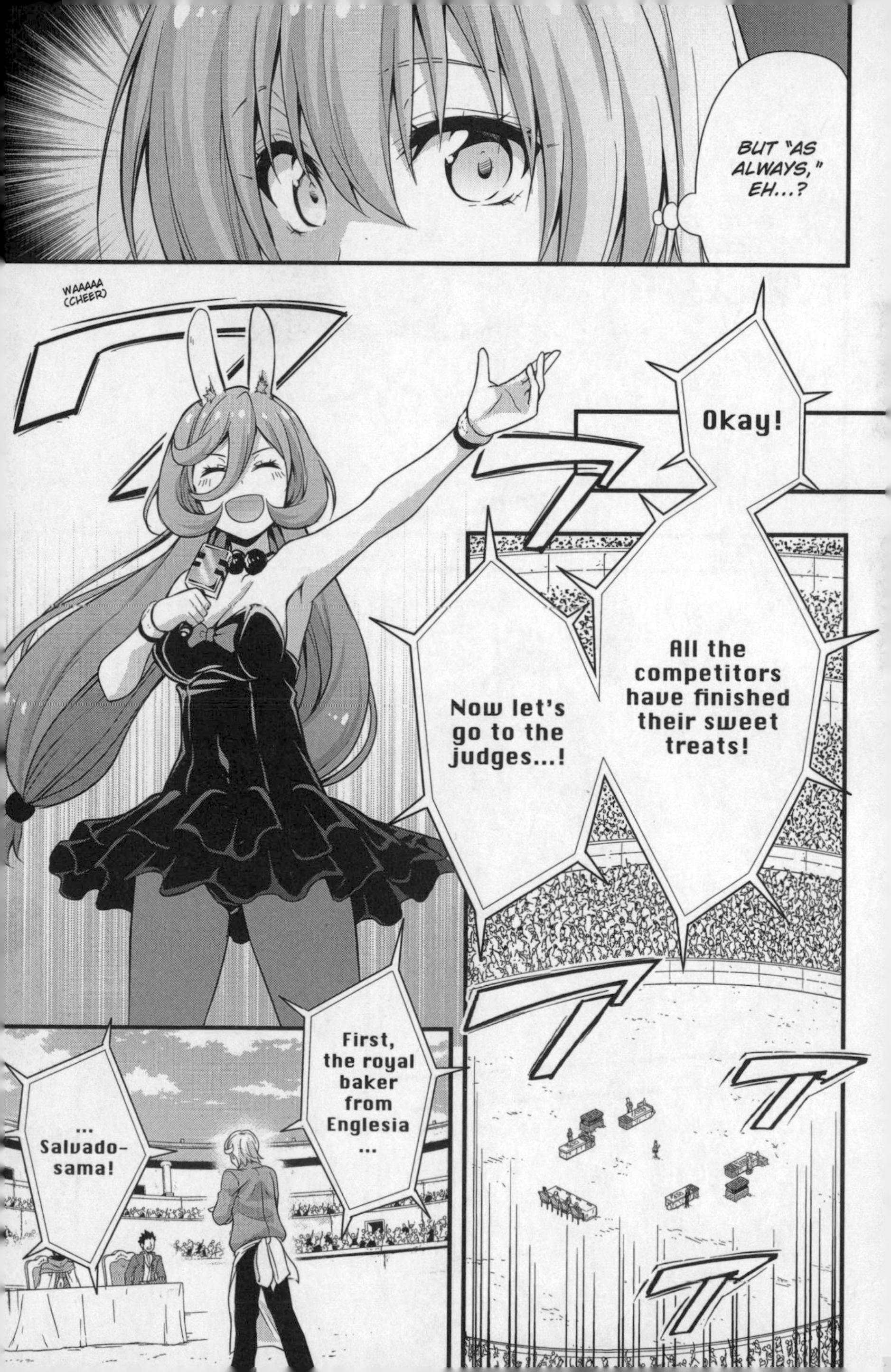
BUT "AS ALWAYS," EH...?
Okay!
All the competitors have finished their sweet treats!
Now let's go to the judges...!
WAAAAA (CHEER)
First, the royal baker from Englesia ...
... Salvado-sama!

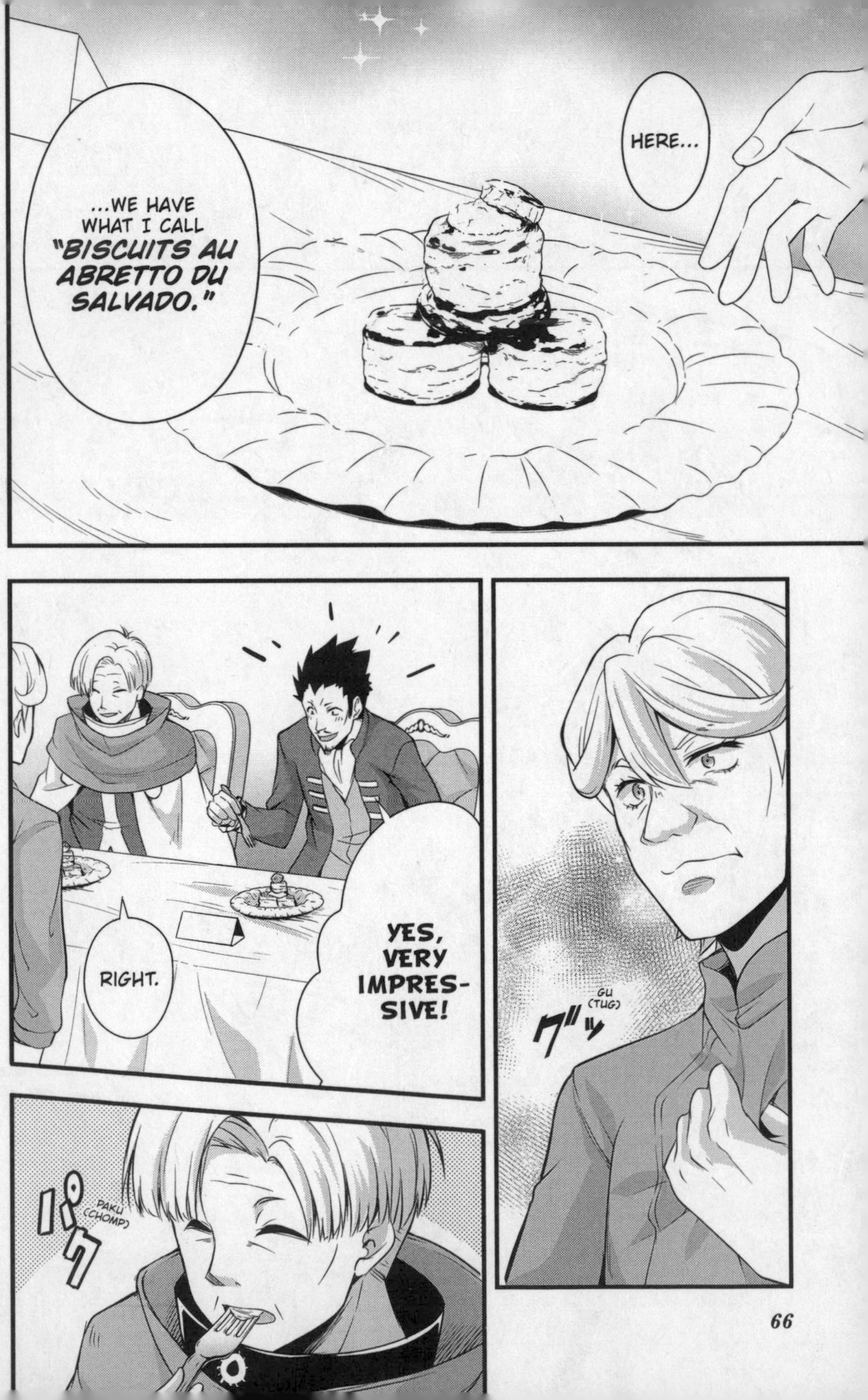
HERE...
...WE HAVE WHAT I CALL "BISCUITS AU ABRETTO DU SALVADO."
GU (TUG)
YES, VERY IMPRES-SIVE!
RIGHT.
PAKU (CHOMP)

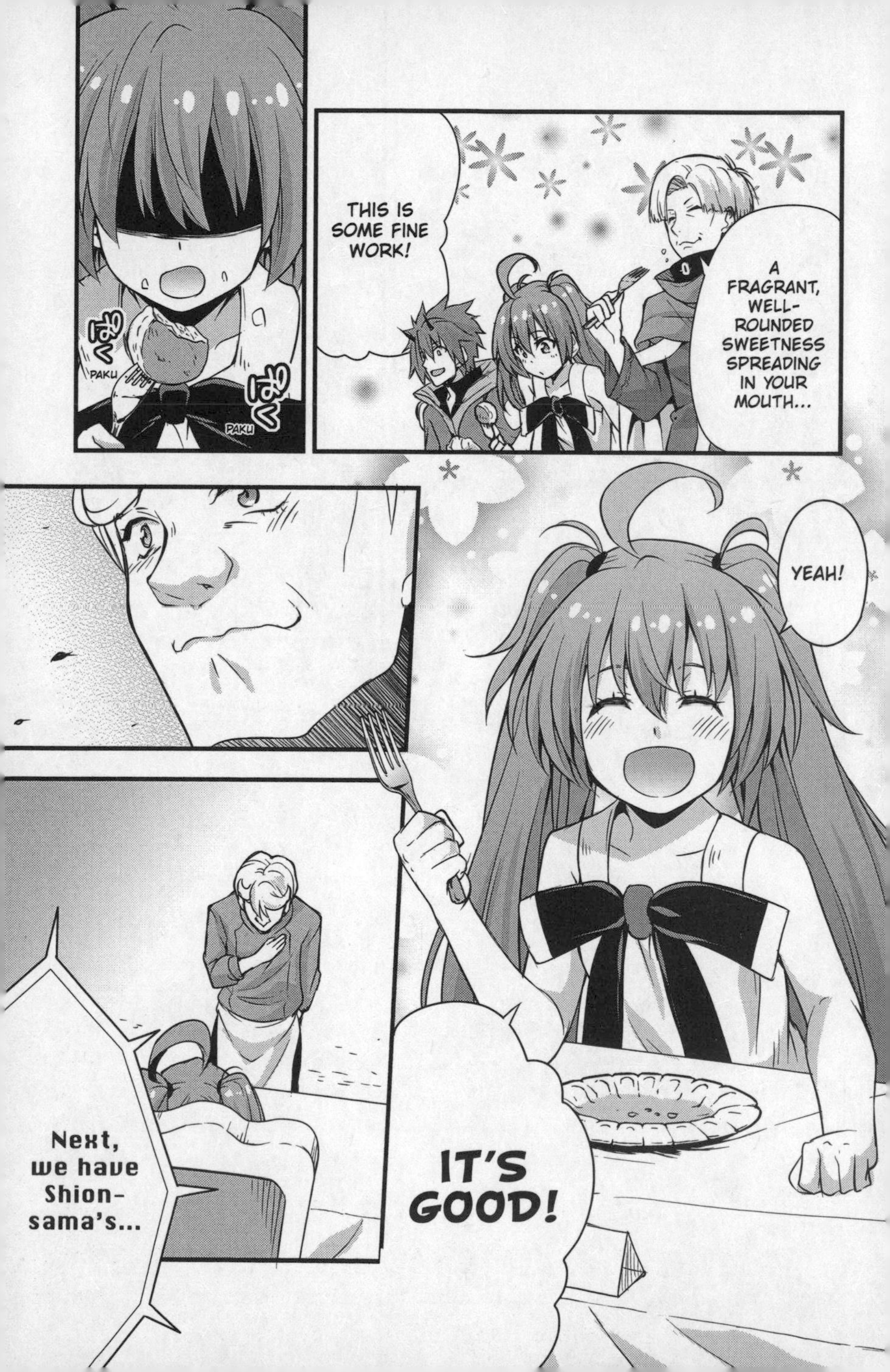
A FRAGRANT, WELL-ROUNDED SWEETNESS SPREADING IN YOUR MOUTH...
THIS IS SOME FINE WORK!
ぱく
PAKU
ぱく
PAKU
YEAH!
IT'S GOOD!
Next, we have Shion-sama's...

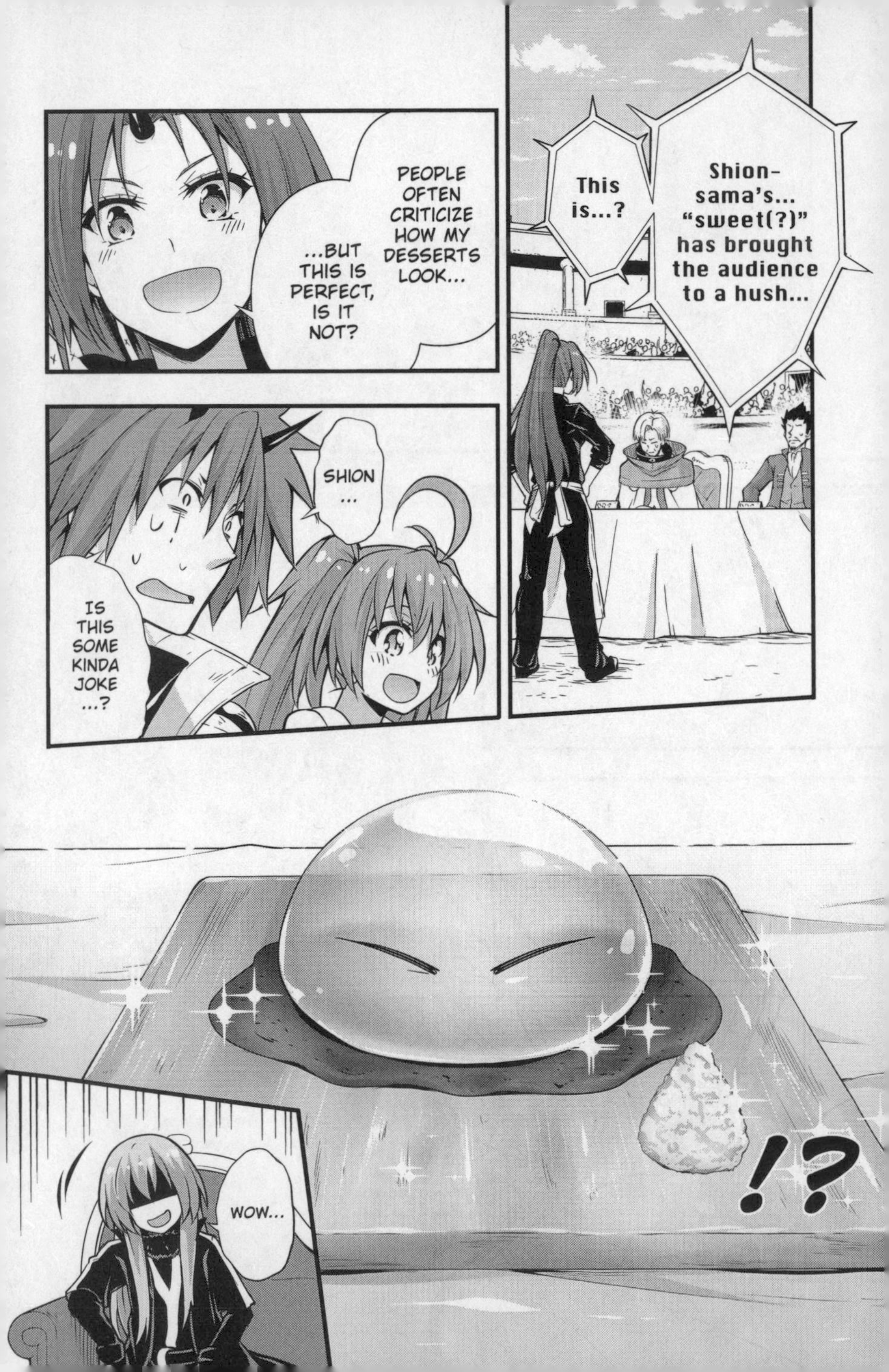
Shion-sama's... "sweet(?)" has brought the audience to a hush...
This is...?
PEOPLE OFTEN CRITICIZE HOW MY DESSERTS LOOK...
...BUT THIS IS PERFECT, IS IT NOT?
SHION...
IS THIS SOME KINDA JOKE...?
!?
WOW...

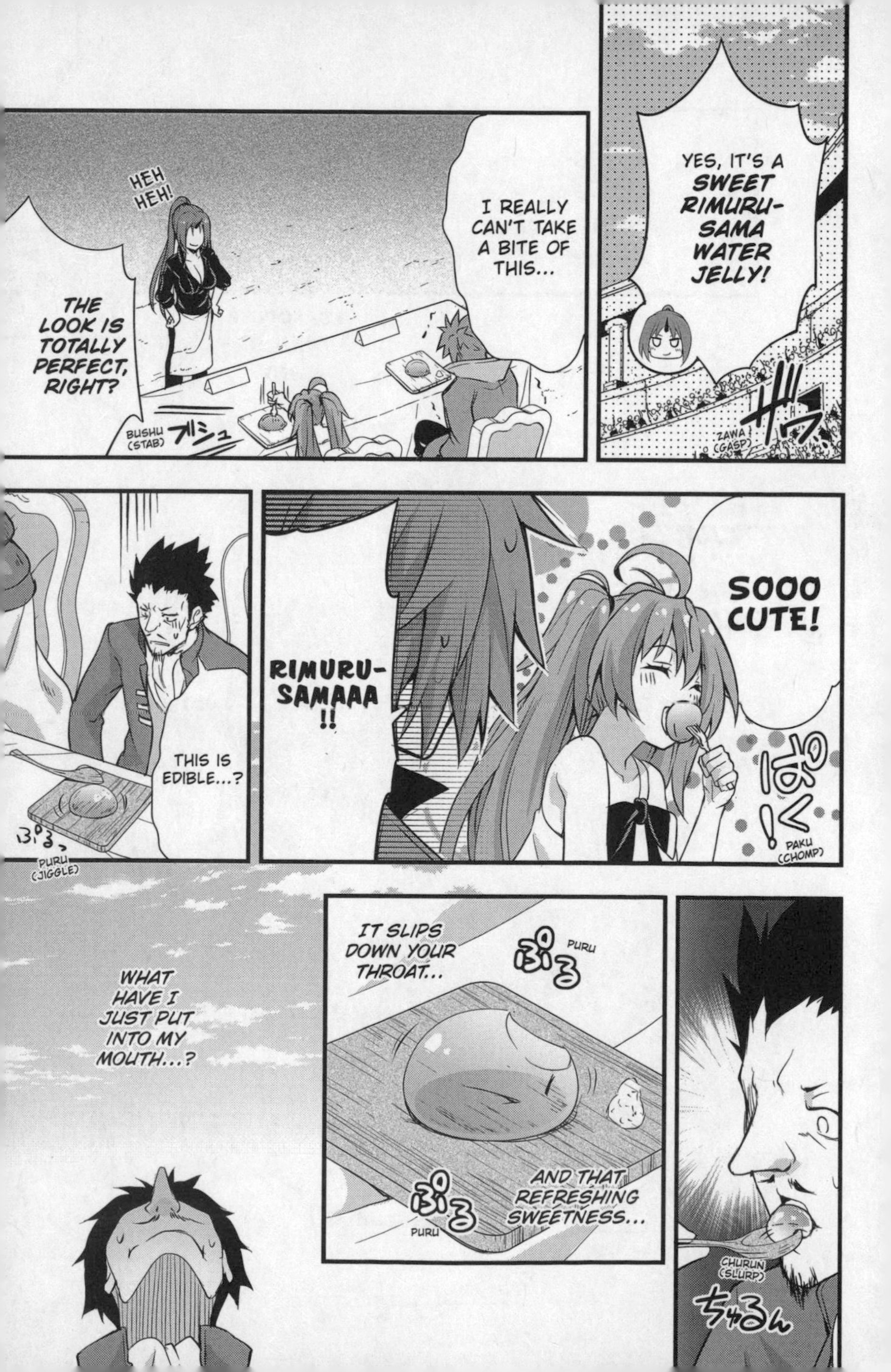
YES, IT'S A SWEET RIMURU-SAMA WATER JELLY!
ザワ
ZAWA (GASP)
I REALLY CAN'T TAKE A BITE OF THIS...
HEH HEH!
THE LOOK IS TOTALLY PERFECT, RIGHT?
BUSHU (STAB) ブシュ
SOOO CUTE!
RIMURU-SAMAAA!!
ぱく!
PAKU (CHOMP)
THIS IS EDIBLE...?
ぷるっ
PURU (JIGGLE)
CHURUN (SLURP)
ちゅるん
IT SLIPS DOWN YOUR THROAT...
ぷる
PURU
AND THAT REFRESHING SWEETNESS...
ぷる
PURU
WHAT HAVE I JUST PUT INTO MY MOUTH...?

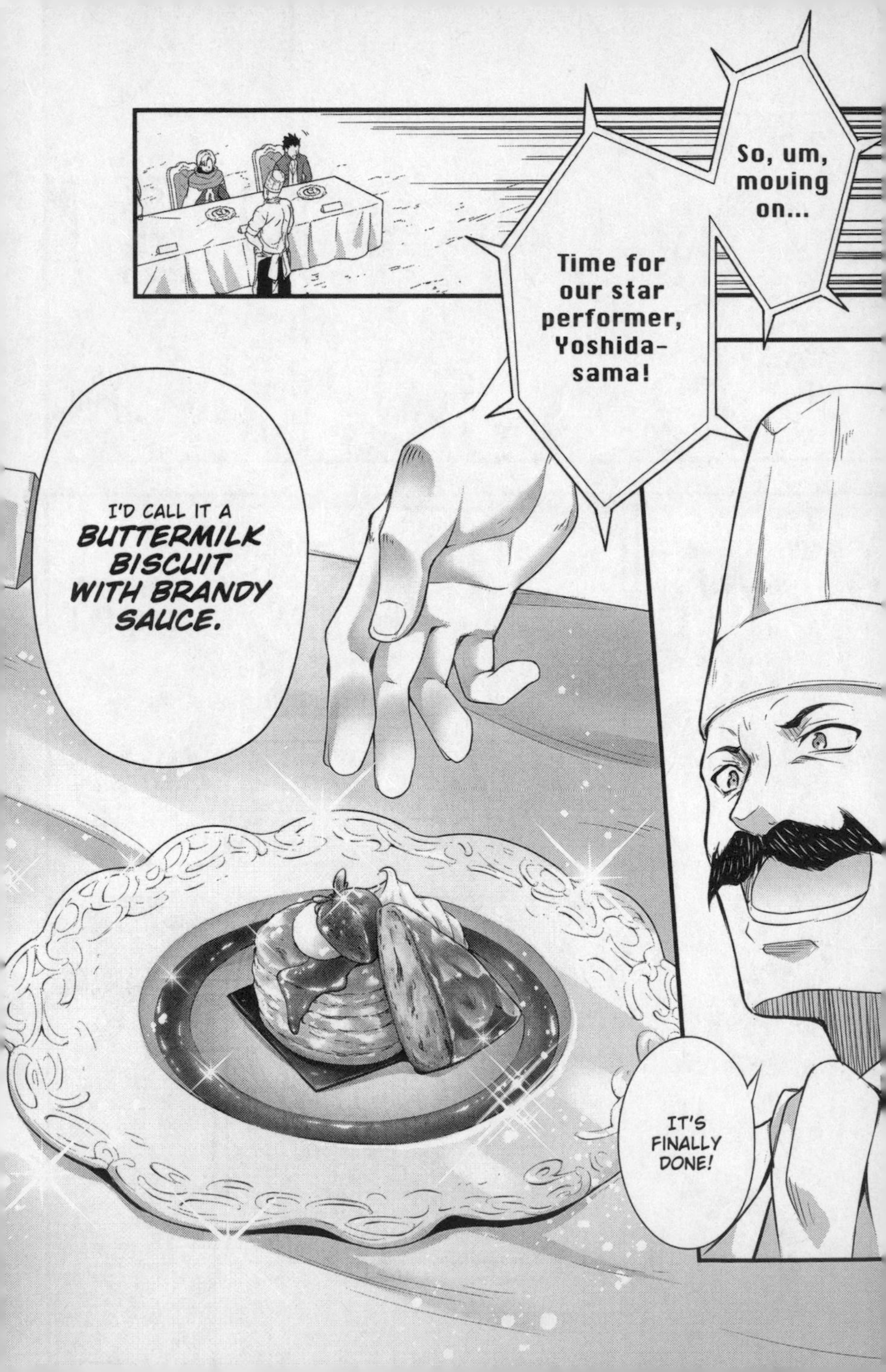
So, um, moving on...
Time for our star performer, Yoshida-sama!
IT'S FINALLY DONE!
I'D CALL IT A BUTTERMILK BISCUIT WITH BRANDY SAUCE.

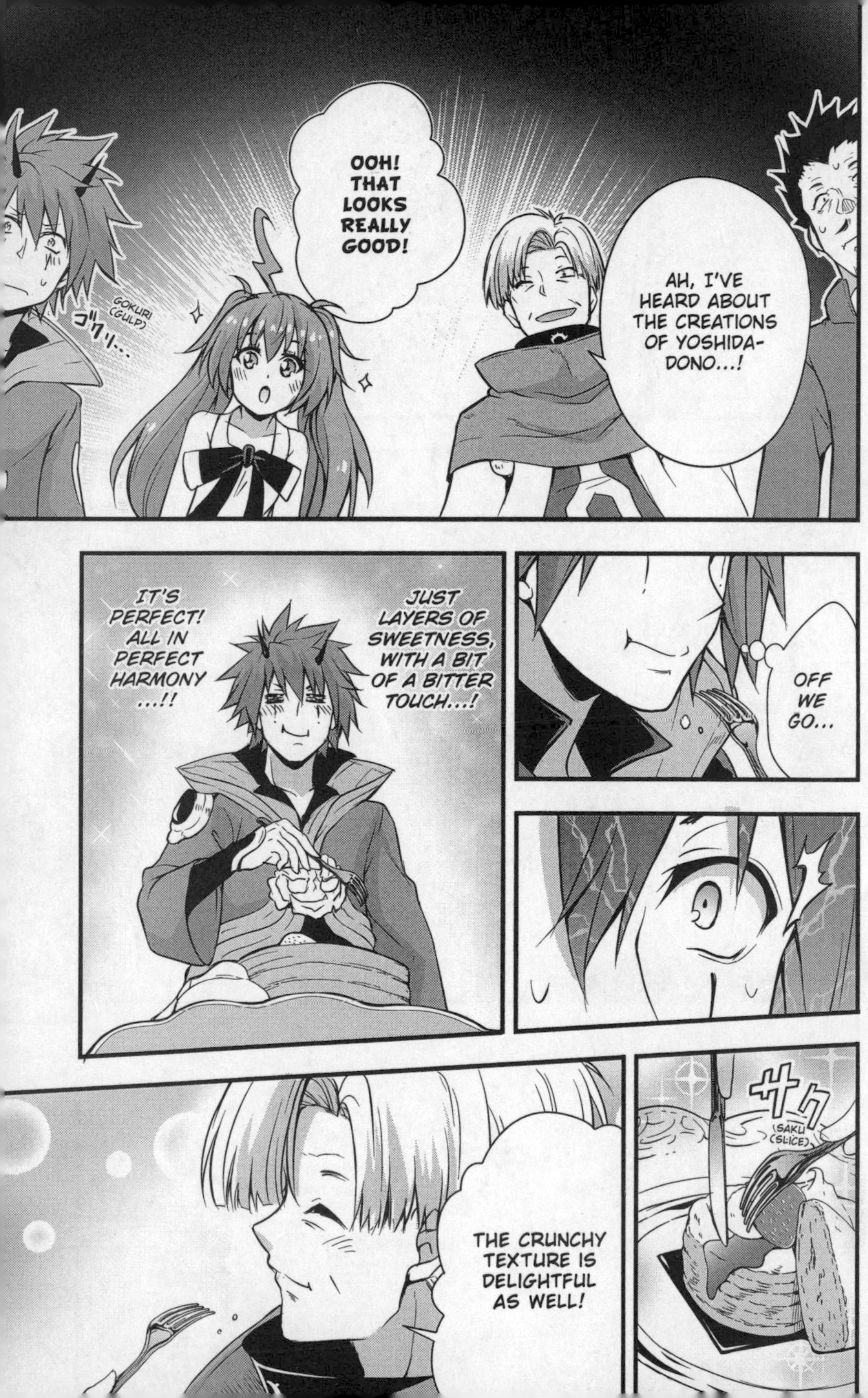
AH, I'VE HEARD ABOUT THE CREATIONS OF YOSHIDA-DONO...!
OOH! THAT LOOKS REALLY GOOD!
ゴクリ…
GOKURI (GULP)
OFF WE GO...
JUST LAYERS OF SWEETNESS, WITH A BIT OF A BITTER TOUCH...!
IT'S PERFECT! ALL IN PERFECT HARMONY...!!
サク
(SAKU) (SLICE)
THE CRUNCHY TEXTURE IS DELIGHTFUL AS WELL!

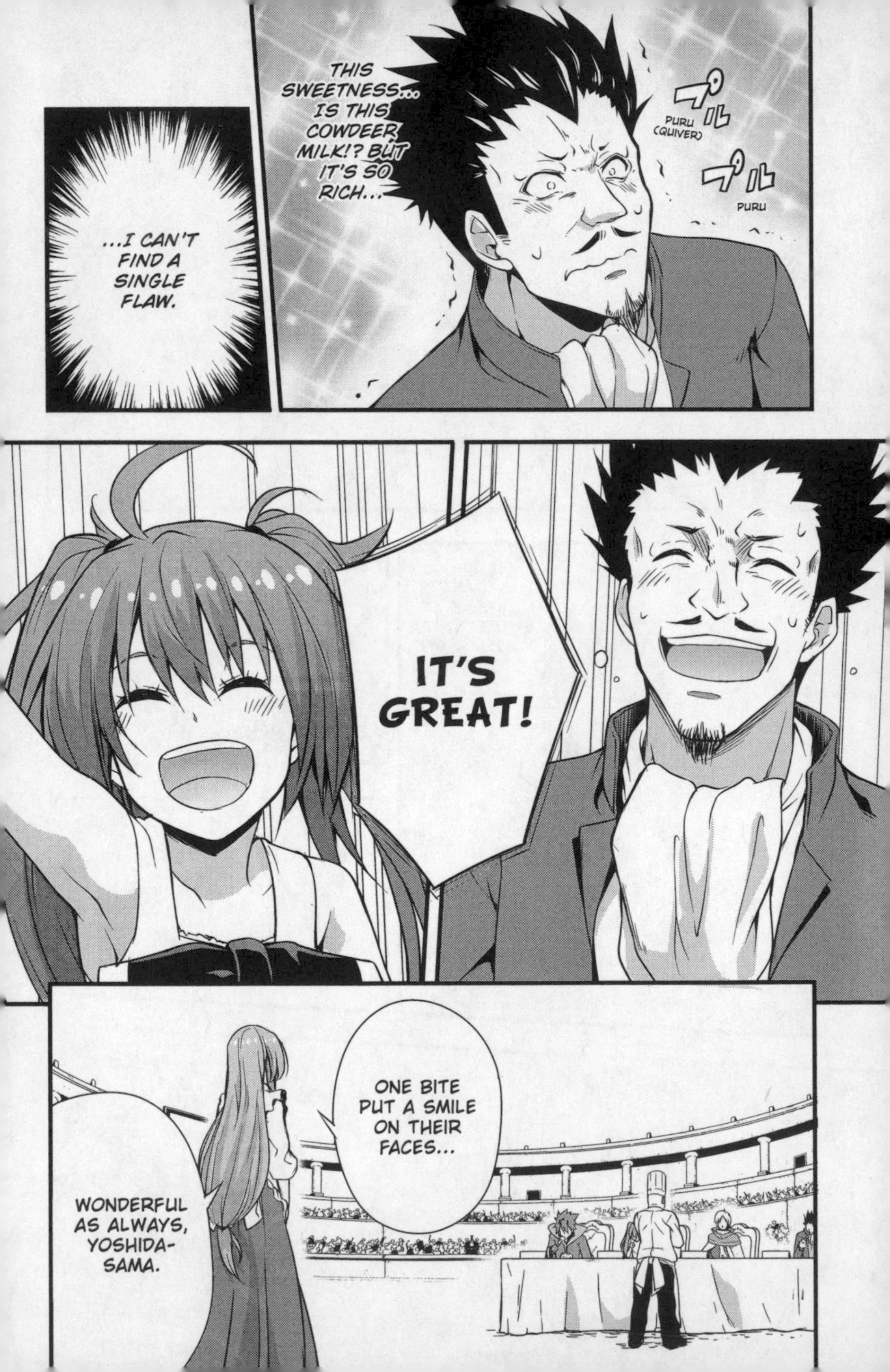
THIS SWEETNESS... IS THIS COWDEER MILK!? BUT IT'S SO RICH...
プル
PURU (QUIVER)
プル
PURU
...I CAN'T FIND A SINGLE FLAW.
IT'S GREAT!
ONE BITE PUT A SMILE ON THEIR FACES...
WONDERFUL AS ALWAYS, YOSHIDA-SAMA.

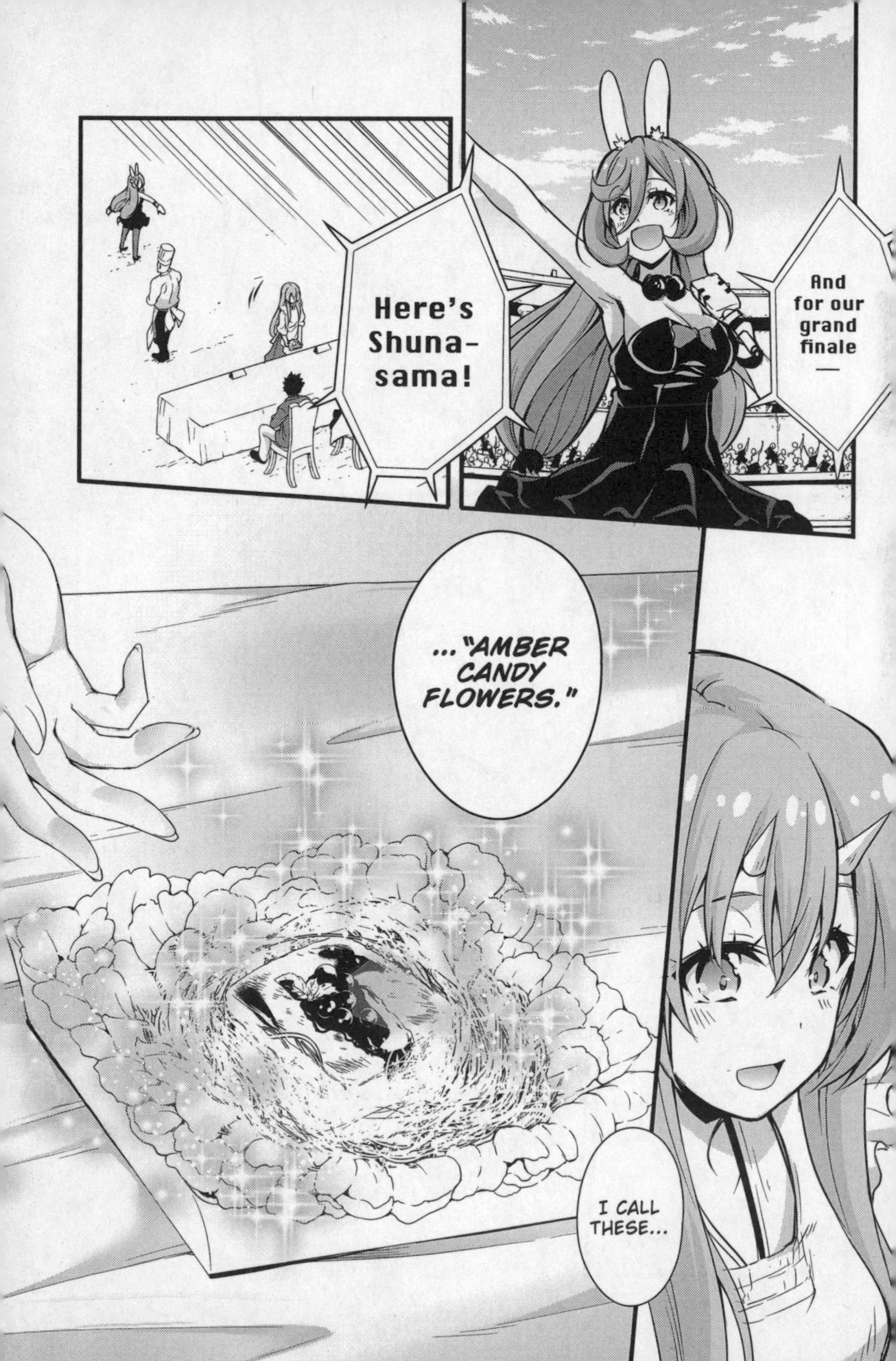
And for our grand finale —
Here's Shuna-sama!
I CALL THESE...
..."AMBER CANDY FLOWERS."

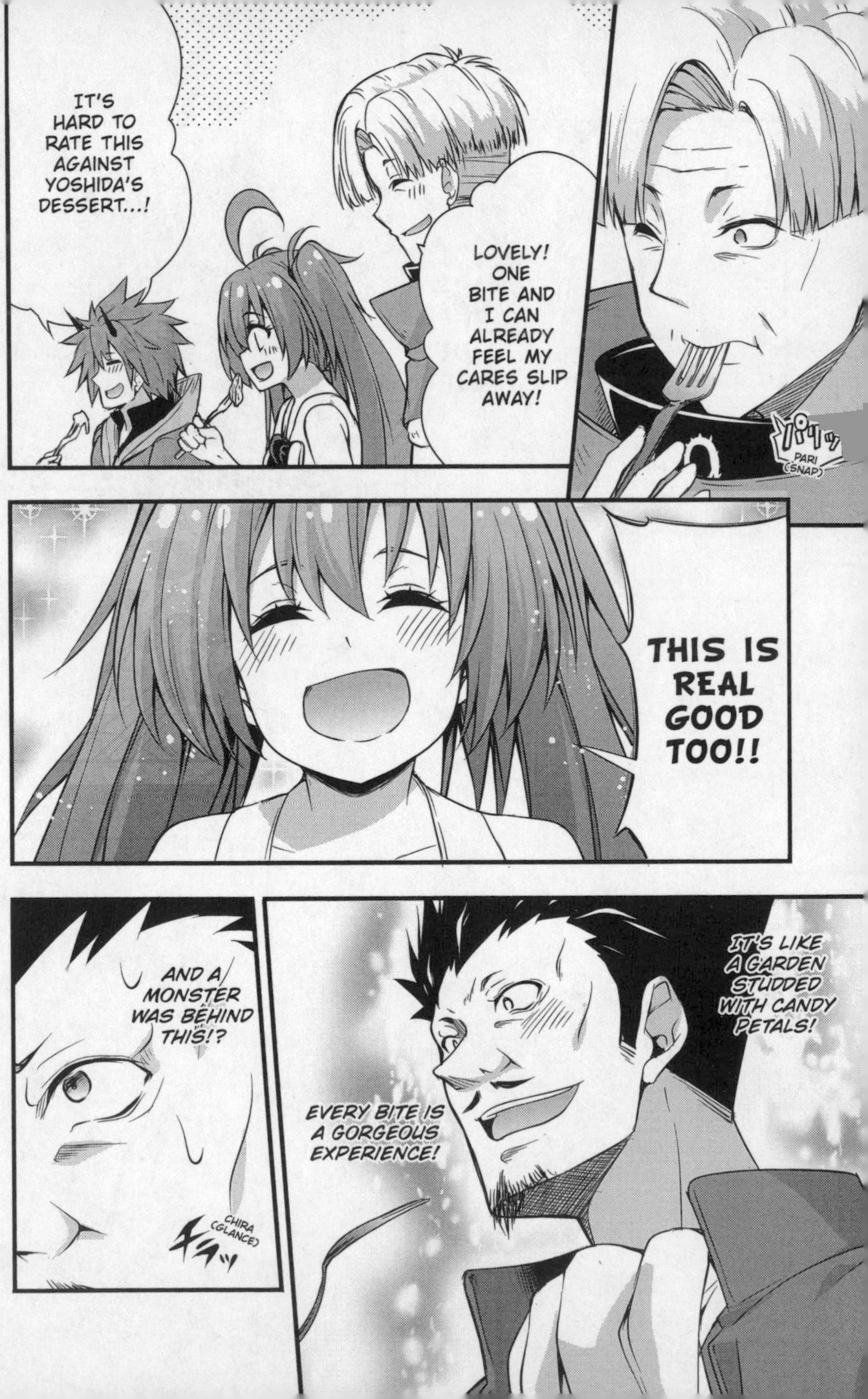
パリッ
PARI (SNAP)
LOVELY! ONE BITE AND I CAN ALREADY FEEL MY CARES SLIP AWAY!
IT'S HARD TO RATE THIS AGAINST YOSHIDA'S DESSERT...!
THIS IS REAL GOOD TOO!!
IT'S LIKE A GARDEN STUDDED WITH CANDY PETALS!
EVERY BITE IS A GORGEOUS EXPERIENCE!
AND A MONSTER WAS BEHIND THIS!?
チラッ
CHIRA (GLANCE)

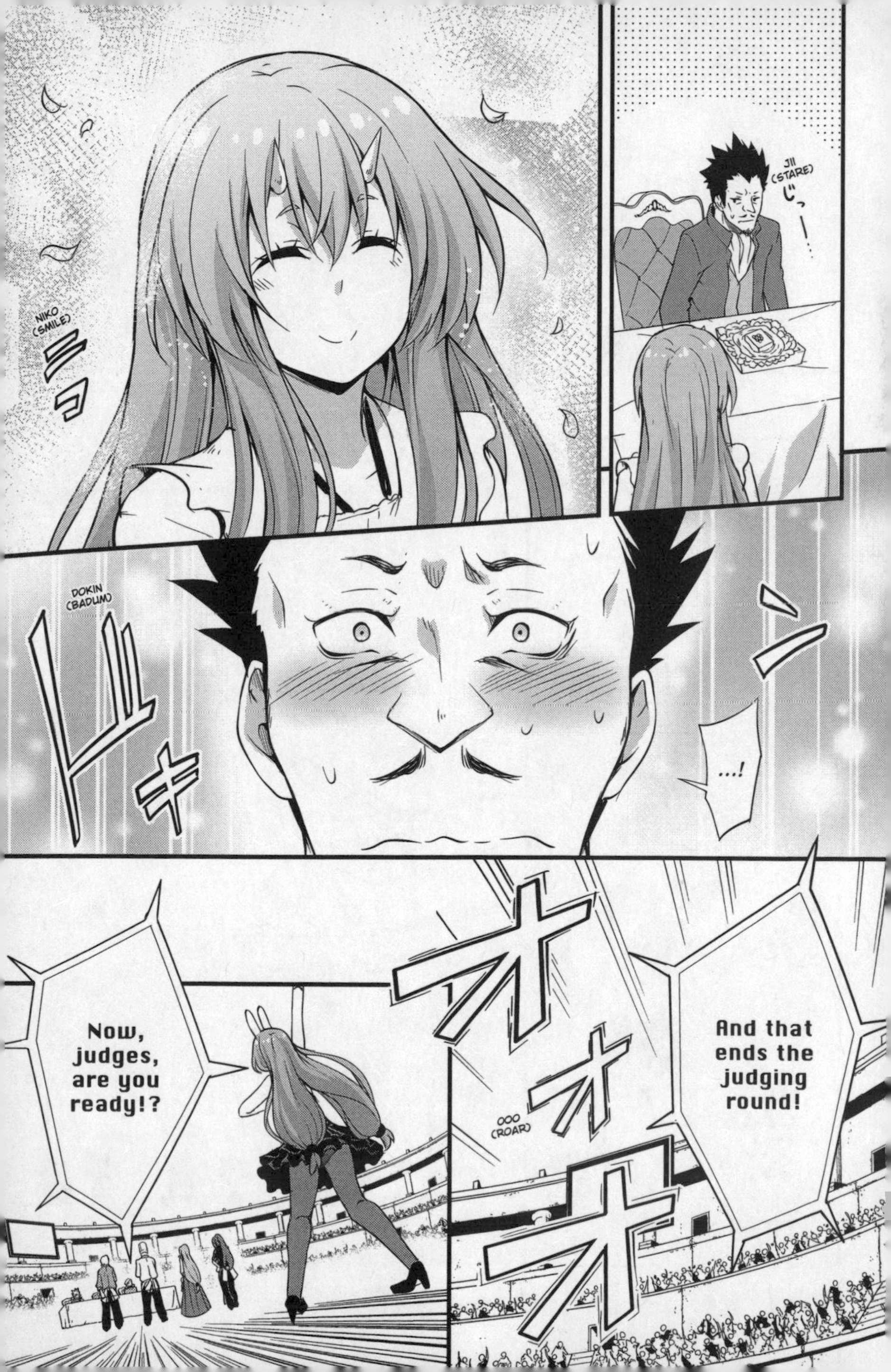

JII (STARE)
じっ
NIKO (SMILE)
ニコッ
DOKIN (BADUM)
ドキッ
...!
And that ends the judging round!
OOO (ROAR)
オオオオ
Now, judges, are you ready!?

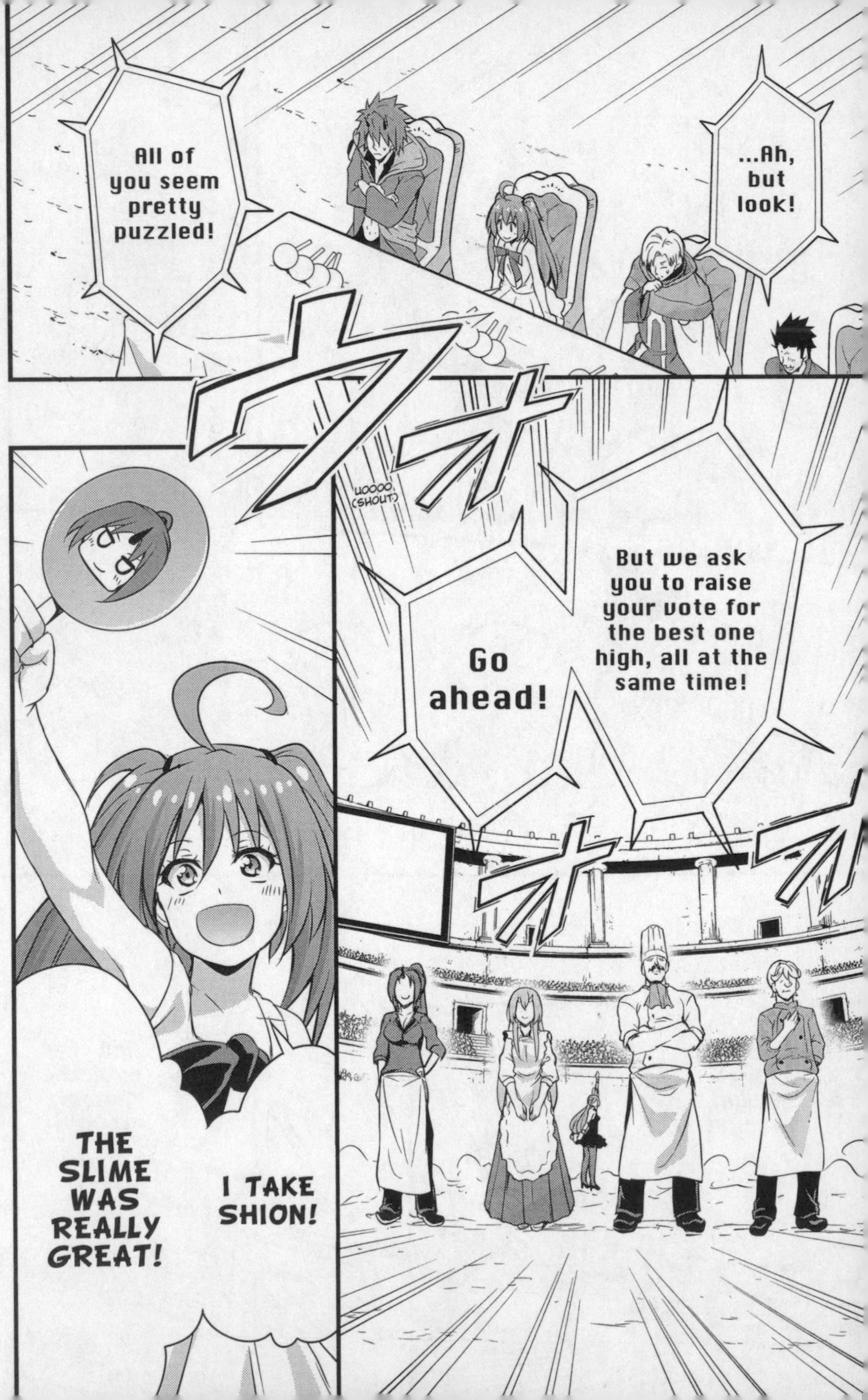
...Ah, but look!
All of you seem pretty puzzled!
UOOOO (SHOUT)
But we ask you to raise your vote for the best one high, all at the same time!
Go ahead!
I TAKE SHION!
THE SLIME WAS REALLY GREAT!

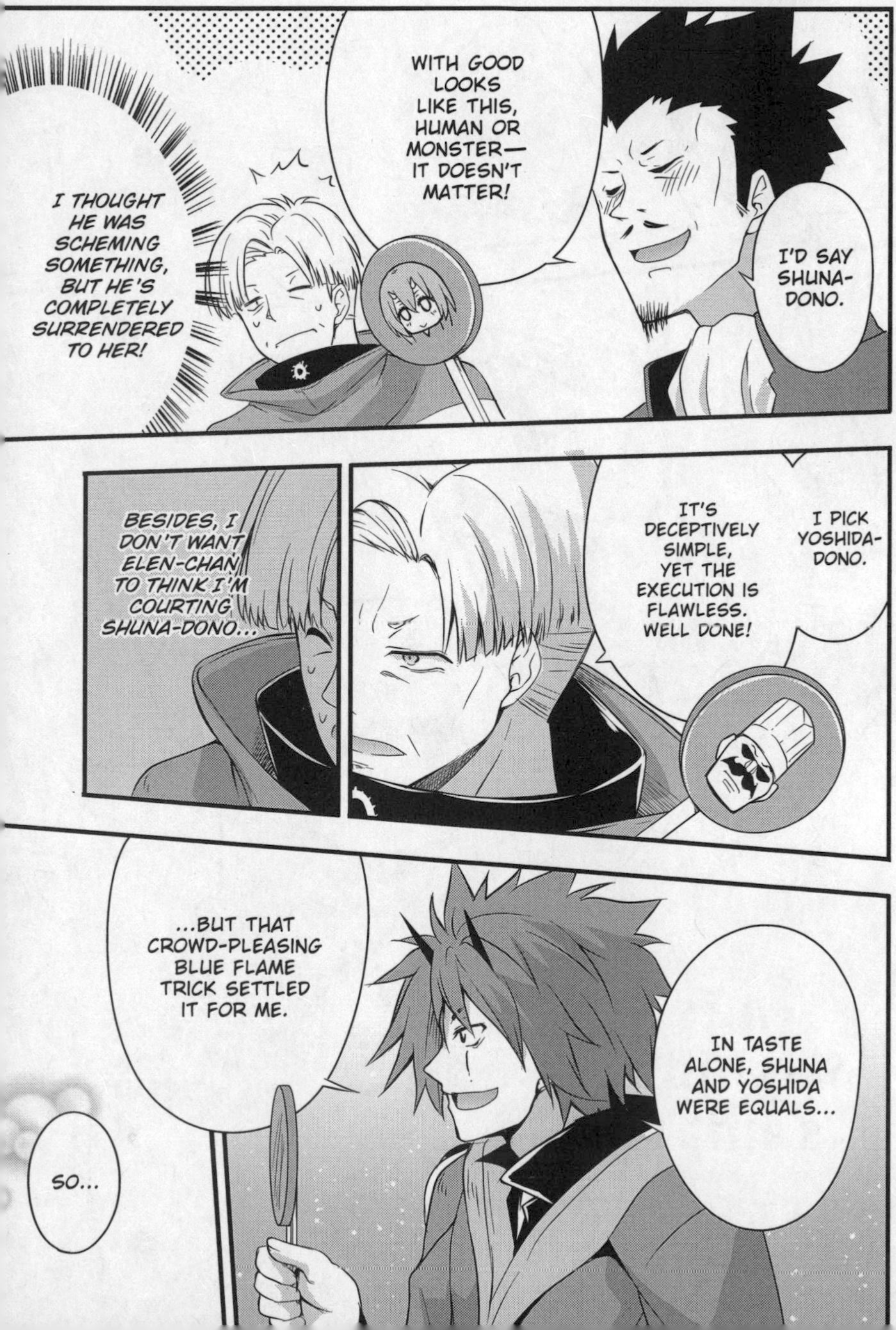
I'D SAY SHUNA-DONO.
WITH GOOD LOOKS LIKE THIS, HUMAN OR MONSTER— IT DOESN'T MATTER!
I THOUGHT HE WAS SCHEMING SOMETHING, BUT HE'S COMPLETELY SURRENDERED TO HER!
I PICK YOSHIDA-DONO.
IT'S DECEPTIVELY SIMPLE, YET THE EXECUTION IS FLAWLESS. WELL DONE!
BESIDES, I DON'T WANT ELEN-CHAN TO THINK I'M COURTING SHUNA-DONO...
IN TASTE ALONE, SHUNA AND YOSHIDA WERE EQUALS...
...BUT THAT CROWD-PLEASING BLUE FLAME TRICK SETTLED IT FOR ME.
SO...

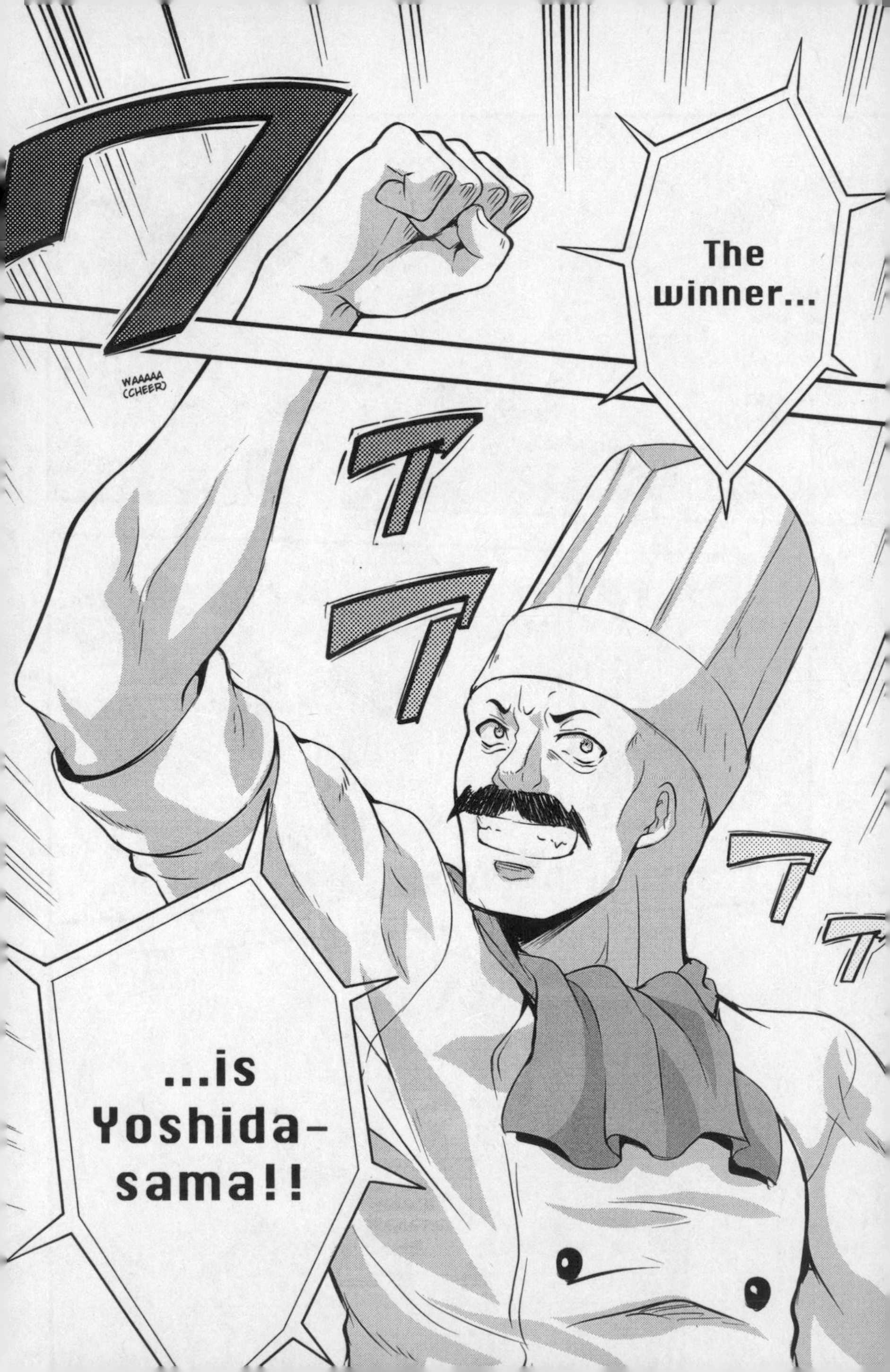
The winner...
WAAAAA (CHEER)
...is Yoshida-sama!!

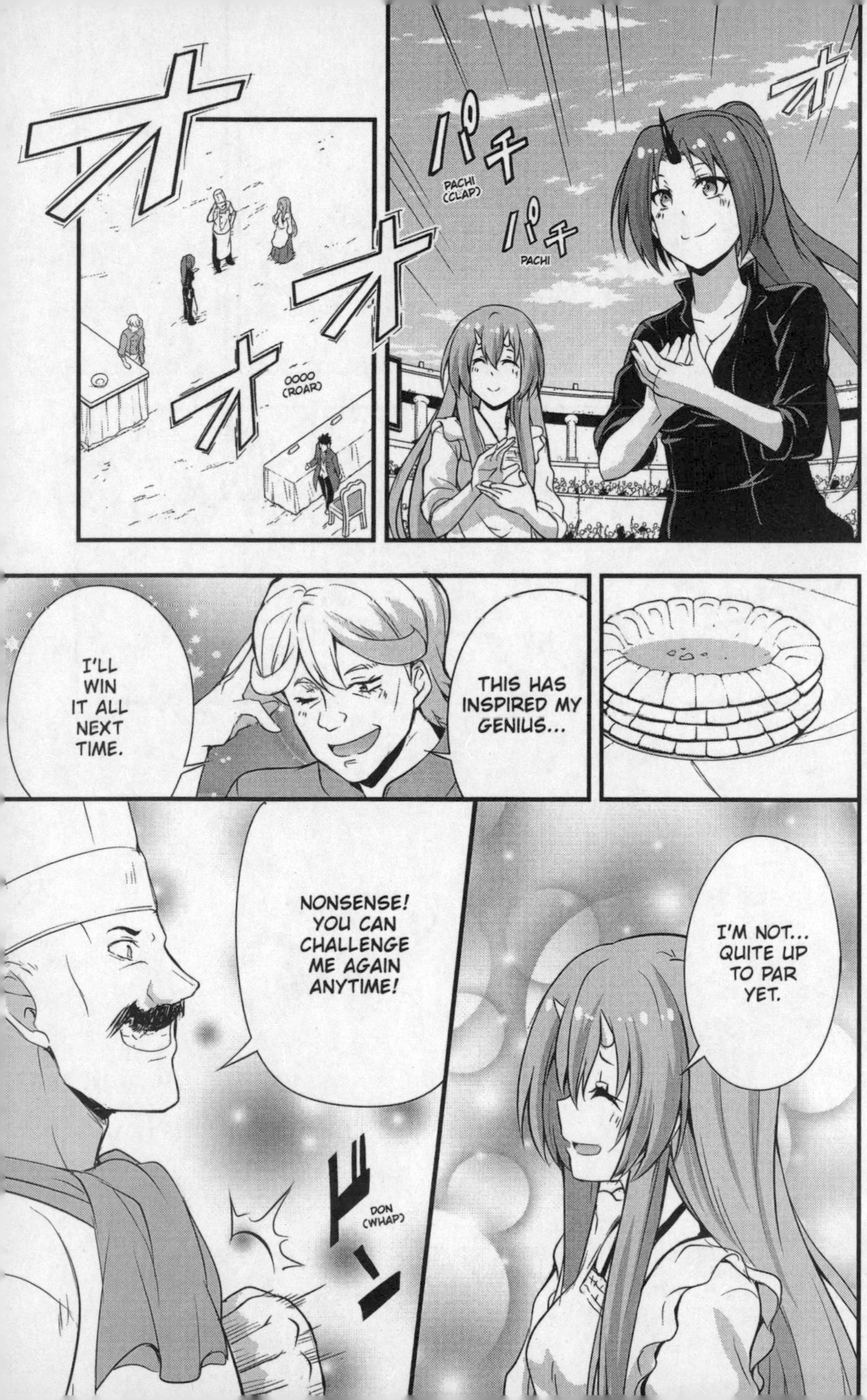
オ
パチ
PACHI (CLAP)
パチ
PACHI
オオオオ
OOOO (ROAR)
THIS HAS INSPIRED MY GENIUS...
I'LL WIN IT ALL NEXT TIME.
I'M NOT... QUITE UP TO PAR YET.
NONSENSE! YOU CAN CHALLENGE ME AGAIN ANYTIME!
ドーン
DON (WHAP)

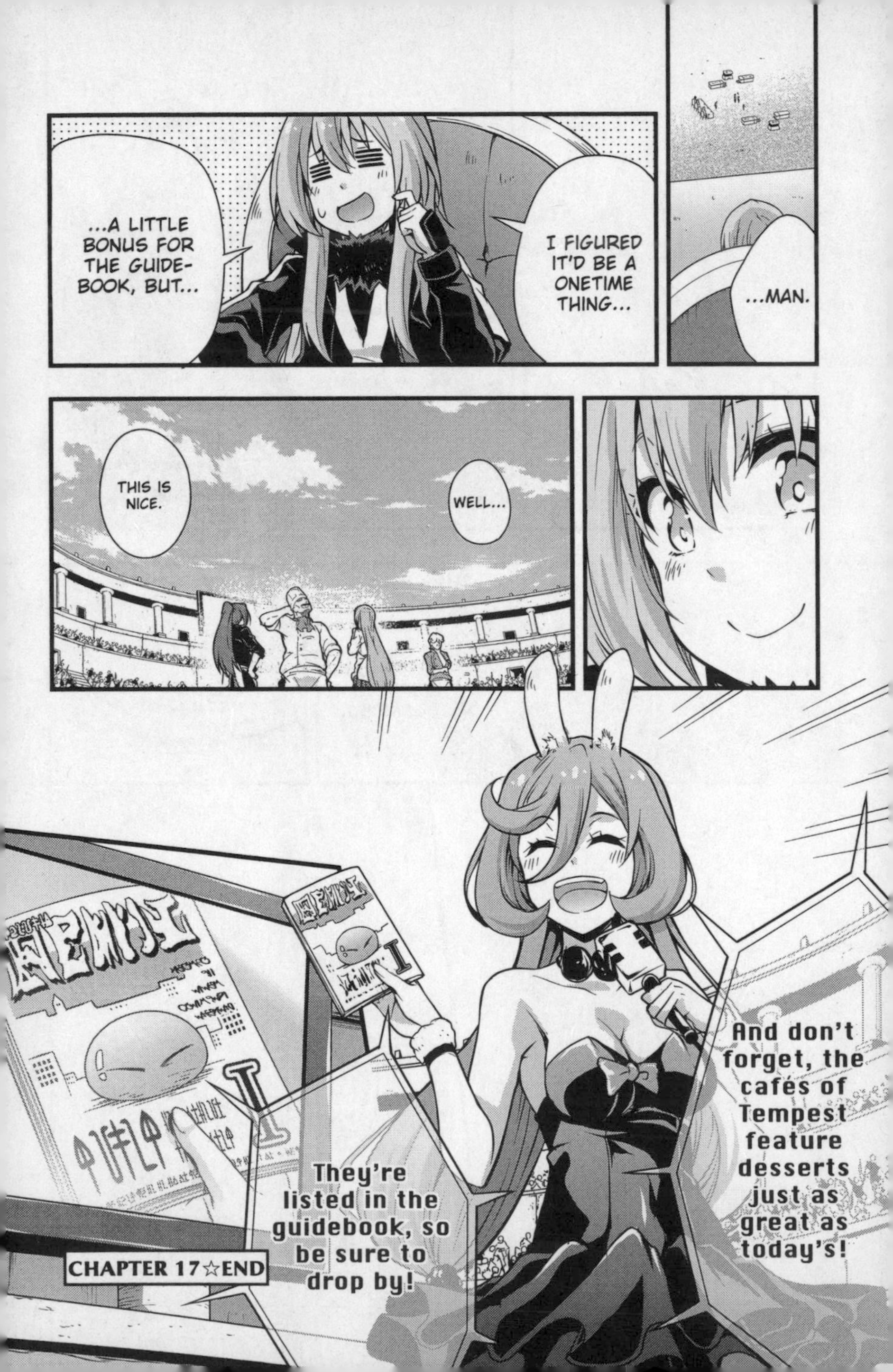
...MAN.
I FIGURED IT'D BE A ONETIME THING...
...A LITTLE BONUS FOR THE GUIDE-BOOK, BUT...
WELL...
THIS IS NICE.
And don't forget, the cafés of Tempest feature desserts just as great as today's!
They're listed in the guidebook, so be sure to drop by!
CHAPTER 17☆END

That **Time I Got
Reìncarnated
as SLIME**
The Ways of the Monster Nation

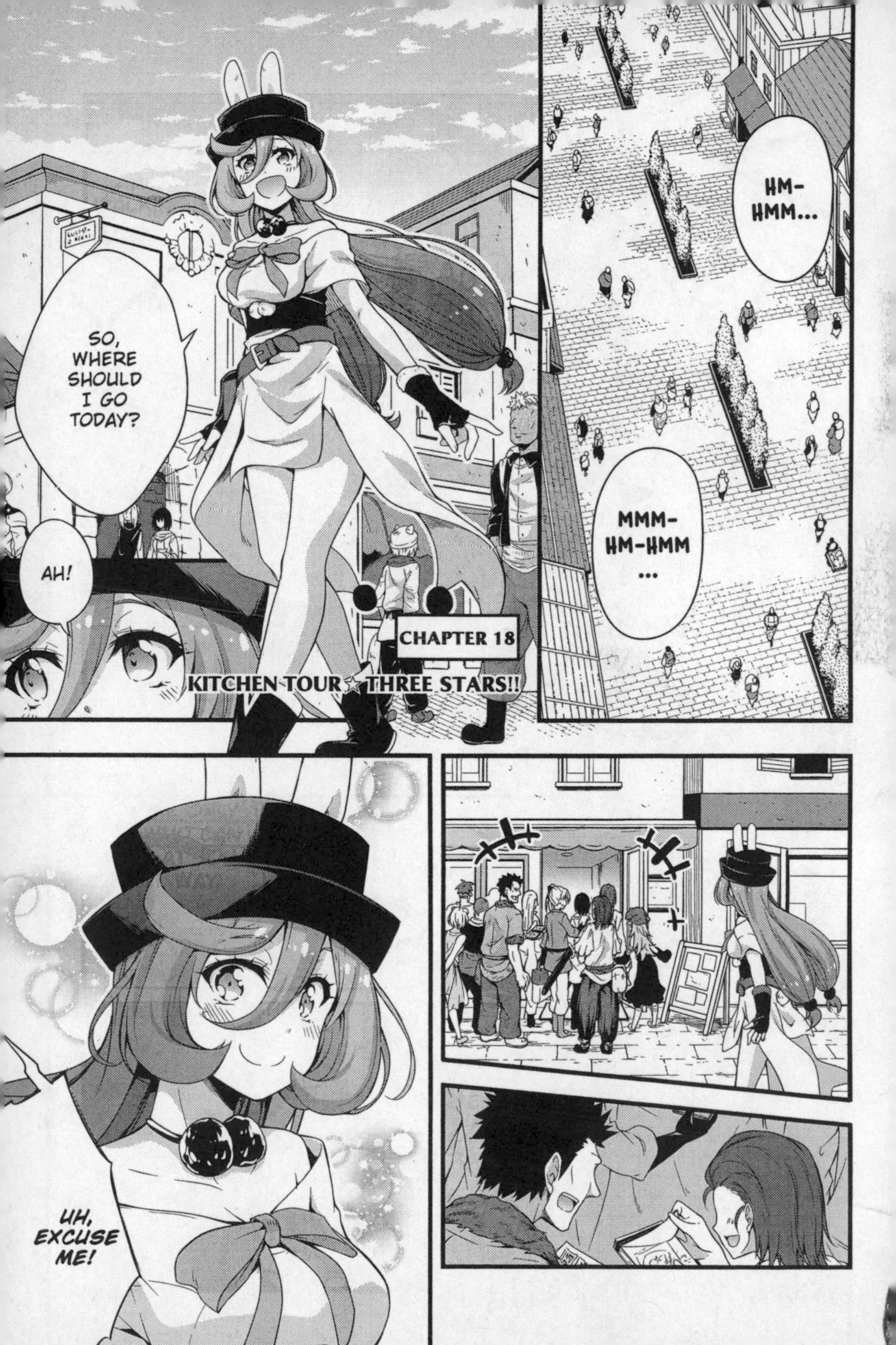
HM-HMM...
MMM-HM-HMM...
SO, WHERE SHOULD I GO TODAY?
AH!
CHAPTER 18
KITCHEN TOUR☆THREE STARS!!
UH, EXCUSE ME!

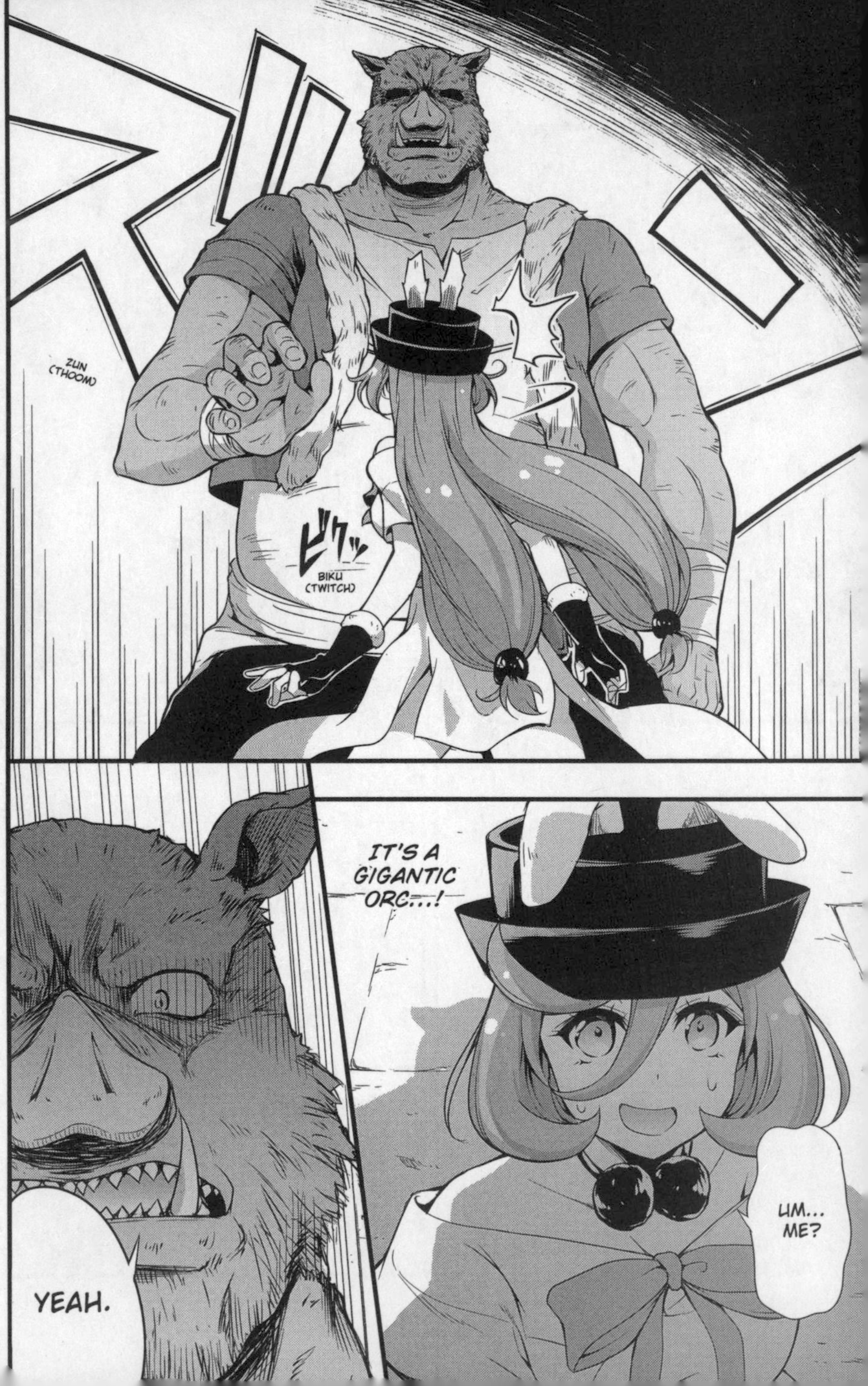
ZUN
(THOOM)
ビクッ
BIKU
(TWITCH)
IT'S A GIGANTIC ORC...!
UM... ME?
YEAH.

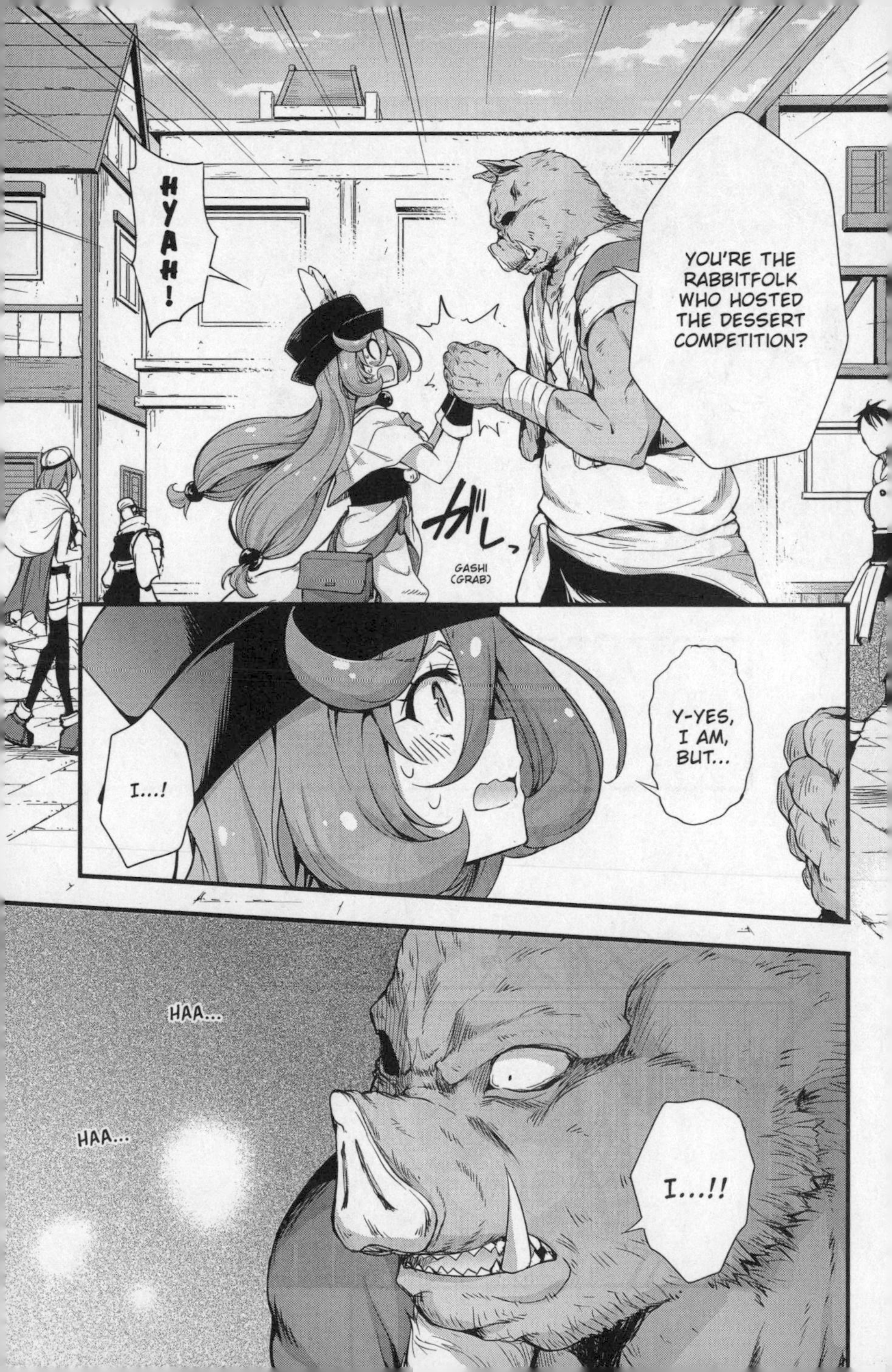
YOU'RE THE RABBITFOLK WHO HOSTED THE DESSERT COMPETITION?
HYAH!
GASHI (GRAB)
Y-YES, I AM, BUT...
I...!
I...!!
HAA...
HAA...

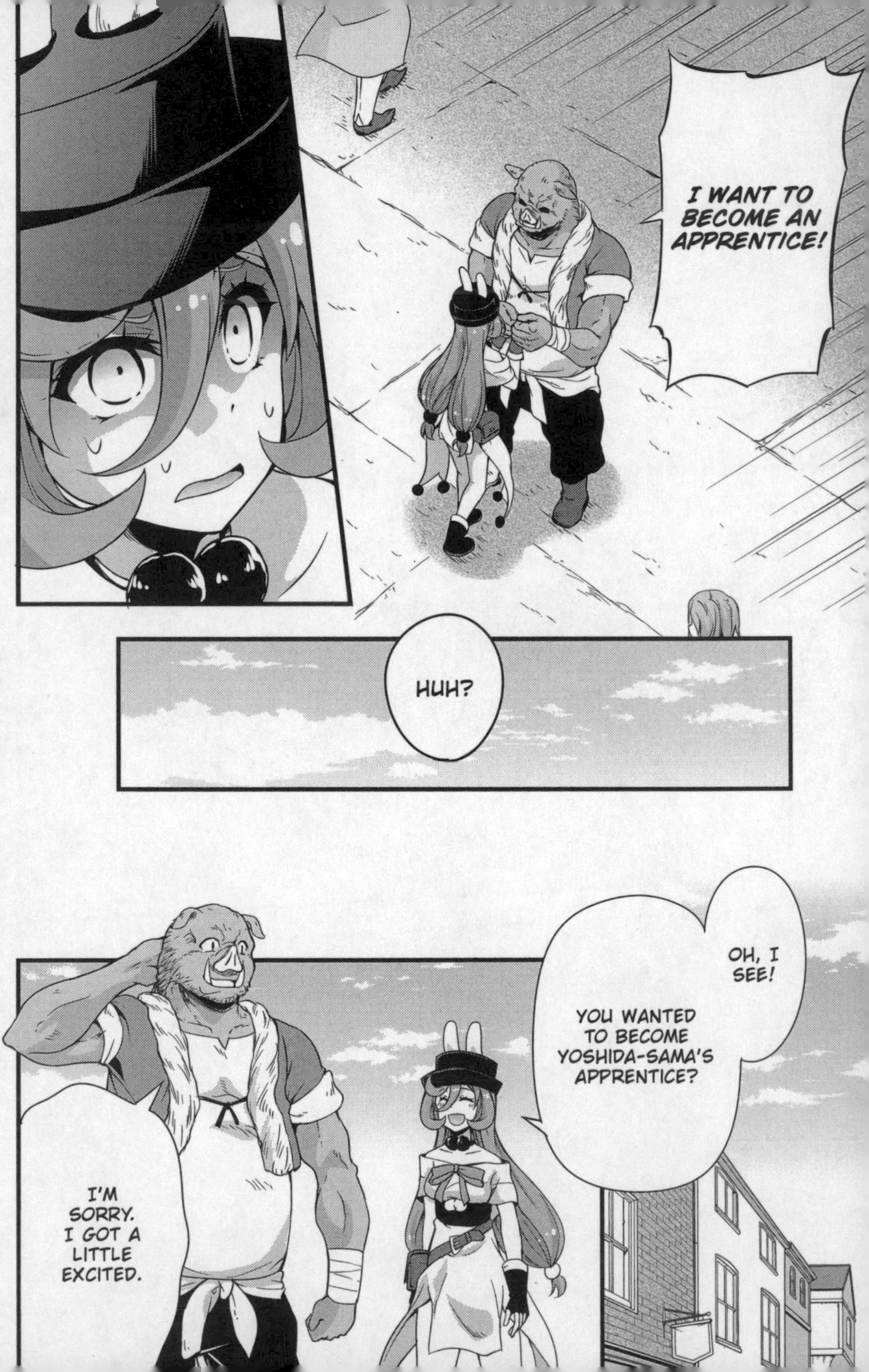
I WANT TO BECOME AN APPRENTICE!
HUH?
OH, I SEE!
YOU WANTED TO BECOME YOSHIDA-SAMA'S APPRENTICE?
I'M SORRY. I GOT A LITTLE EXCITED.

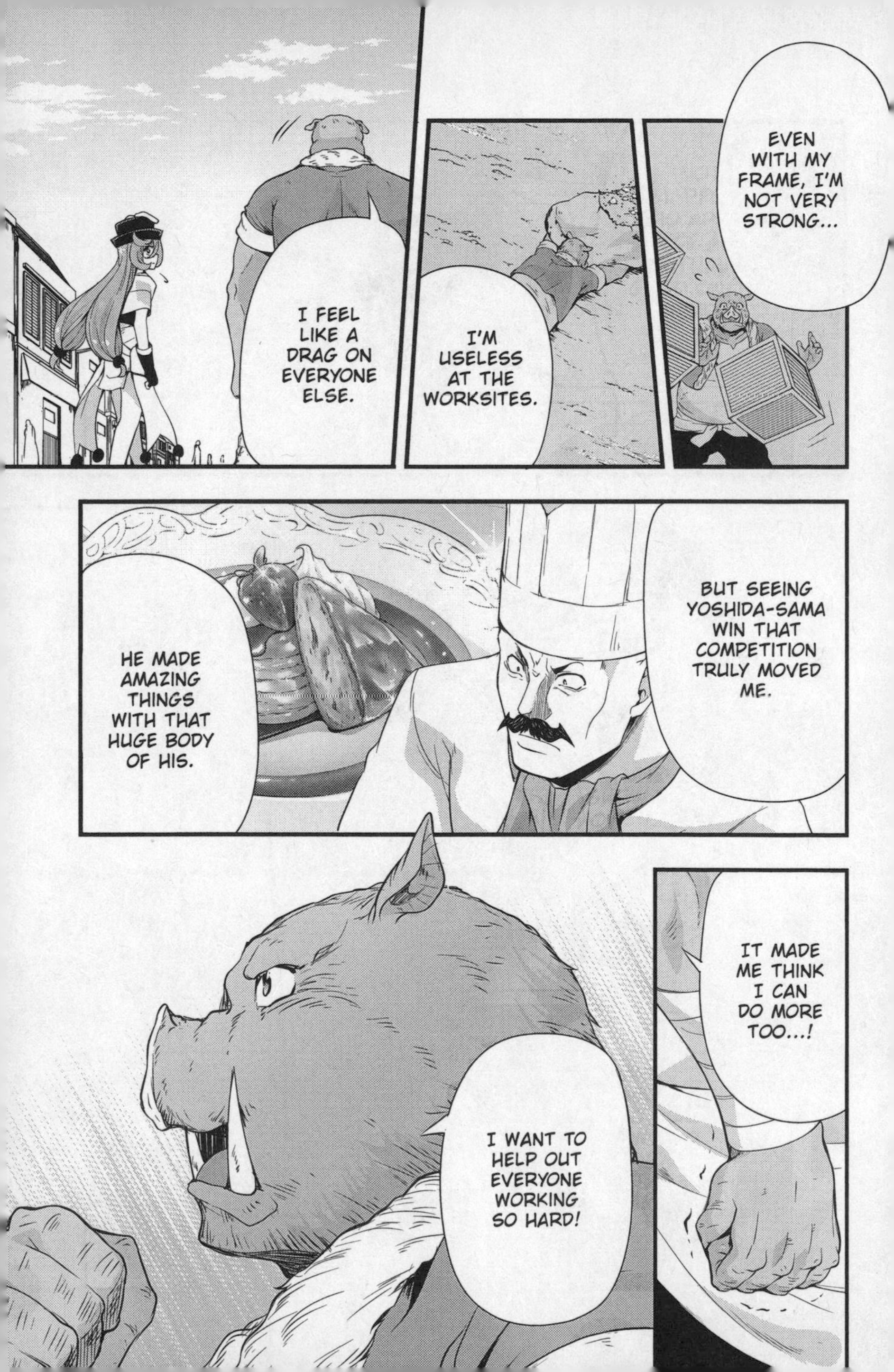
EVEN WITH MY FRAME, I'M NOT VERY STRONG...
I'M USELESS AT THE WORKSITES.
I FEEL LIKE A DRAG ON EVERYONE ELSE.
BUT SEEING YOSHIDA-SAMA WIN THAT COMPETITION TRULY MOVED ME.
HE MADE AMAZING THINGS WITH THAT HUGE BODY OF HIS.
IT MADE ME THINK I CAN DO MORE TOO...!
I WANT TO HELP OUT EVERYONE WORKING SO HARD!

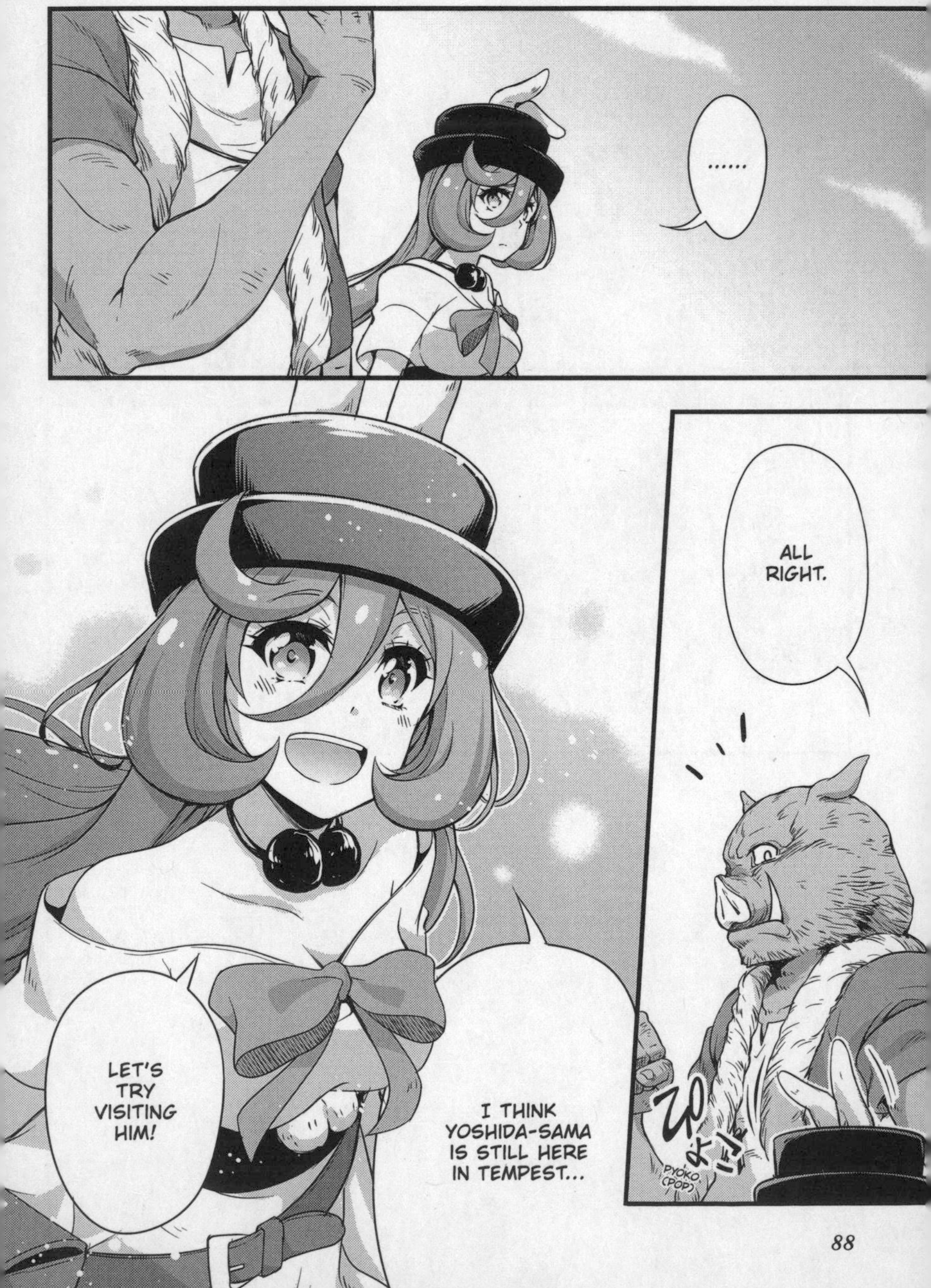
......
ALL RIGHT.
PYOKO (POP)
I THINK YOSHIDA-SAMA IS STILL HERE IN TEMPEST...
LET'S TRY VISITING HIM!

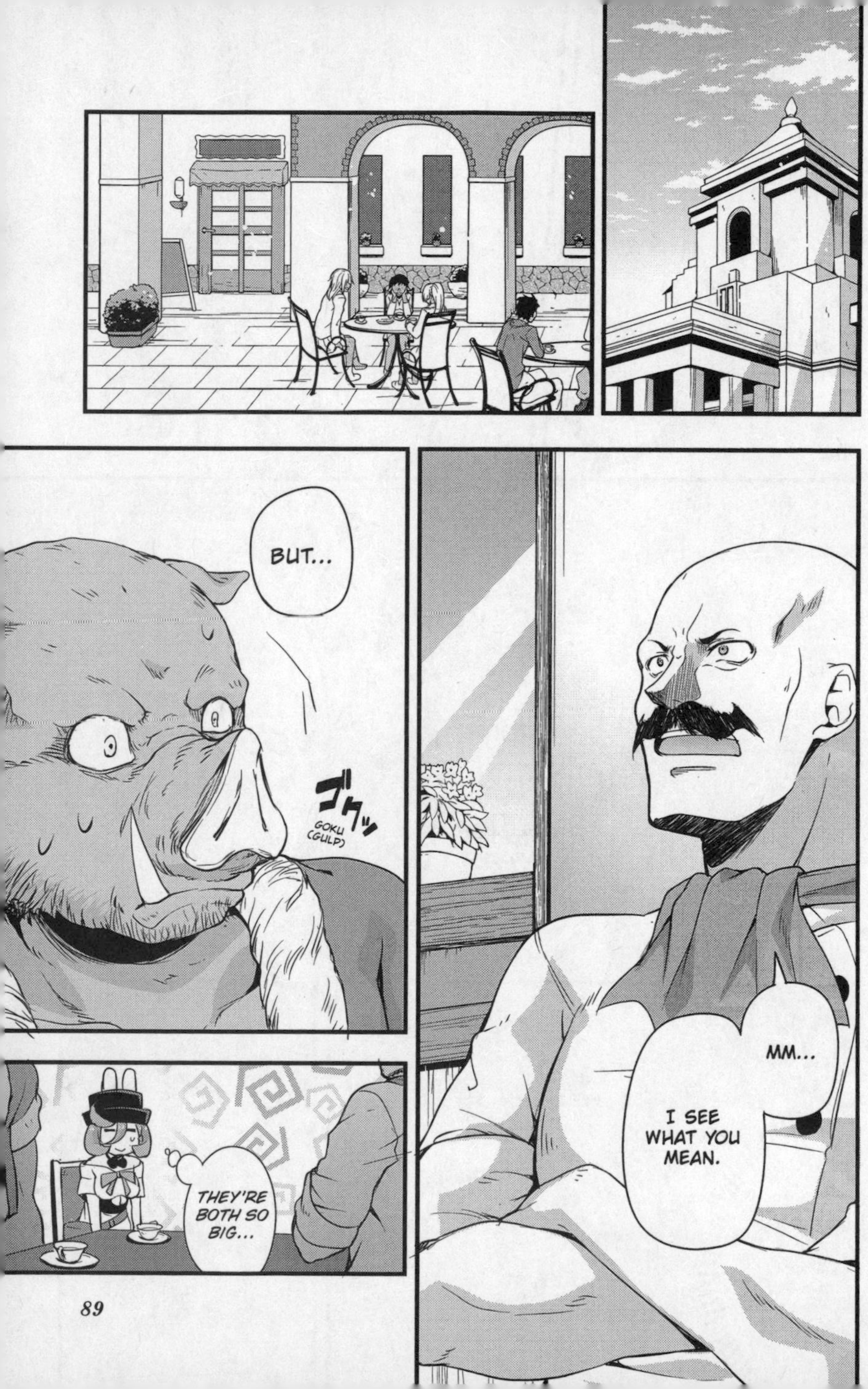
MM...
I SEE WHAT YOU MEAN.
BUT...
ゴクッ
GOKU (GULP)
THEY'RE BOTH SO BIG...

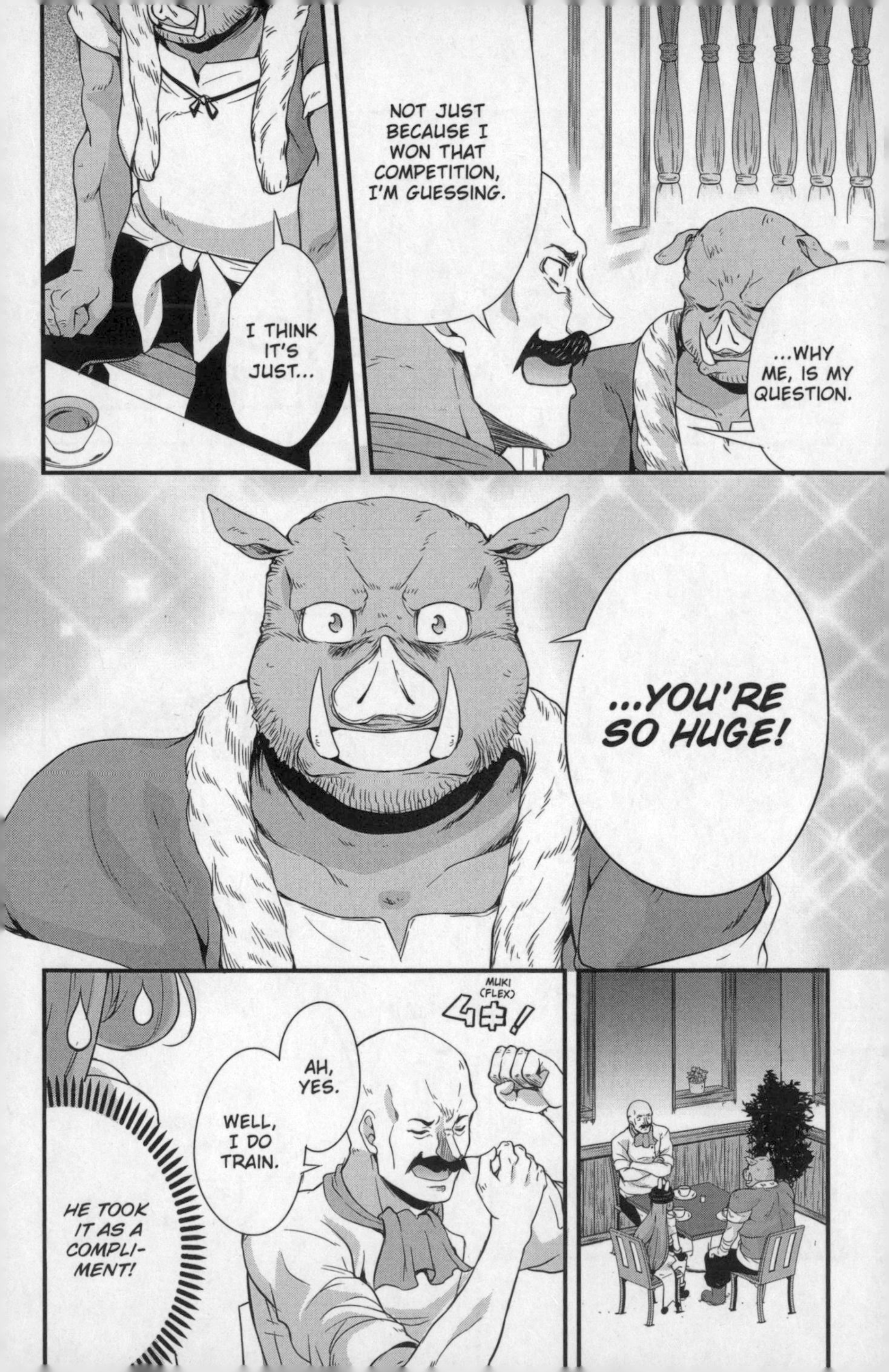
NOT JUST BECAUSE I WON THAT COMPETITION, I'M GUESSING.
...WHY ME, IS MY QUESTION.
I THINK IT'S JUST...
...YOU'RE SO HUGE!
MUKI (FLEX)
ムキ!
AH, YES.
WELL, I DO TRAIN.
HE TOOK IT AS A COMPLIMENT!

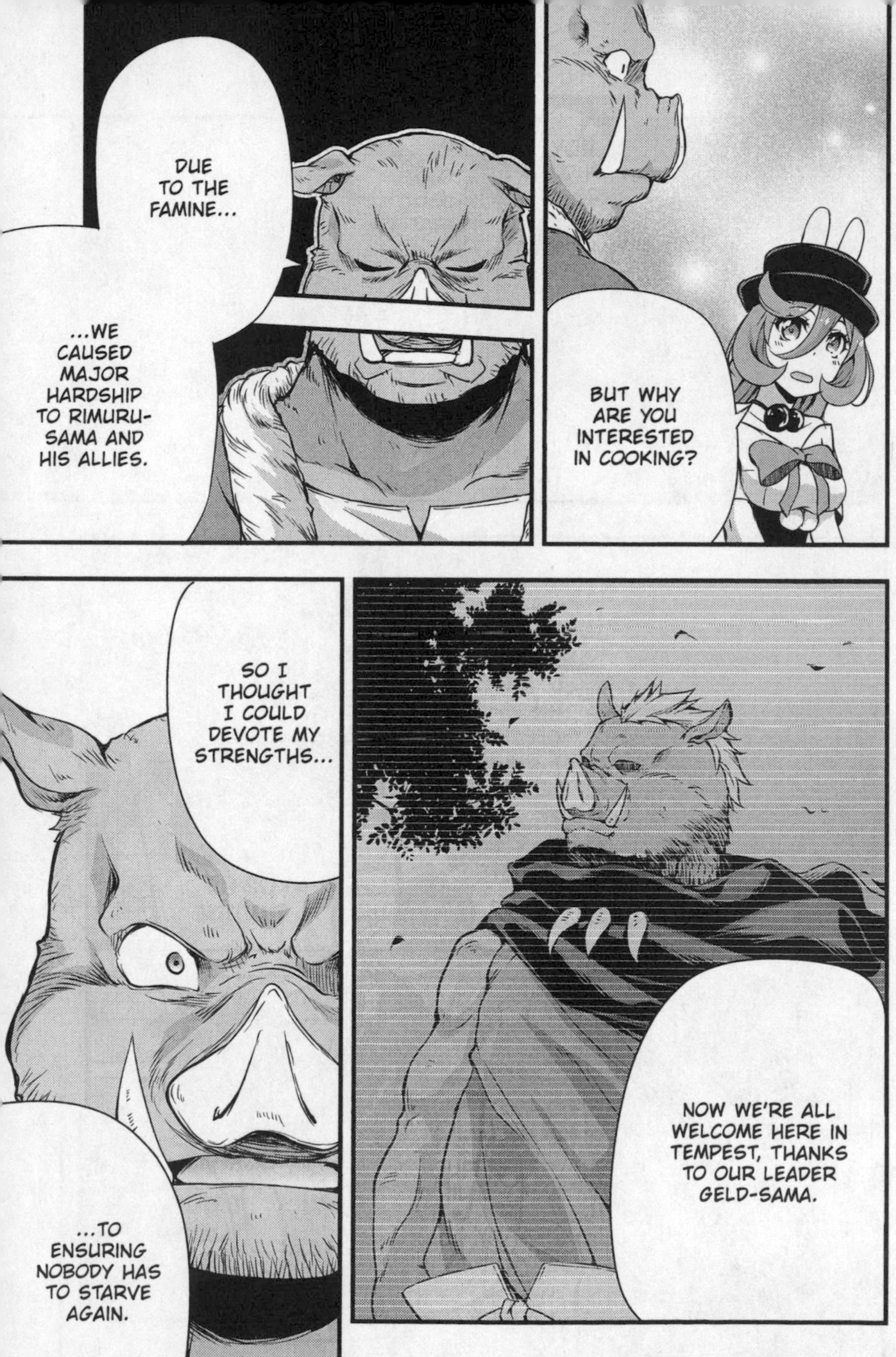
BUT WHY ARE YOU INTERESTED IN COOKING?
DUE TO THE FAMINE...
...WE CAUSED MAJOR HARDSHIP TO RIMURU-SAMA AND HIS ALLIES.
NOW WE'RE ALL WELCOME HERE IN TEMPEST, THANKS TO OUR LEADER GELD-SAMA.
SO I THOUGHT I COULD DEVOTE MY STRENGTHS...
...TO ENSURING NOBODY HAS TO STARVE AGAIN.

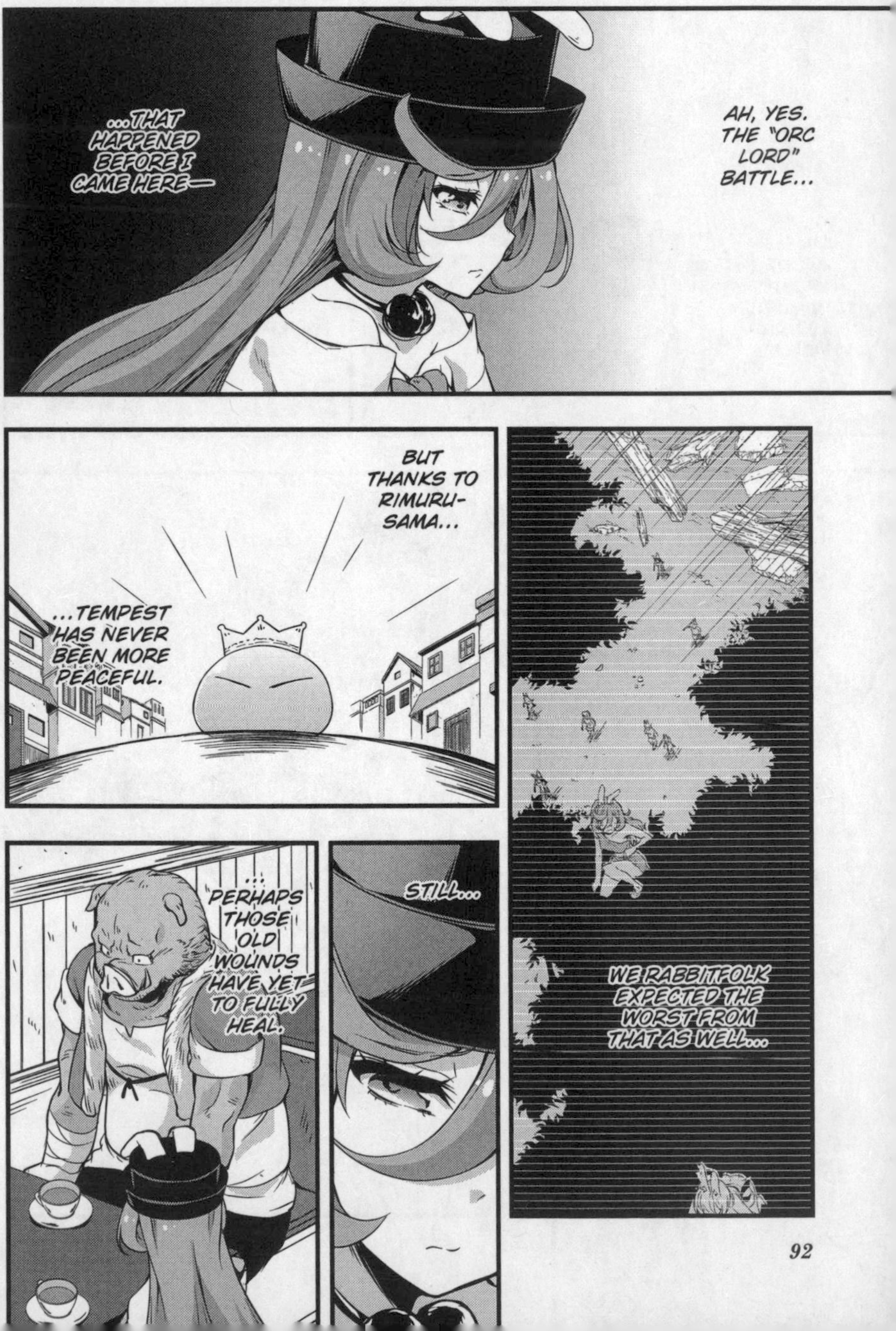
AH, YES. THE "ORC LORD" BATTLE...
...THAT HAPPENED BEFORE I CAME HERE—
WE RABBITFOLK EXPECTED THE WORST FROM THAT AS WELL...
BUT THANKS TO RIMURU-SAMA...
...TEMPEST HAS NEVER BEEN MORE PEACEFUL.
STILL...
...PERHAPS THOSE OLD WOUNDS HAVE YET TO FULLY HEAL.

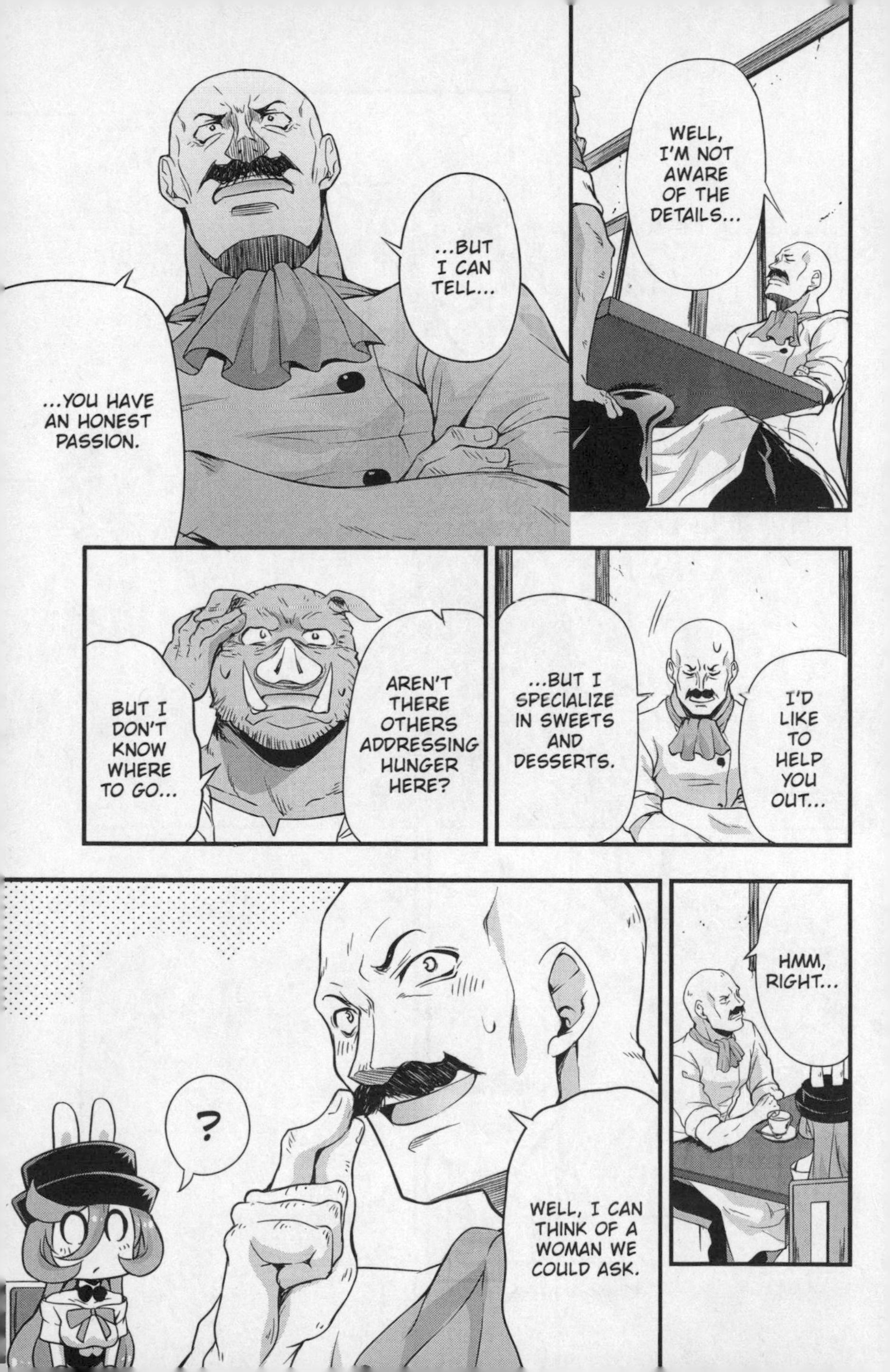
WELL, I'M NOT AWARE OF THE DETAILS...
...BUT I CAN TELL...
...YOU HAVE AN HONEST PASSION.
I'D LIKE TO HELP YOU OUT...
...BUT I SPECIALIZE IN SWEETS AND DESSERTS.
AREN'T THERE OTHERS ADDRESSING HUNGER HERE?
BUT I DON'T KNOW WHERE TO GO...
HMM, RIGHT...
WELL, I CAN THINK OF A WOMAN WE COULD ASK.
?

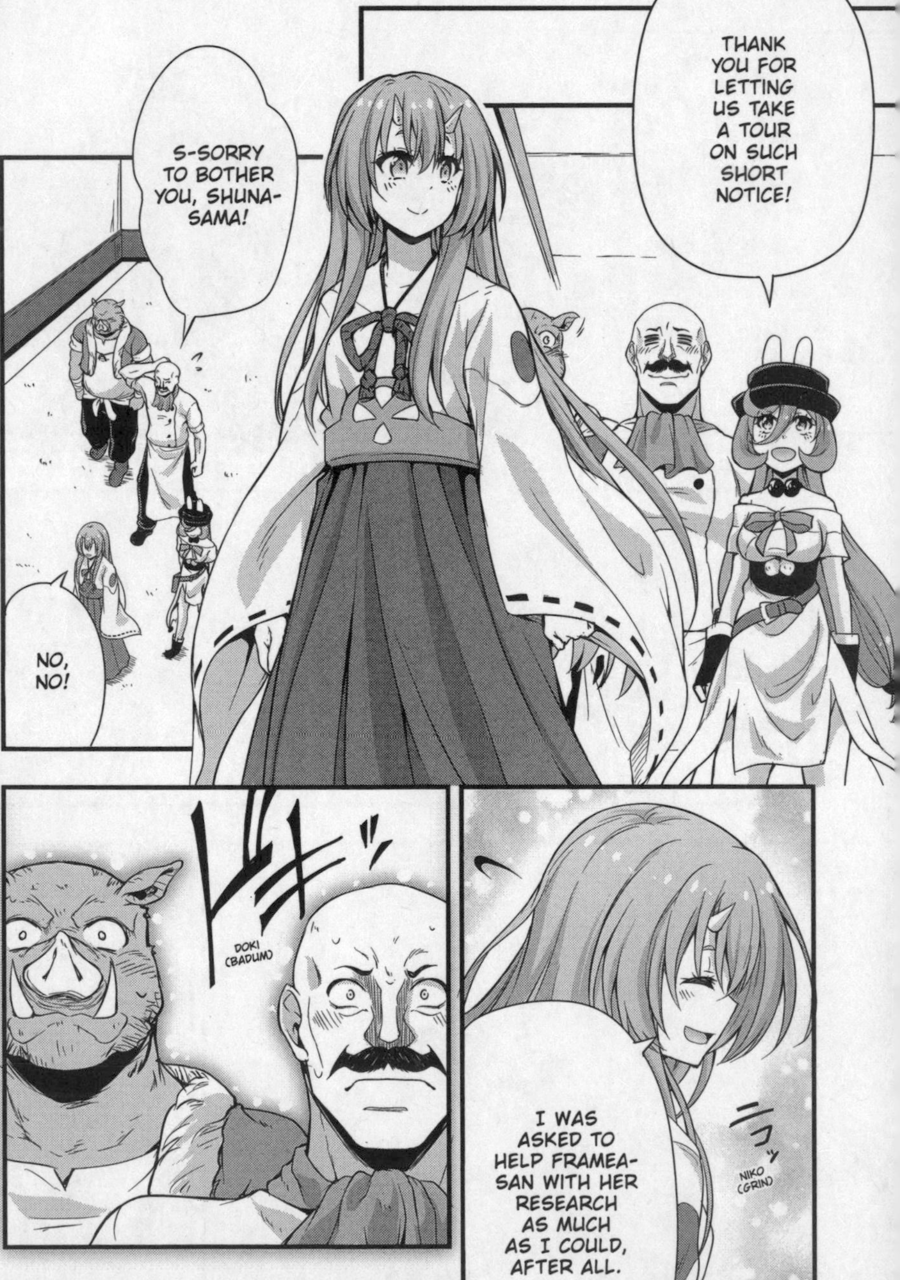
THANK YOU FOR LETTING US TAKE A TOUR ON SUCH SHORT NOTICE!
S-SORRY TO BOTHER YOU, SHUNA-SAMA!
NO, NO!
I WAS ASKED TO HELP FRAMEA-SAN WITH HER RESEARCH AS MUCH AS I COULD, AFTER ALL.
NIKO (GRIN)
DOKI (BADUM)

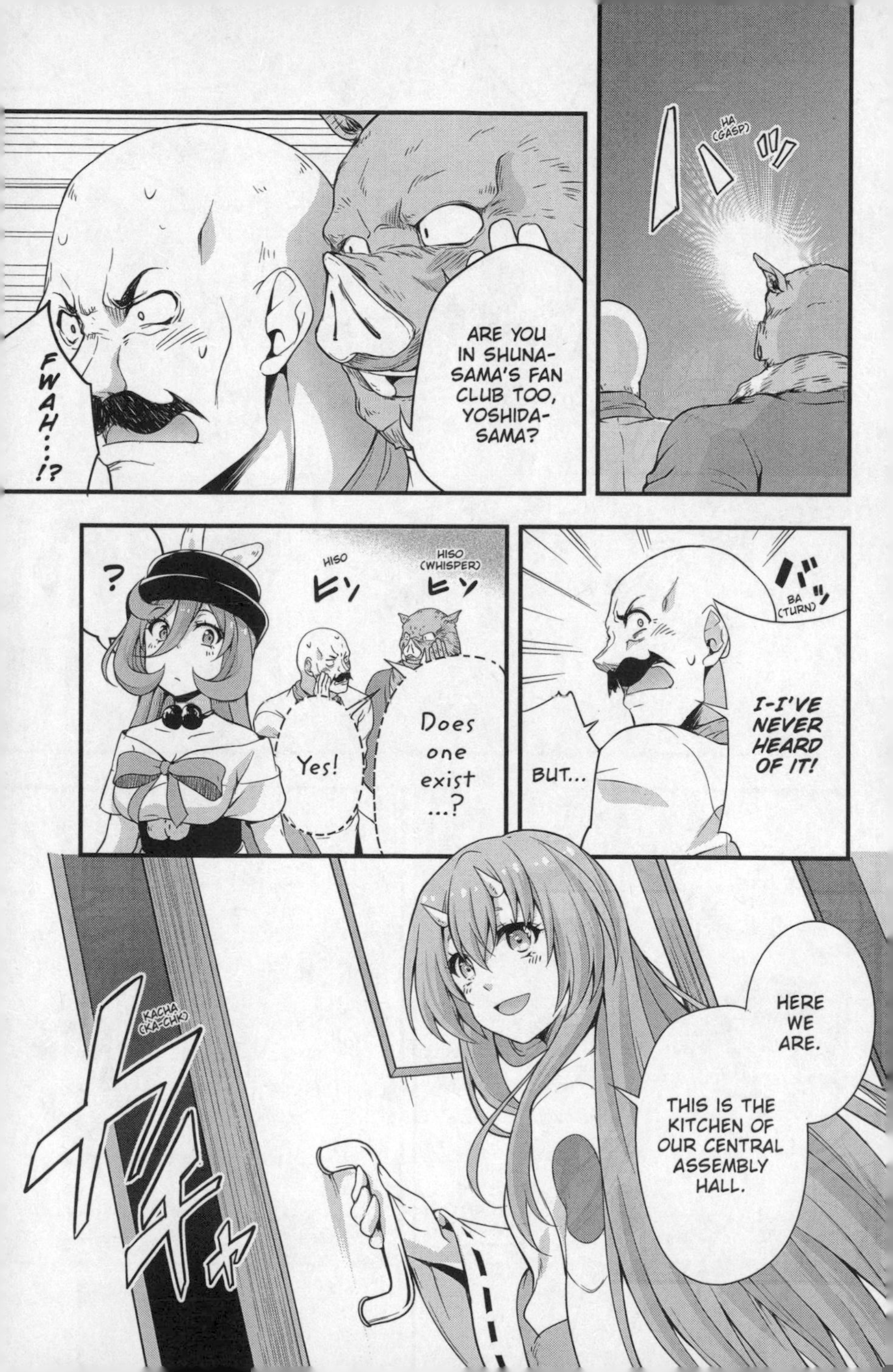
HA (GASP)
ARE YOU IN SHUNA-SAMA'S FAN CLUB TOO, YOSHIDA-SAMA?
FWAH...!?
BA (TURN)
I-I'VE NEVER HEARD OF IT!
BUT...
HISO (WHISPER)
HISO
Does one exist...?
Yes!
?
HERE WE ARE.
THIS IS THE KITCHEN OF OUR CENTRAL ASSEMBLY HALL.
KACHA (KA-CHK)

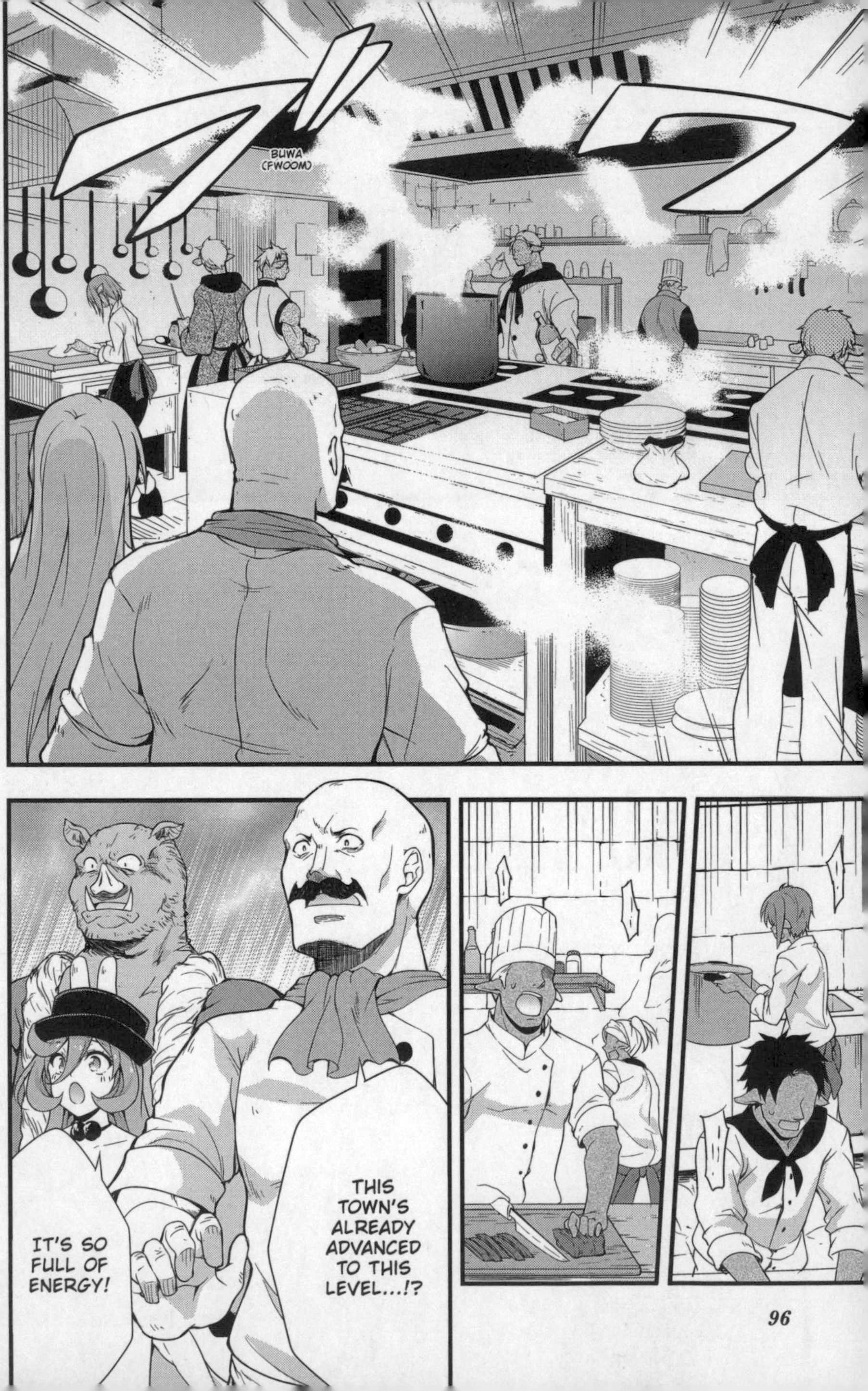
BUWA
(FWOOM)
THIS TOWN'S ALREADY ADVANCED TO THIS LEVEL...!?
IT'S SO FULL OF ENERGY!

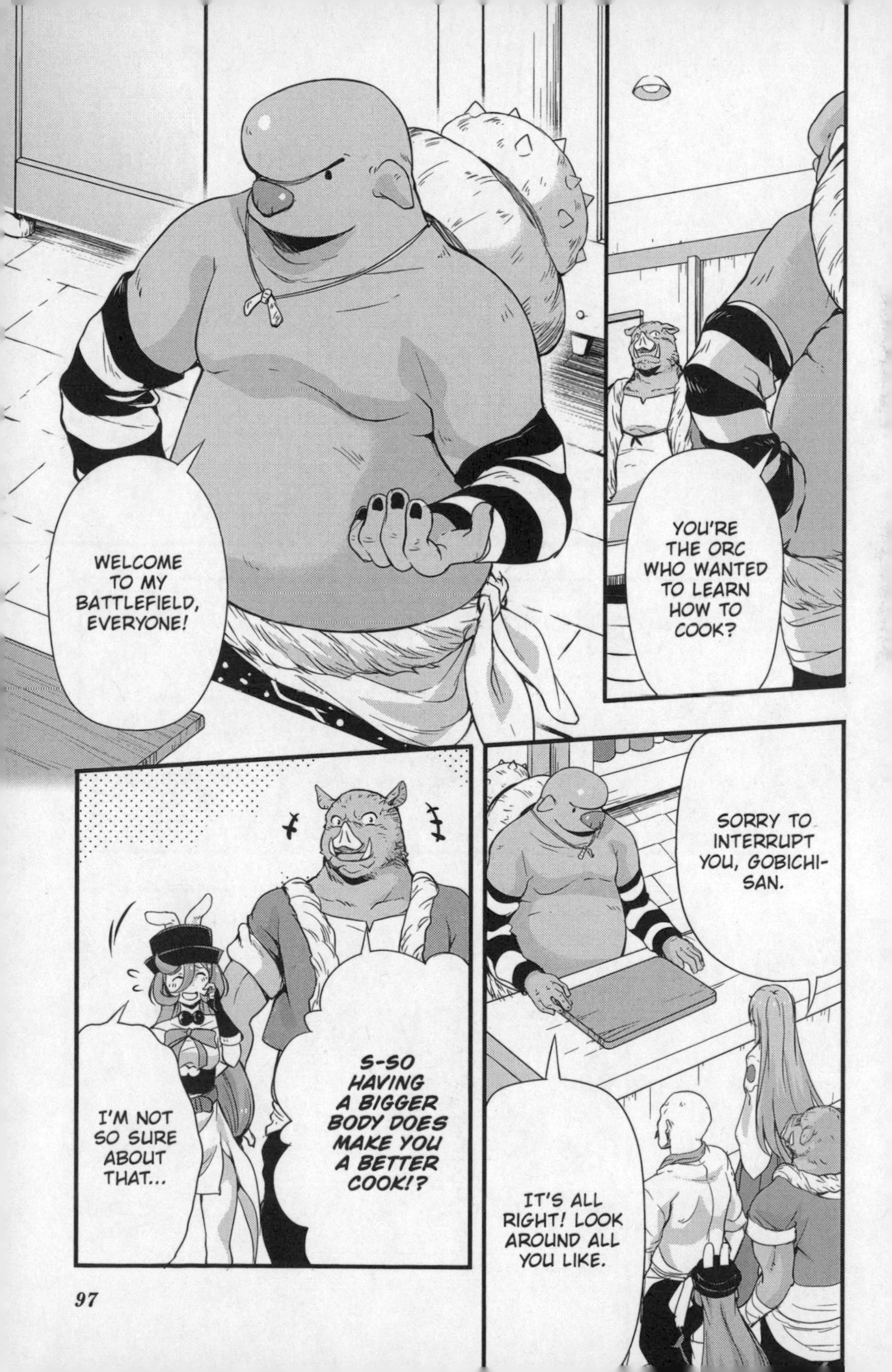
YOU'RE THE ORC WHO WANTED TO LEARN HOW TO COOK?
WELCOME TO MY BATTLEFIELD, EVERYONE!
SORRY TO INTERRUPT YOU, GOBICHI-SAN.
IT'S ALL RIGHT! LOOK AROUND ALL YOU LIKE.
S-SO HAVING A BIGGER BODY DOES MAKE YOU A BETTER COOK!?
I'M NOT SO SURE ABOUT THAT...

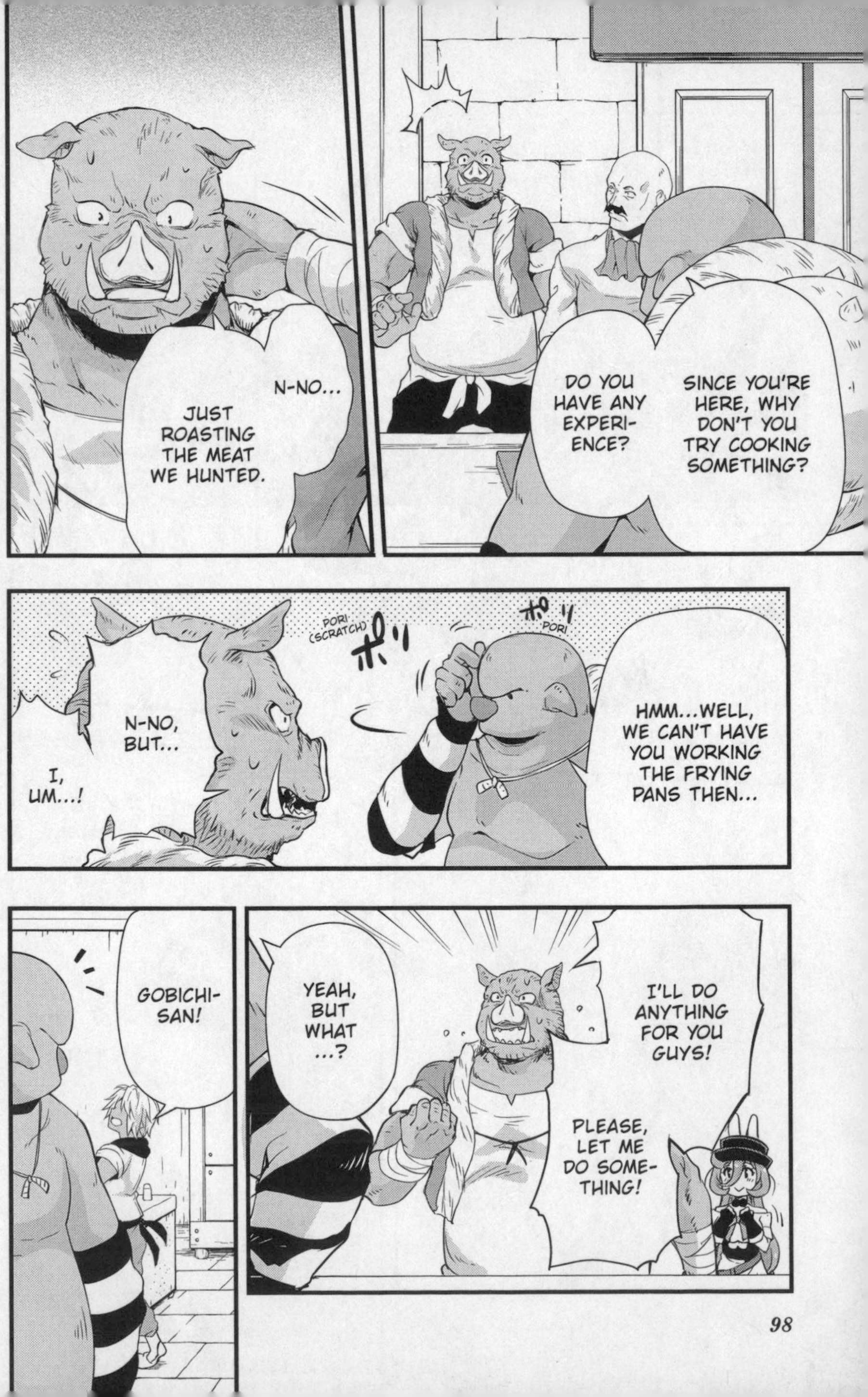
SINCE YOU'RE HERE, WHY DON'T YOU TRY COOKING SOMETHING?
DO YOU HAVE ANY EXPERI-ENCE?
N-NO...
JUST ROASTING THE MEAT WE HUNTED.
HMM...WELL, WE CAN'T HAVE YOU WORKING THE FRYING PANS THEN...
PORI
PORI (SCRATCH)
N-NO, BUT...
I, UM...!
I'LL DO ANYTHING FOR YOU GUYS!
PLEASE, LET ME DO SOME-THING!
YEAH, BUT WHAT ...?
GOBICHI-SAN!

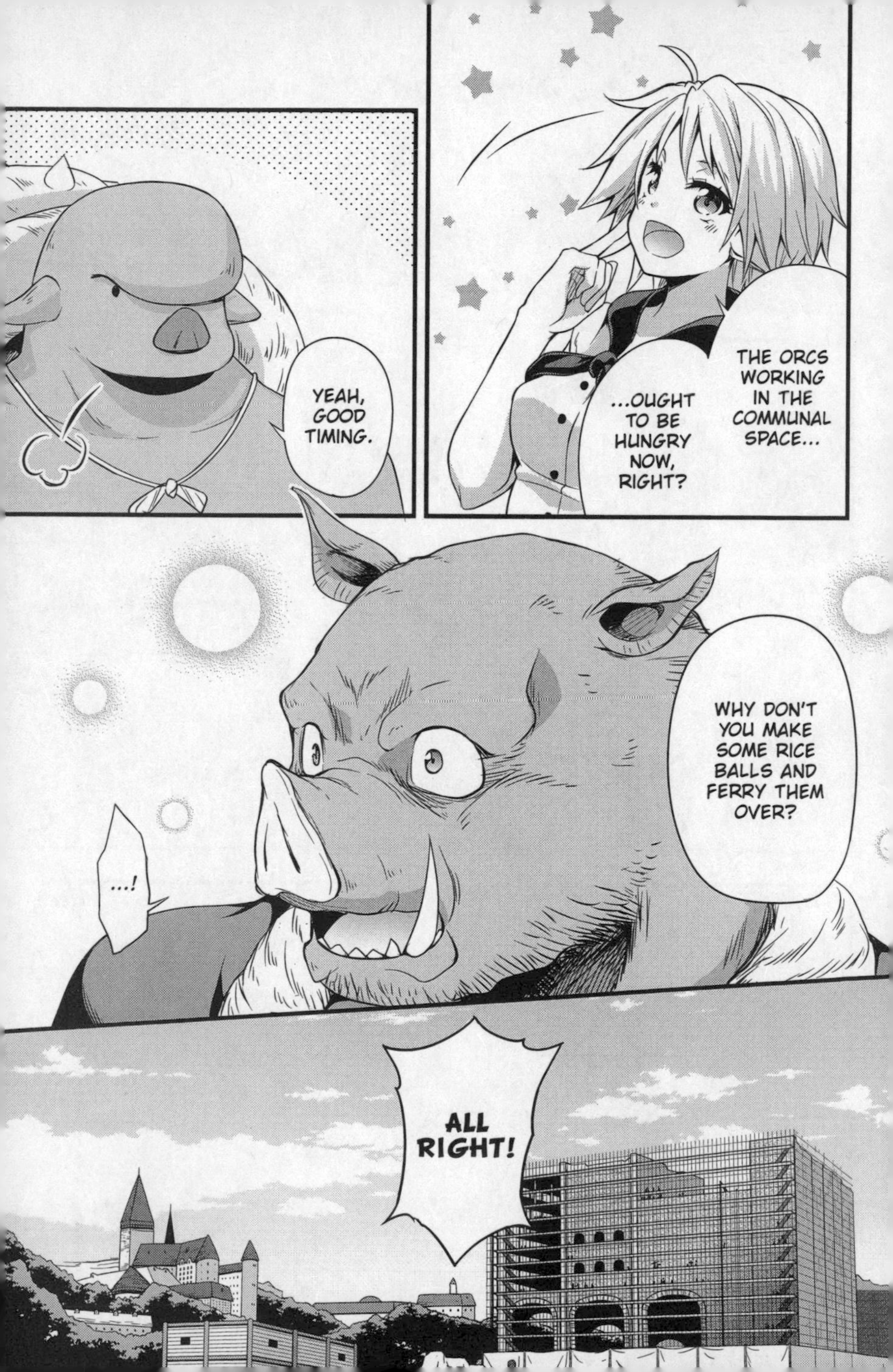

THE ORCS WORKING IN THE COMMUNAL SPACE...
...OUGHT TO BE HUNGRY NOW, RIGHT?
YEAH, GOOD TIMING.
WHY DON'T YOU MAKE SOME RICE BALLS AND FERRY THEM OVER?
...!
ALL RIGHT!

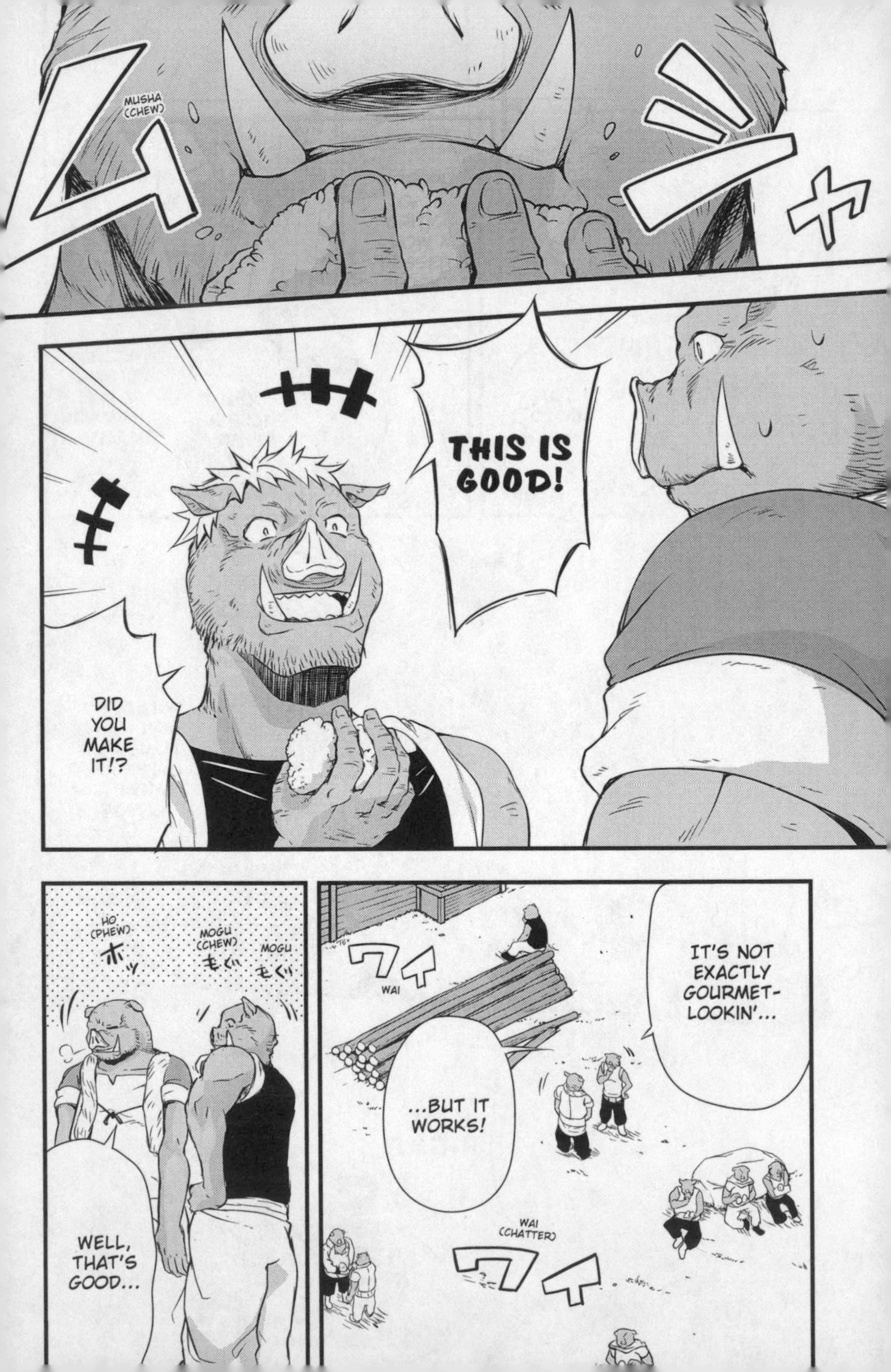
MUSHA (CHEW)
THIS IS GOOD!
DID YOU MAKE IT!?
IT'S NOT EXACTLY GOURMET-LOOKIN'...
...BUT IT WORKS!
WAI
WAI (CHATTER)
HO (PHEW)
MOGU (CHEW)
MOGU
WELL, THAT'S GOOD...

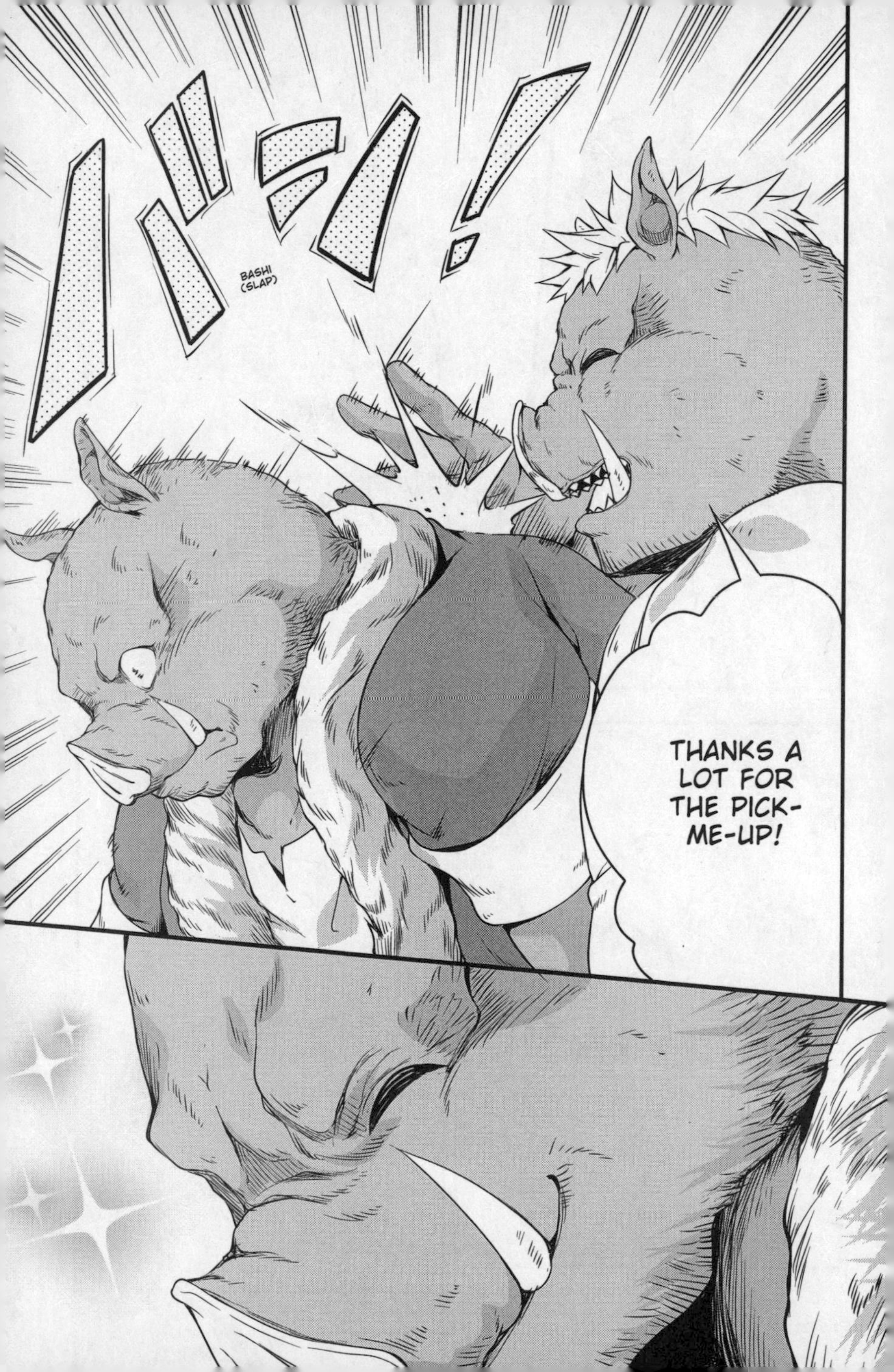
THANKS A LOT FOR THE PICK-ME-UP!
BASHI (SLAP)

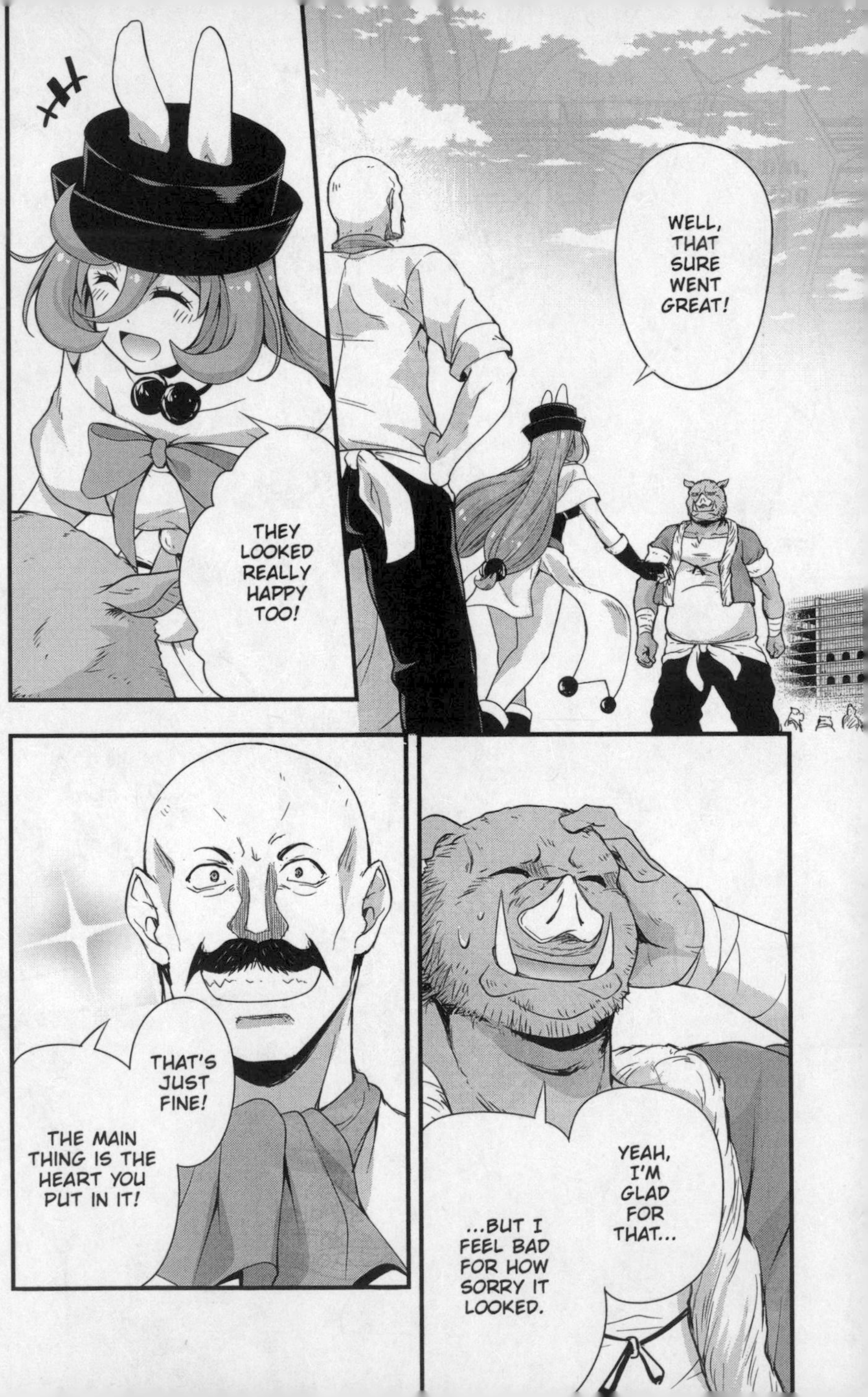
WELL, THAT SURE WENT GREAT!
THEY LOOKED REALLY HAPPY TOO!
YEAH, I'M GLAD FOR THAT...
...BUT I FEEL BAD FOR HOW SORRY IT LOOKED.
THAT'S JUST FINE!
THE MAIN THING IS THE HEART YOU PUT IN IT!

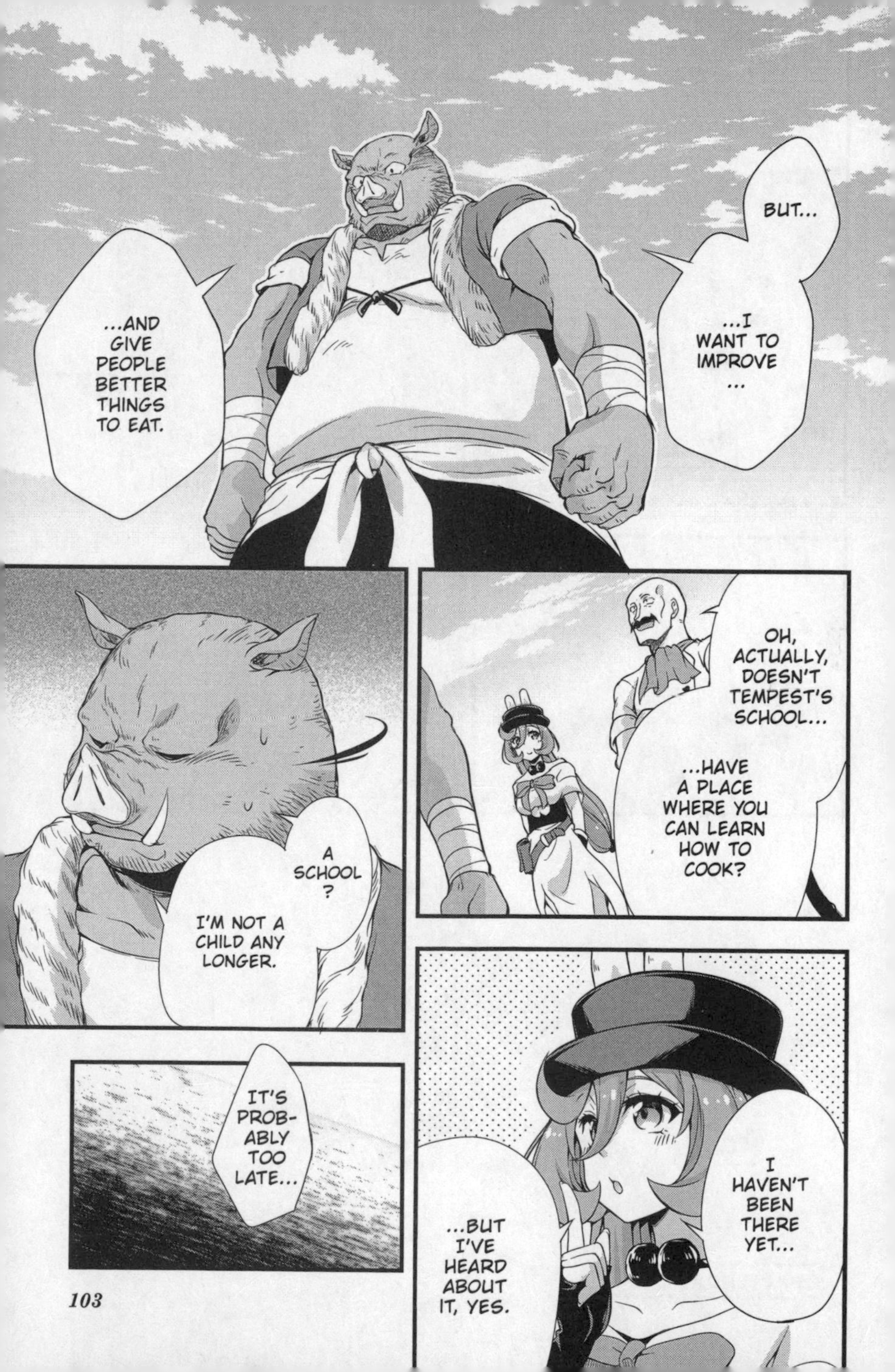
BUT...
...I WANT TO IMPROVE ...
...AND GIVE PEOPLE BETTER THINGS TO EAT.
OH, ACTUALLY, DOESN'T TEMPEST'S SCHOOL...
...HAVE A PLACE WHERE YOU CAN LEARN HOW TO COOK?
A SCHOOL ?
I'M NOT A CHILD ANY LONGER.
IT'S PROB-ABLY TOO LATE...
I HAVEN'T BEEN THERE YET...
...BUT I'VE HEARD ABOUT IT, YES.

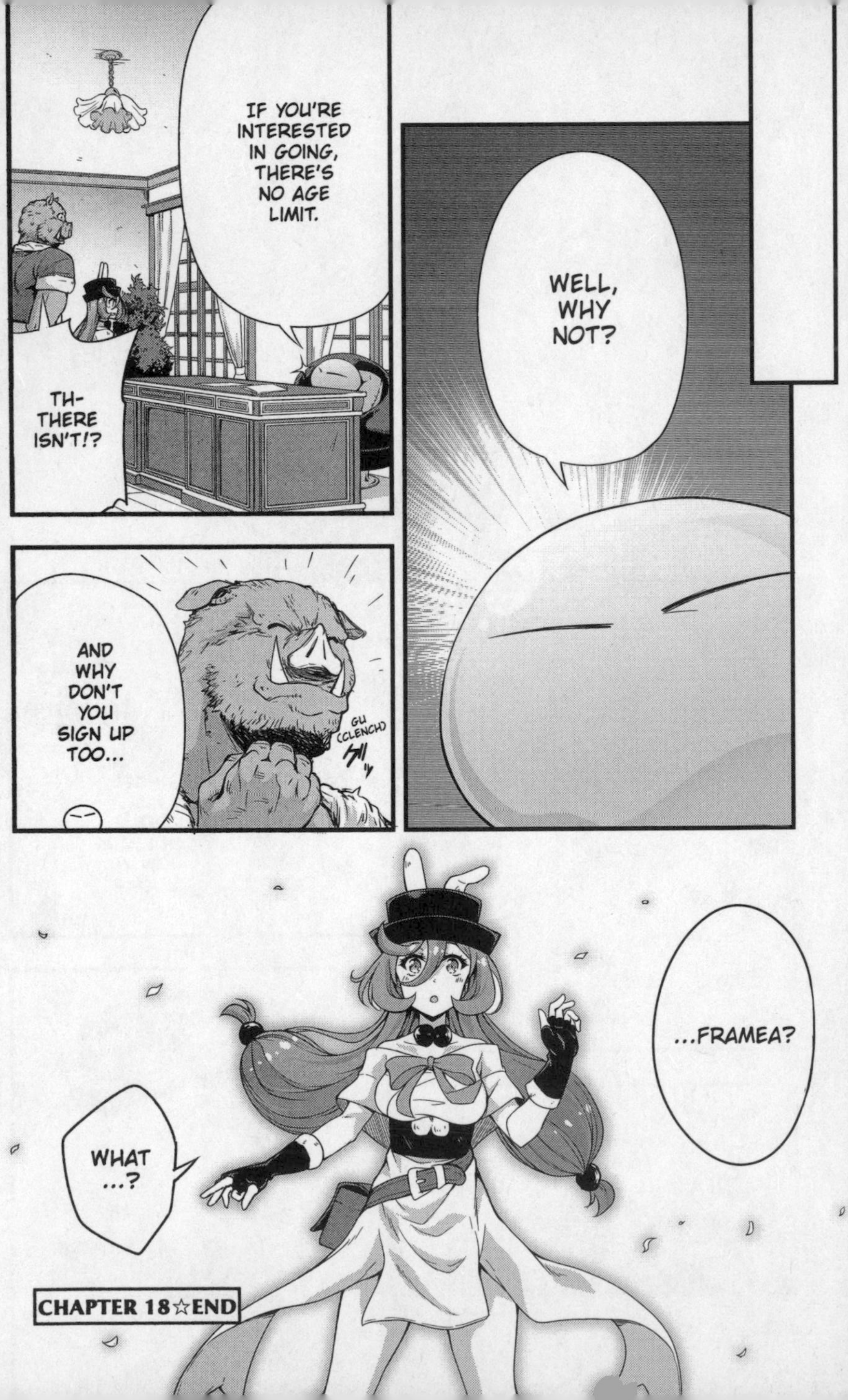
IF YOU'RE INTERESTED IN GOING, THERE'S NO AGE LIMIT.
TH- THERE ISN'T!?
AND WHY DON'T YOU SIGN UP TOO...
GU (CLENCH)
WELL, WHY NOT?
...FRAMEA?
WHAT ...?
CHAPTER 18☆END

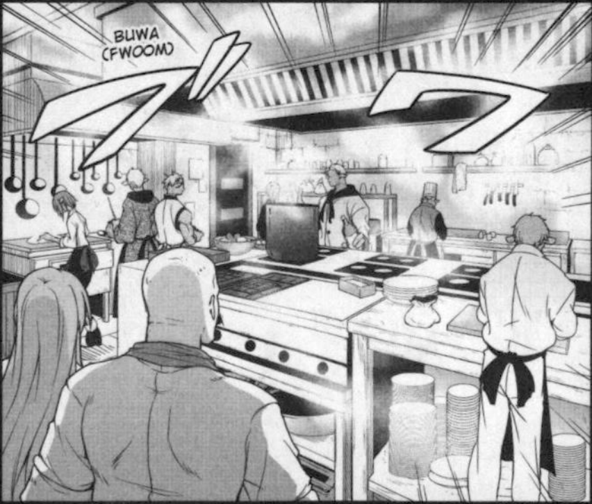
BUWA
(FWOOM)

That Time I Got
Reincarnated
as a SLIME
The Ways of the Monster Nation

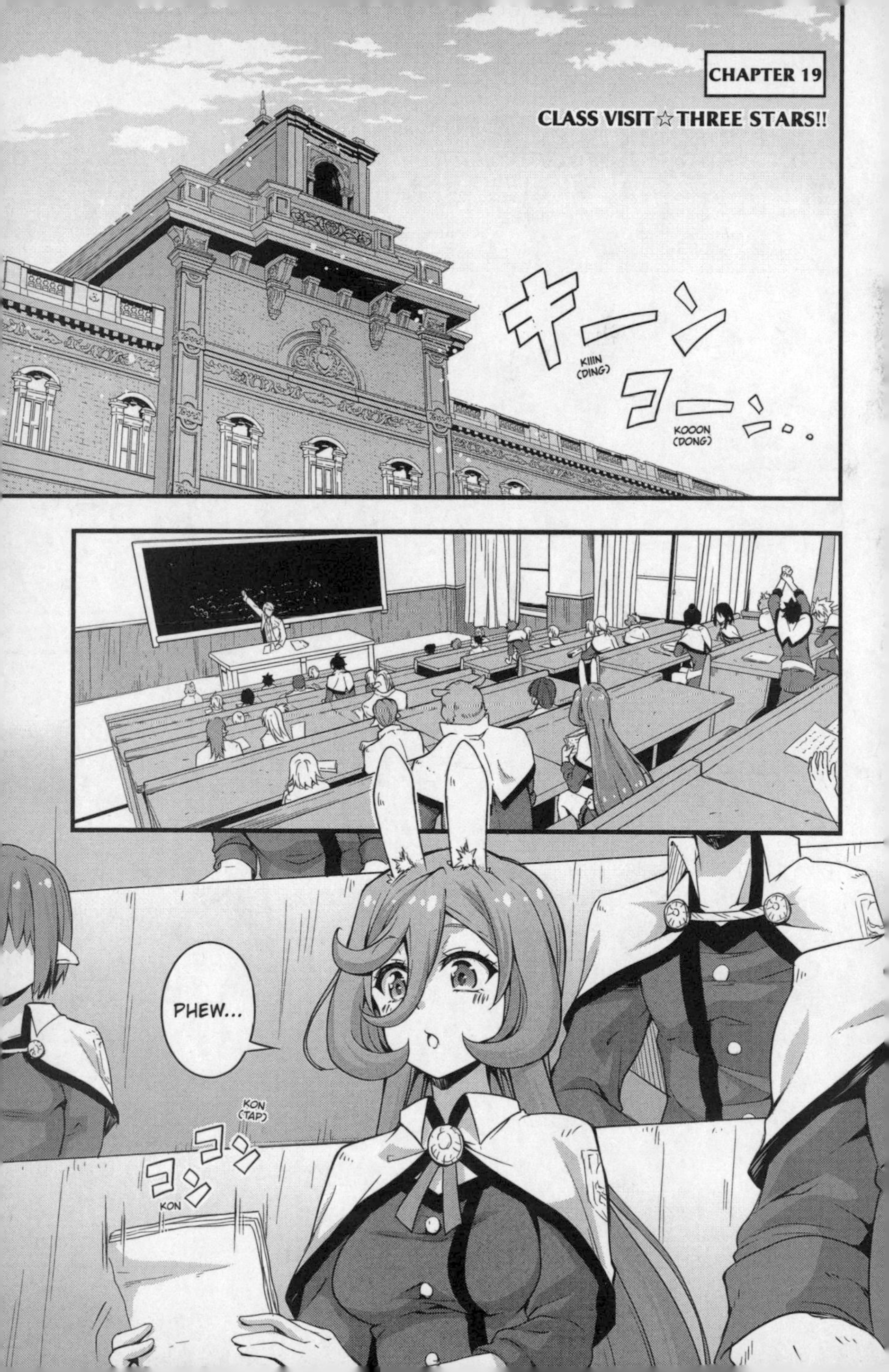
CHAPTER 19
CLASS VISIT☆THREE STARS!!
キーン
KIIIN (DING)
コーン
KOOON (DONG)
PHEW...
コンコン
KON (TAP)
KON

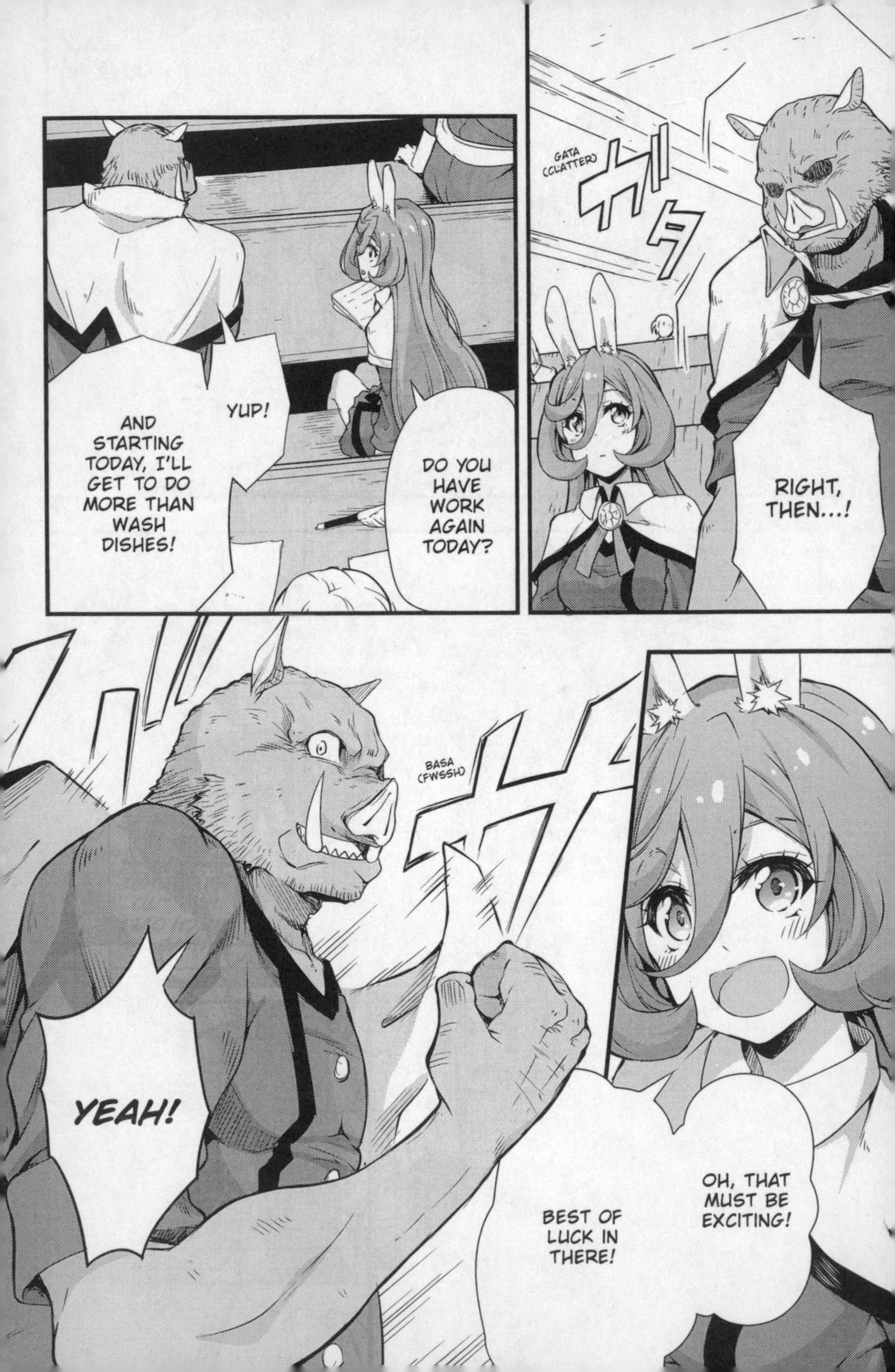
GATA (CLATTER)
RIGHT, THEN...!
DO YOU HAVE WORK AGAIN TODAY?
YUP!
AND STARTING TODAY, I'LL GET TO DO MORE THAN WASH DISHES!
OH, THAT MUST BE EXCITING!
BEST OF LUCK IN THERE!
BASA (FWSSH)
YEAH!

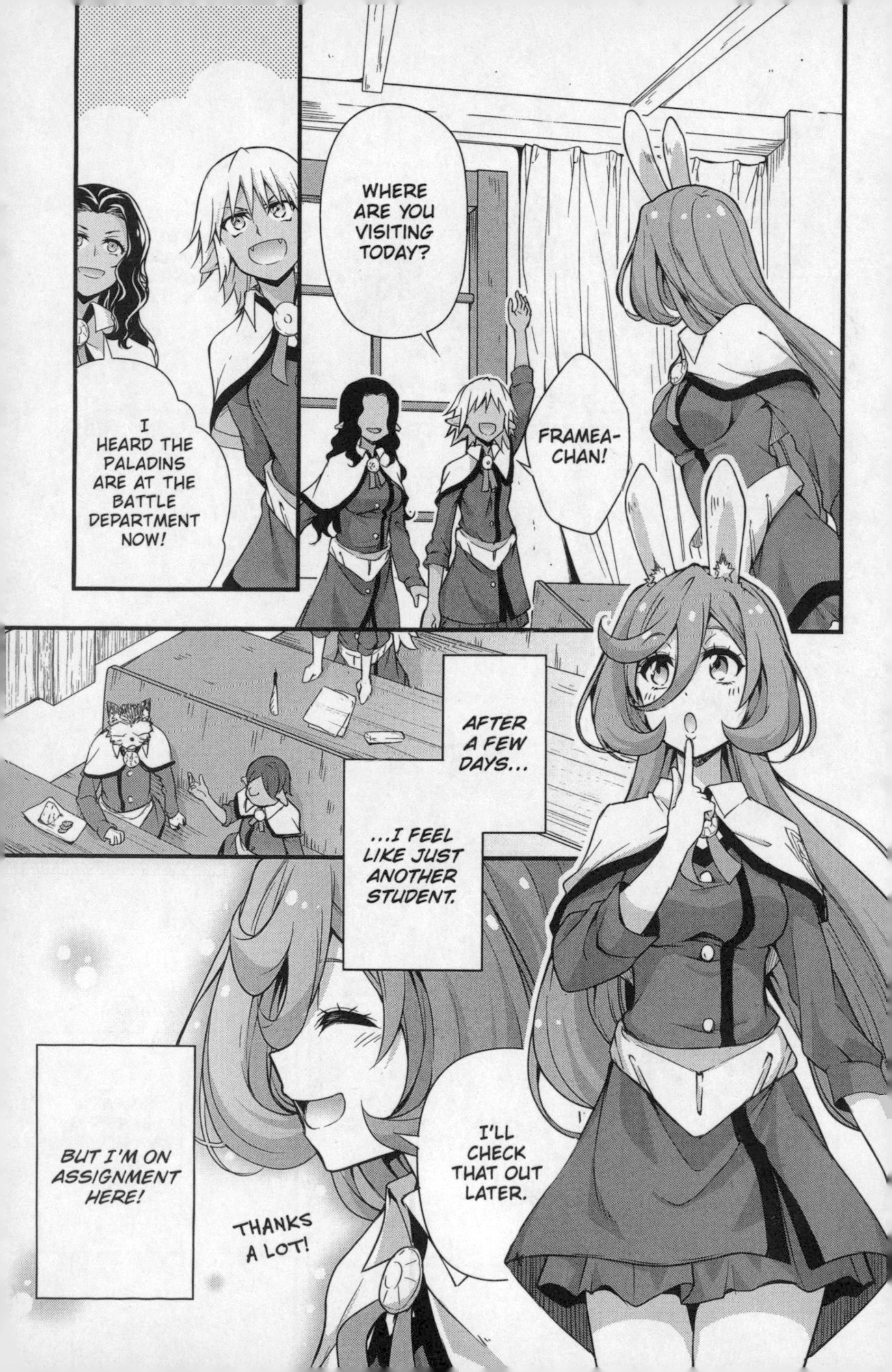
FRAMEA-CHAN!
WHERE ARE YOU VISITING TODAY?
I HEARD THE PALADINS ARE AT THE BATTLE DEPARTMENT NOW!
AFTER A FEW DAYS...
...I FEEL LIKE JUST ANOTHER STUDENT.
I'LL CHECK THAT OUT LATER.
THANKS A LOT!
BUT I'M ON ASSIGNMENT HERE!

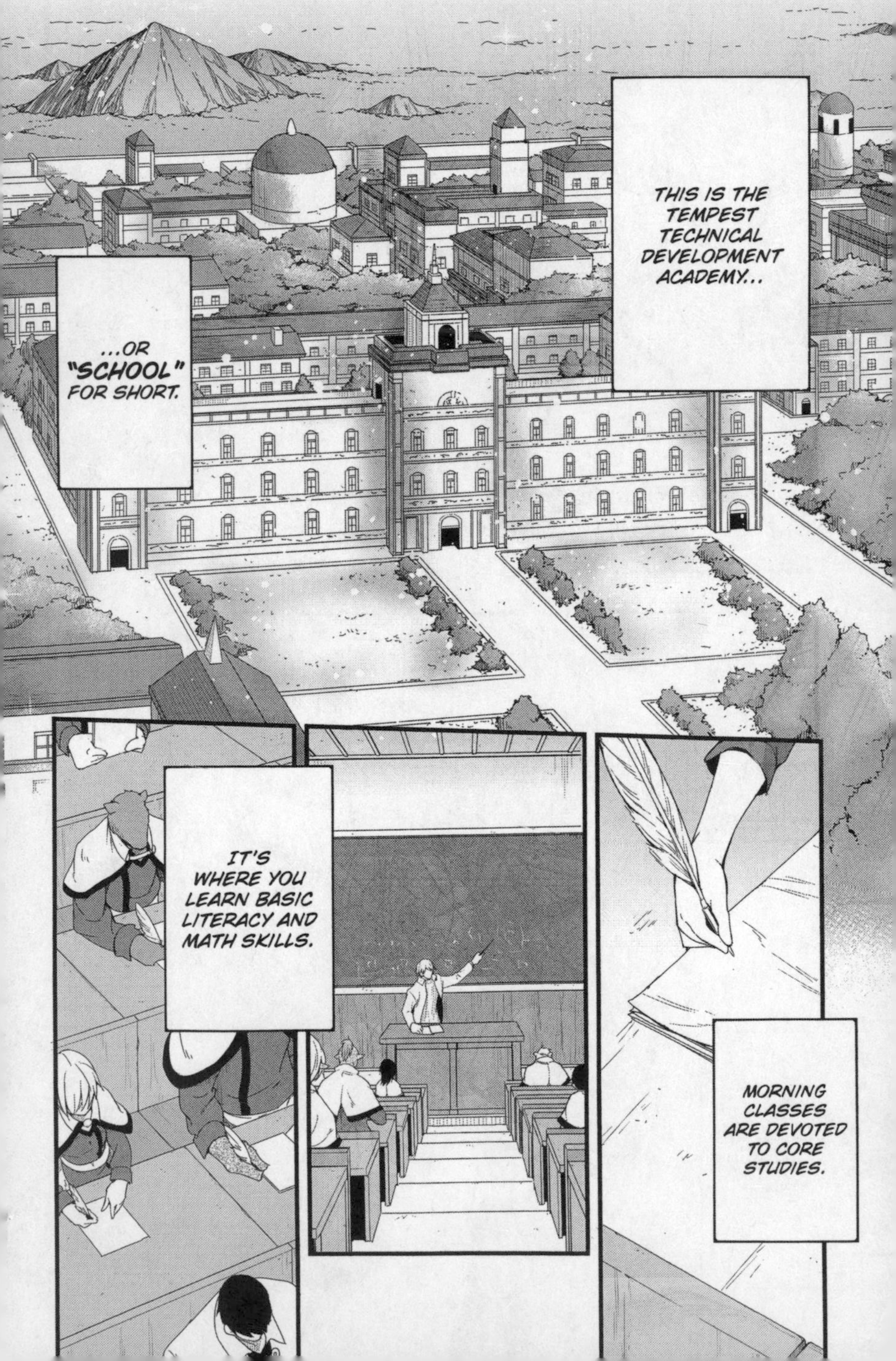
THIS IS THE TEMPEST TECHNICAL DEVELOPMENT ACADEMY...
...OR "SCHOOL" FOR SHORT.
MORNING CLASSES ARE DEVOTED TO CORE STUDIES.
IT'S WHERE YOU LEARN BASIC LITERACY AND MATH SKILLS.

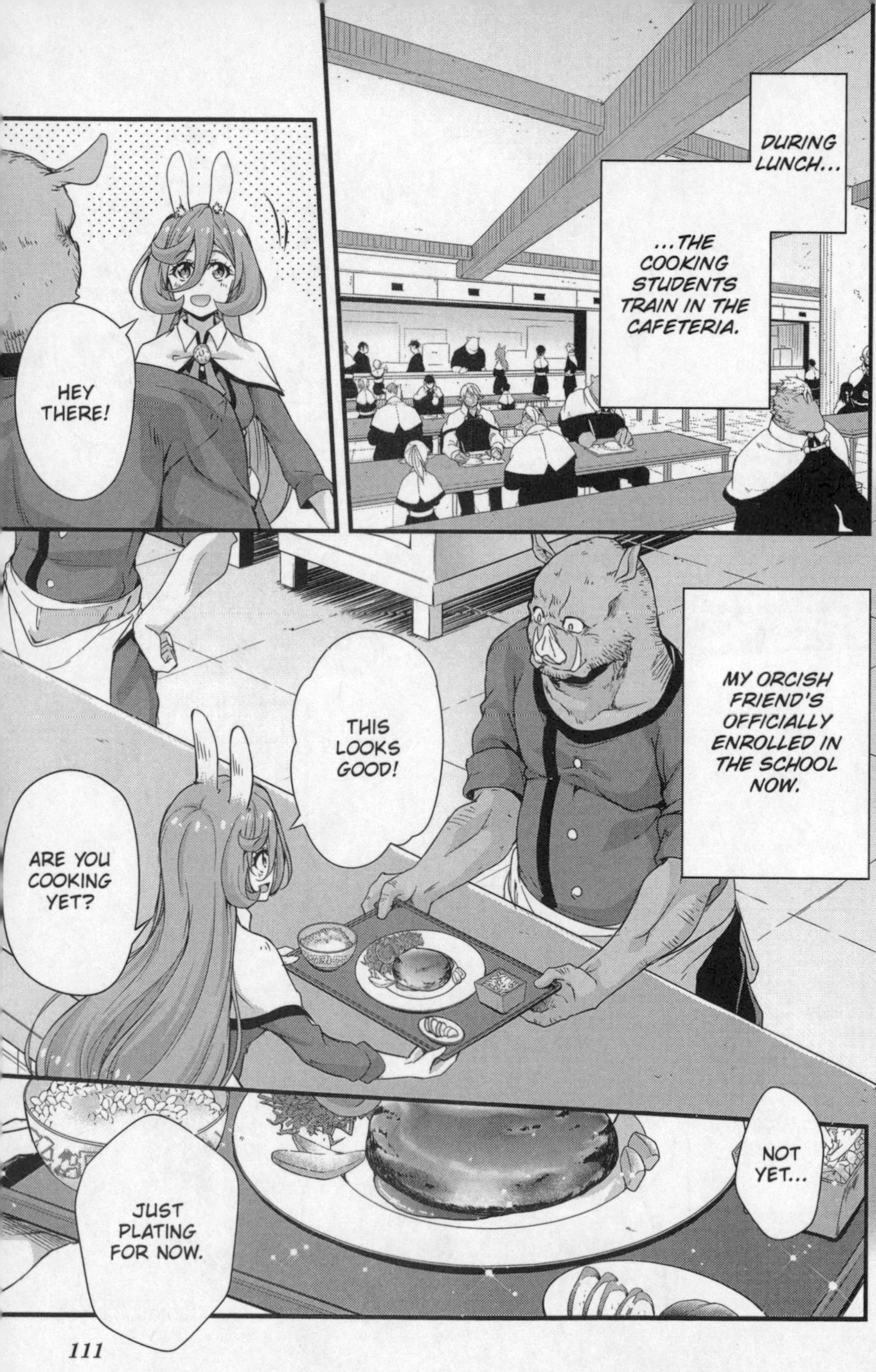
DURING LUNCH...
...THE COOKING STUDENTS TRAIN IN THE CAFETERIA.
HEY THERE!
MY ORCISH FRIEND'S OFFICIALLY ENROLLED IN THE SCHOOL NOW.
THIS LOOKS GOOD!
ARE YOU COOKING YET?
NOT YET...
JUST PLATING FOR NOW.

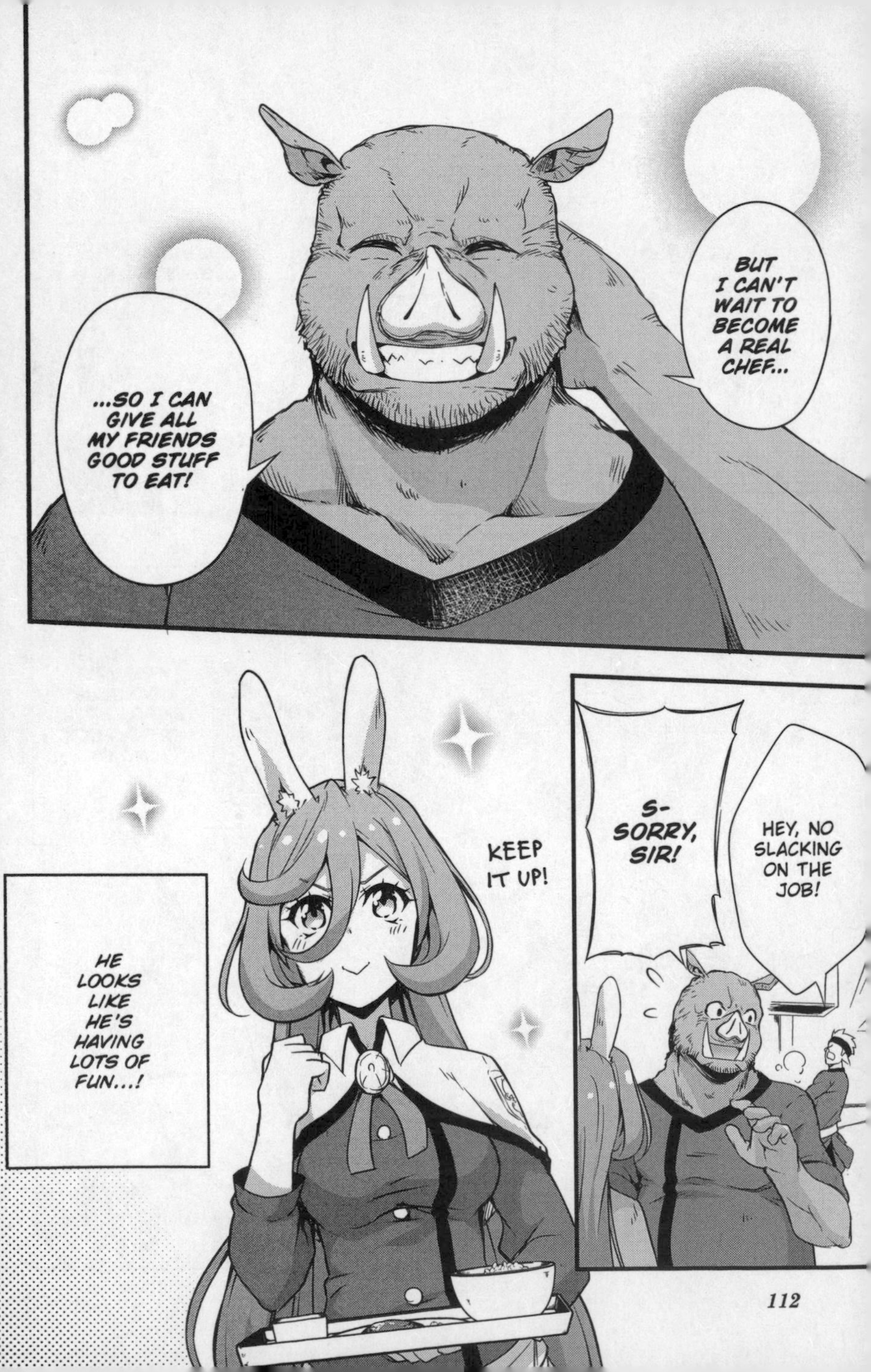
BUT I CAN'T WAIT TO BECOME A REAL CHEF...
...SO I CAN GIVE ALL MY FRIENDS GOOD STUFF TO EAT!
HEY, NO SLACKING ON THE JOB!
S-SORRY, SIR!
KEEP IT UP!
HE LOOKS LIKE HE'S HAVING LOTS OF FUN...!

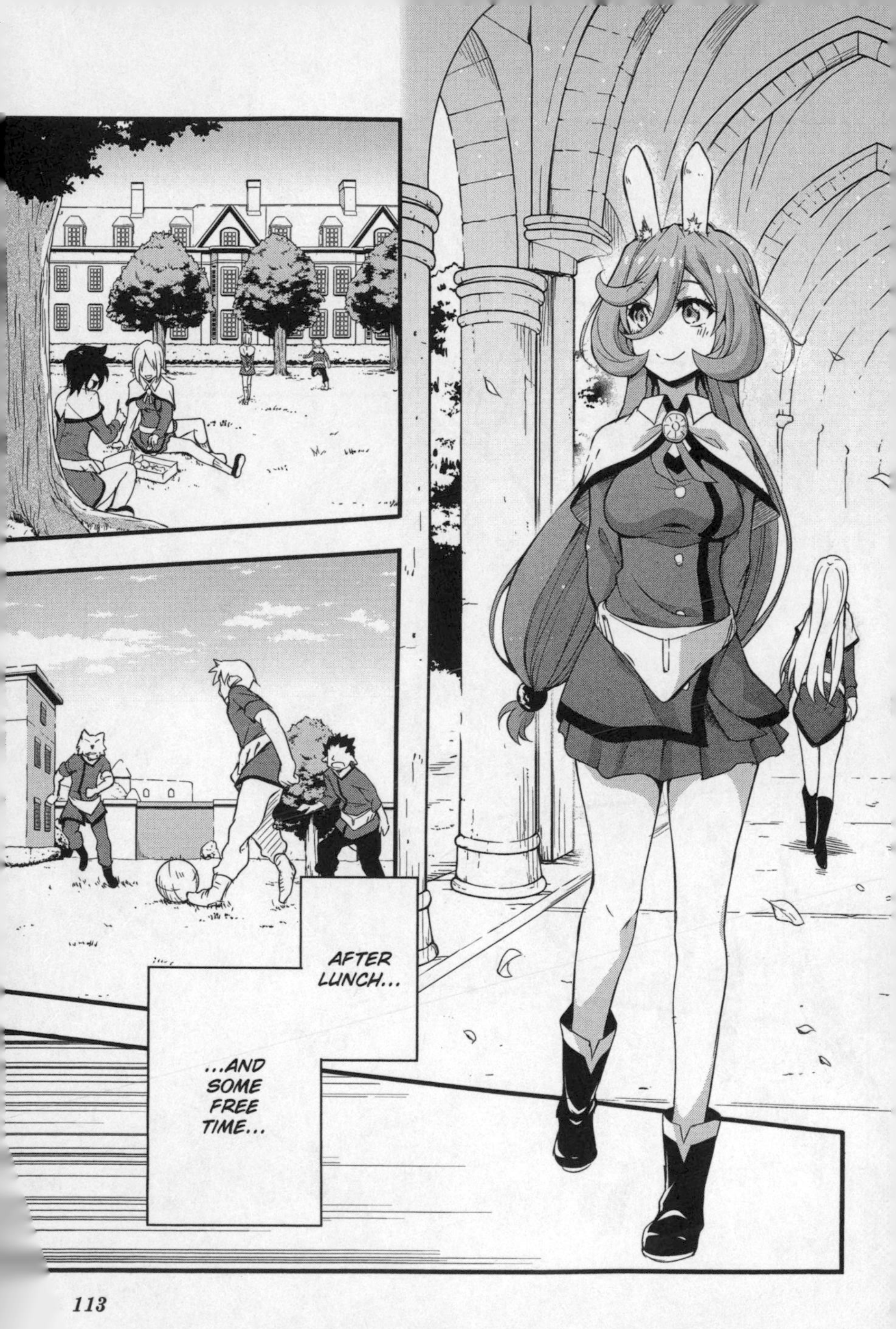
AFTER LUNCH...
...AND SOME FREE TIME...

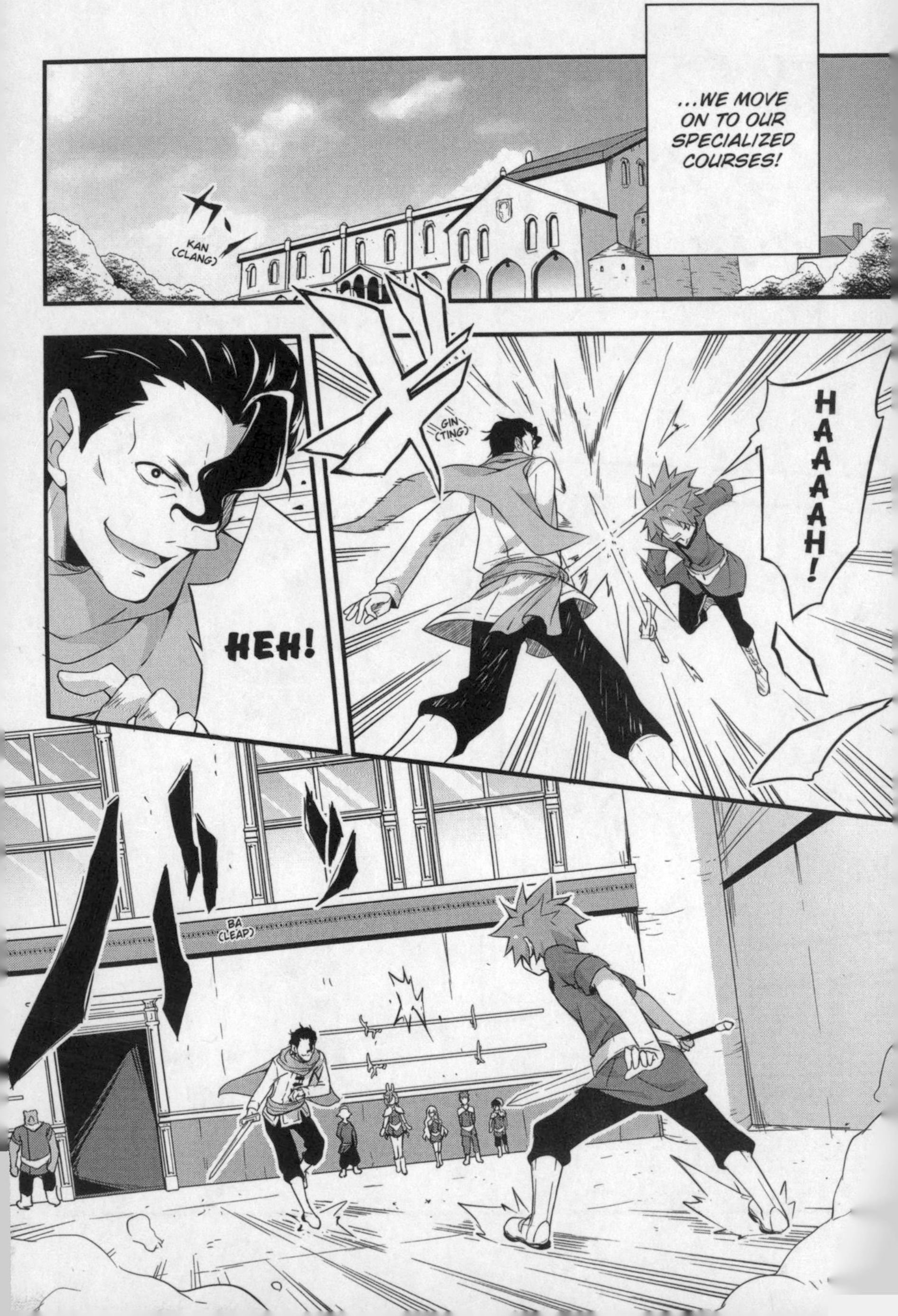
...WE MOVE ON TO OUR SPECIALIZED COURSES!
KAN (CLANG)
HAAAAAH!
GIN (TING)
HEH!
BA (LEAP)

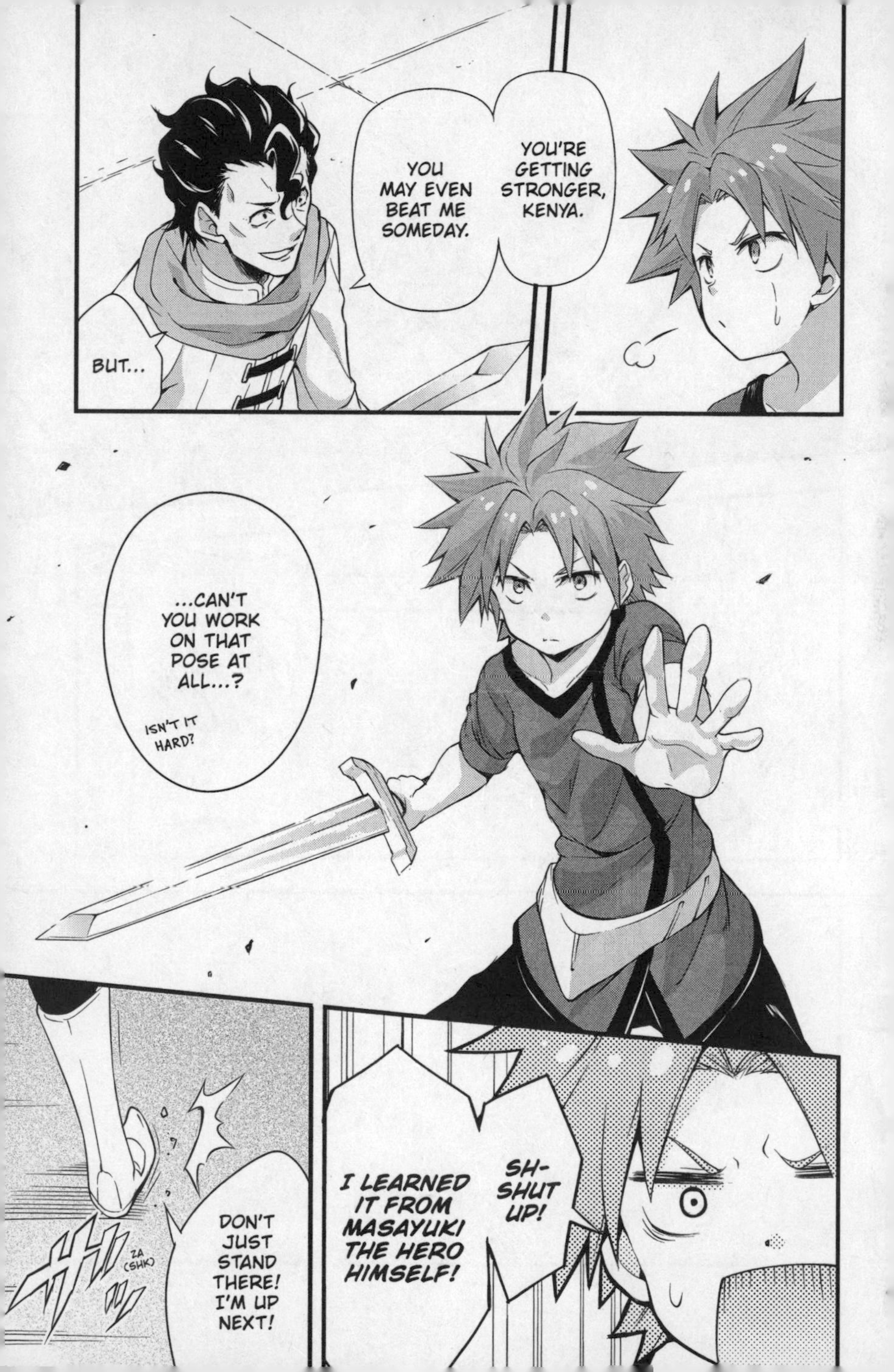
YOU'RE GETTING STRONGER, KENYA.
YOU MAY EVEN BEAT ME SOMEDAY.
BUT...
...CAN'T YOU WORK ON THAT POSE AT ALL...?
ISN'T IT HARD?
SH-SHUT UP!
I LEARNED IT FROM MASAYUKI THE HERO HIMSELF!
ZA (SHK)
DON'T JUST STAND THERE! I'M UP NEXT!

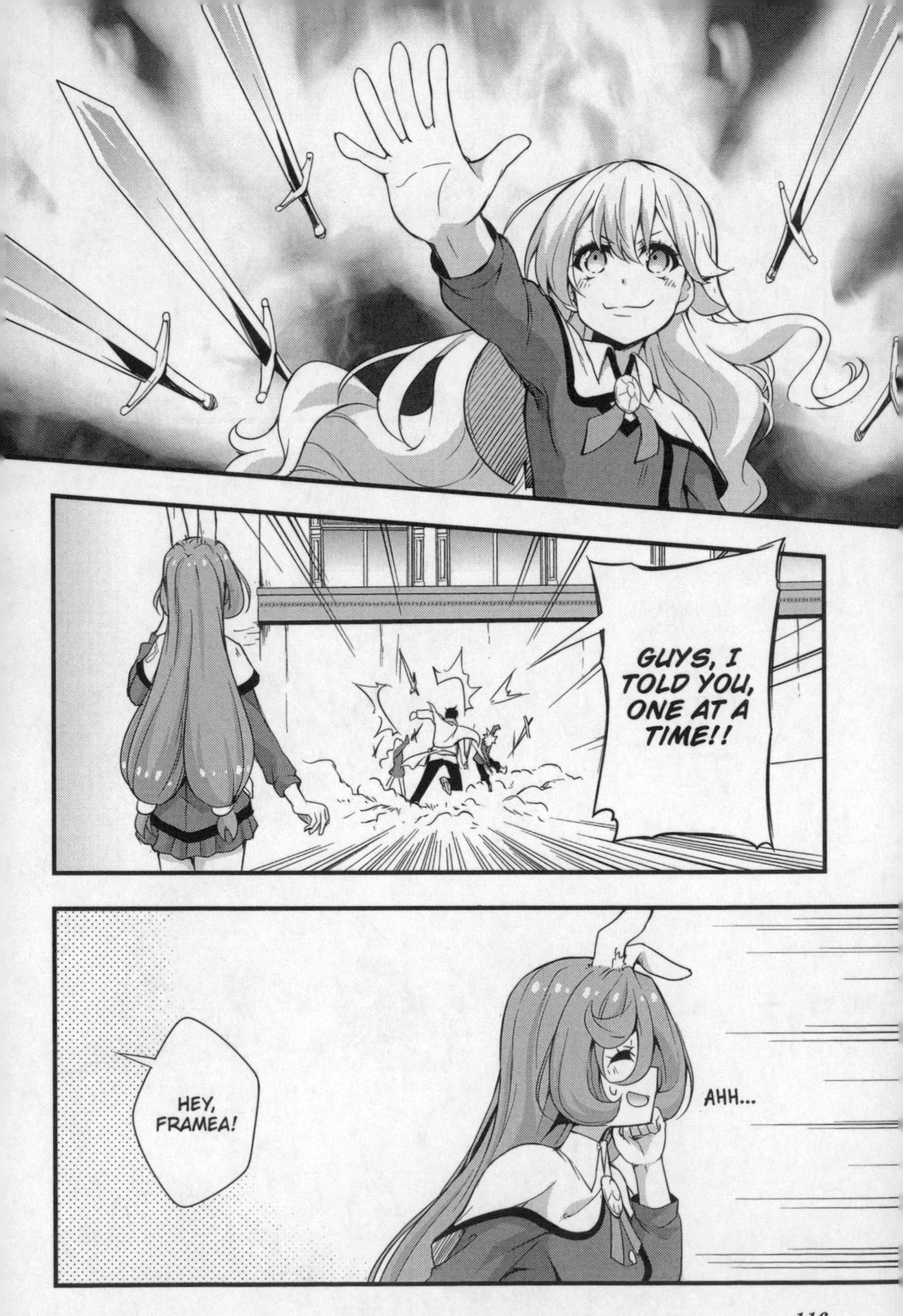
GUYS, I TOLD YOU, ONE AT A TIME!!
AHH...
HEY, FRAMEA!

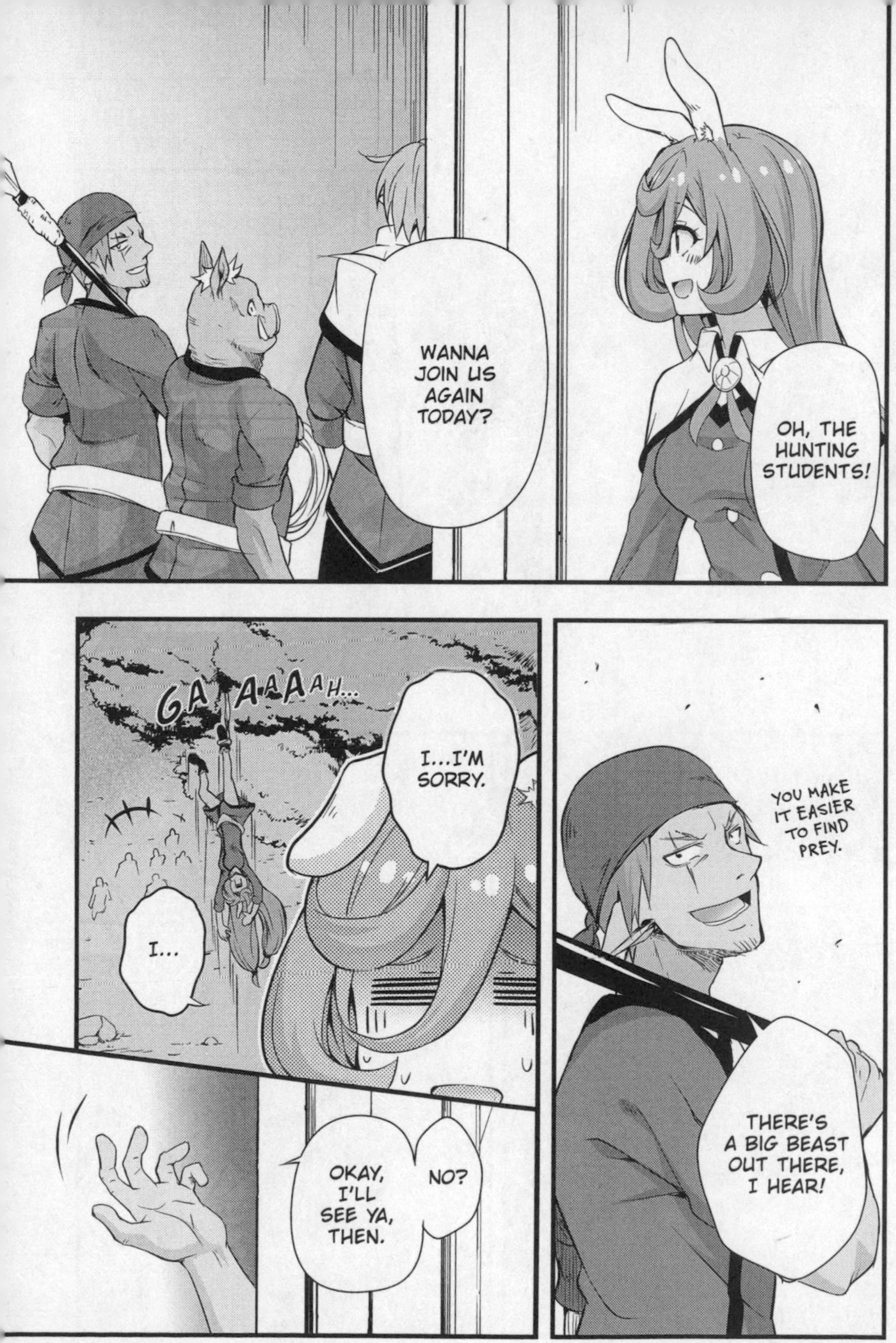

OH, THE HUNTING STUDENTS!
WANNA JOIN US AGAIN TODAY?
YOU MAKE IT EASIER TO FIND PREY.
THERE'S A BIG BEAST OUT THERE, I HEAR!
I...I'M SORRY.
GAAAAAH...
I...
NO?
OKAY, I'LL SEE YA, THEN.

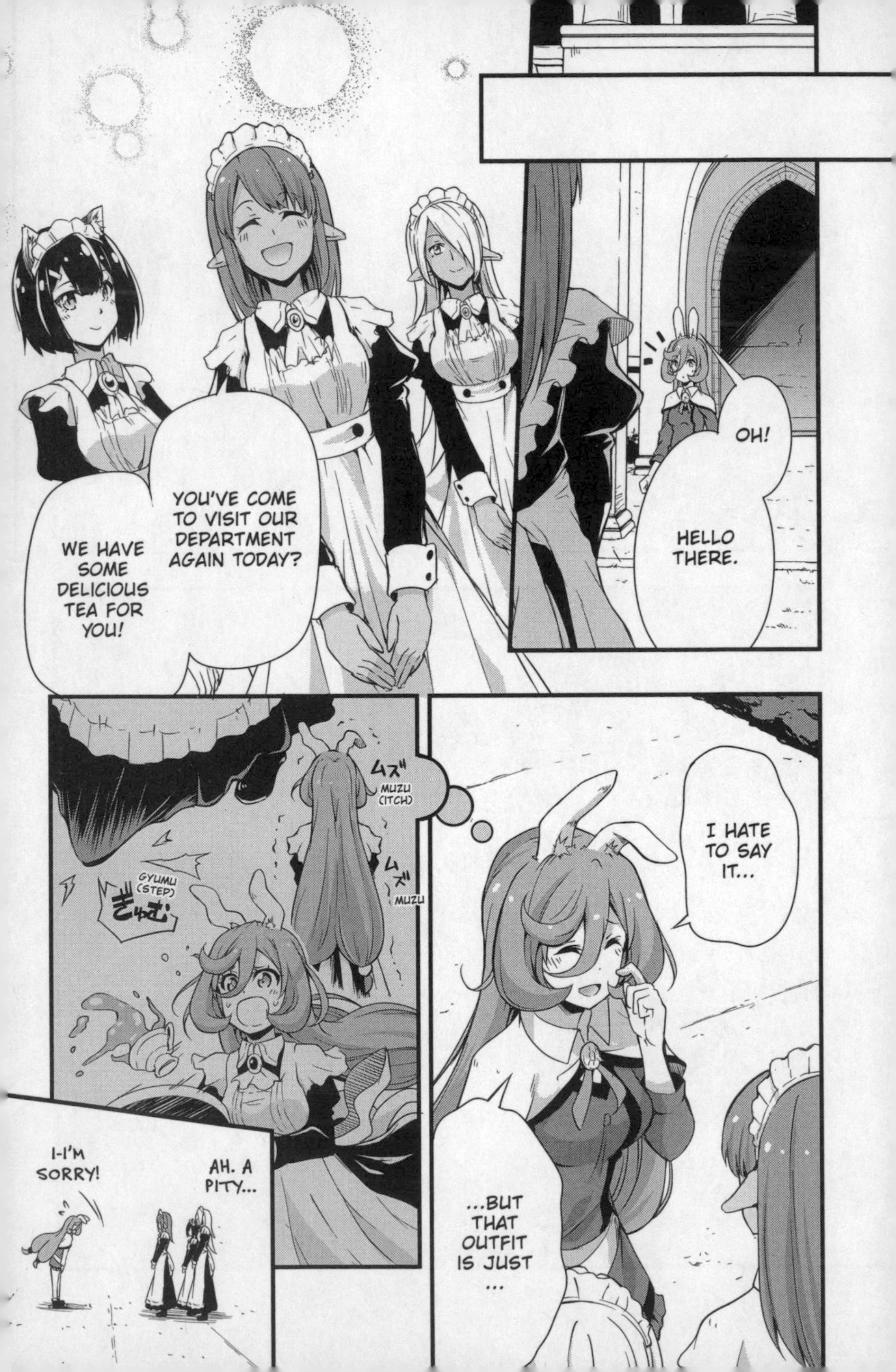
OH!
HELLO THERE.
YOU'VE COME TO VISIT OUR DEPARTMENT AGAIN TODAY?
WE HAVE SOME DELICIOUS TEA FOR YOU!
I HATE TO SAY IT...
...BUT THAT OUTFIT IS JUST ...
ムズ
MUZU (ITCH)
ムズ
MUZU
GYUMU (STEP)
ぎゅむ
I-I'M SORRY!
AH. A PITY...

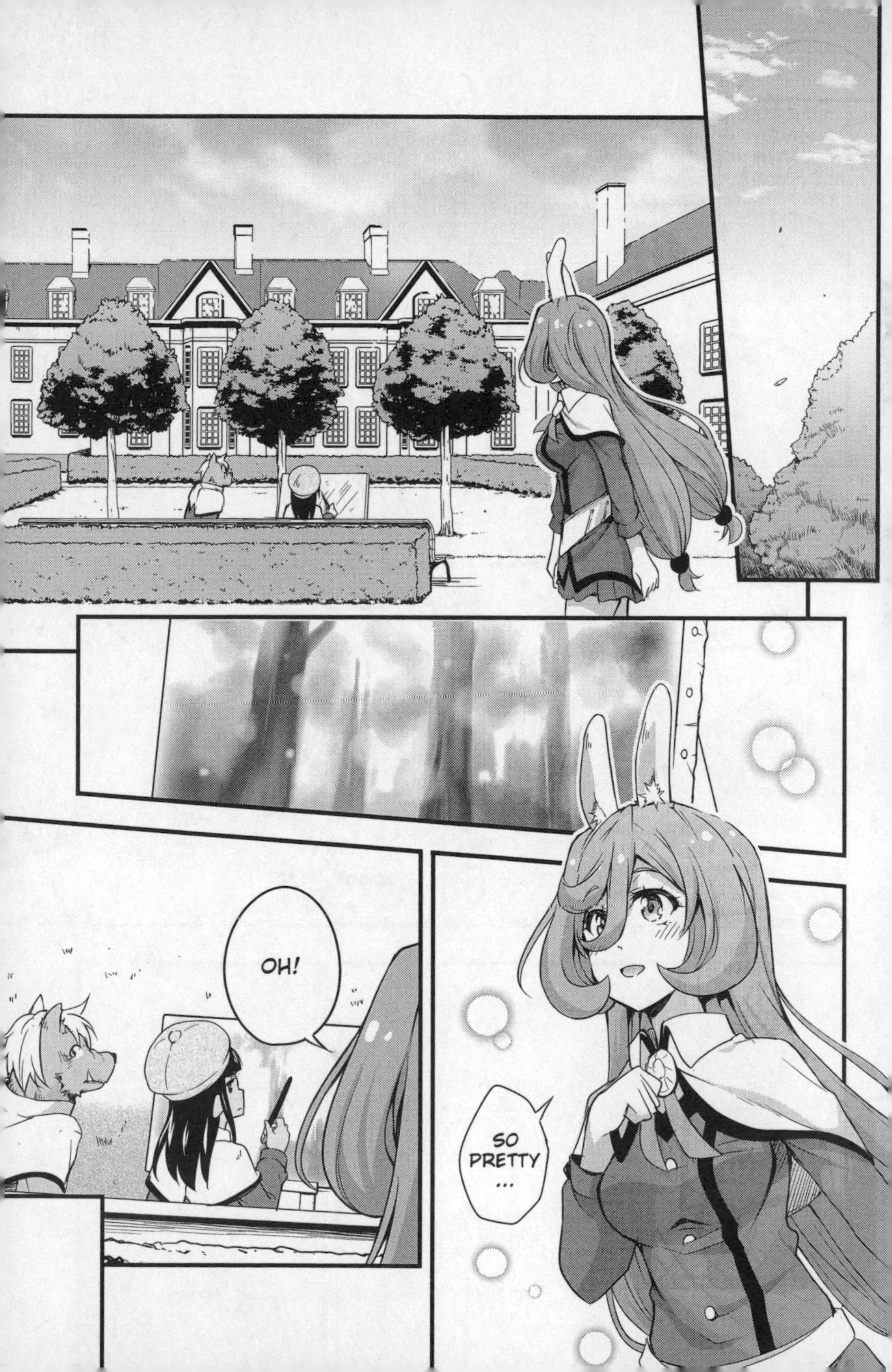
SO PRETTY ...
OH!

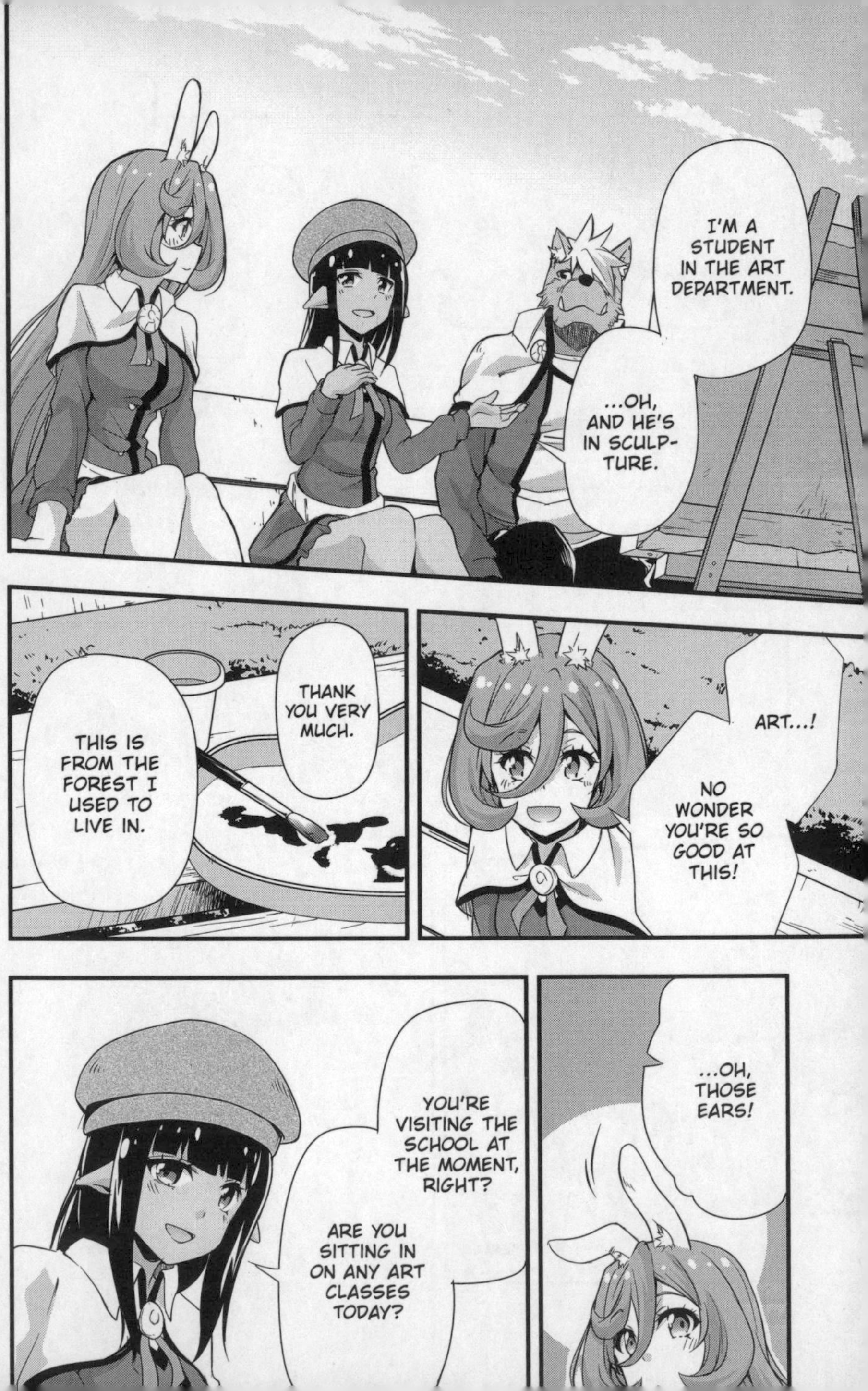
I'M A STUDENT IN THE ART DEPARTMENT.
...OH, AND HE'S IN SCULPTURE.
ART...!
NO WONDER YOU'RE SO GOOD AT THIS!
THANK YOU VERY MUCH.
THIS IS FROM THE FOREST I USED TO LIVE IN.
...OH, THOSE EARS!
YOU'RE VISITING THE SCHOOL AT THE MOMENT, RIGHT?
ARE YOU SITTING IN ON ANY ART CLASSES TODAY?

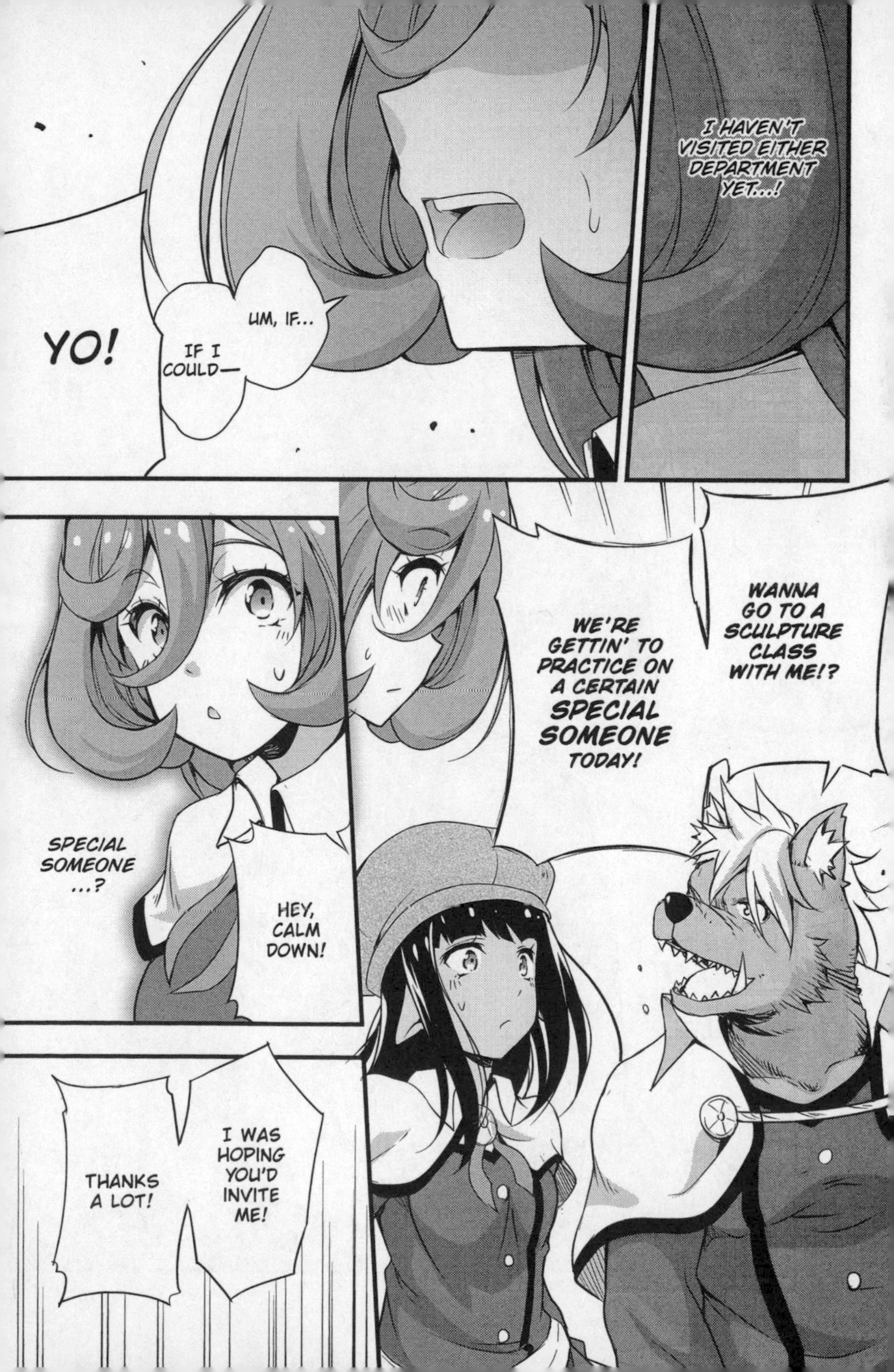
I HAVEN'T VISITED EITHER DEPARTMENT YET...!
UM, IF... IF I COULD—
YO!
WANNA GO TO A SCULPTURE CLASS WITH ME!?
WE'RE GETTIN' TO PRACTICE ON A CERTAIN SPECIAL SOMEONE TODAY!
HEY, CALM DOWN!
SPECIAL SOMEONE ...?
I WAS HOPING YOU'D INVITE ME!
THANKS A LOT!

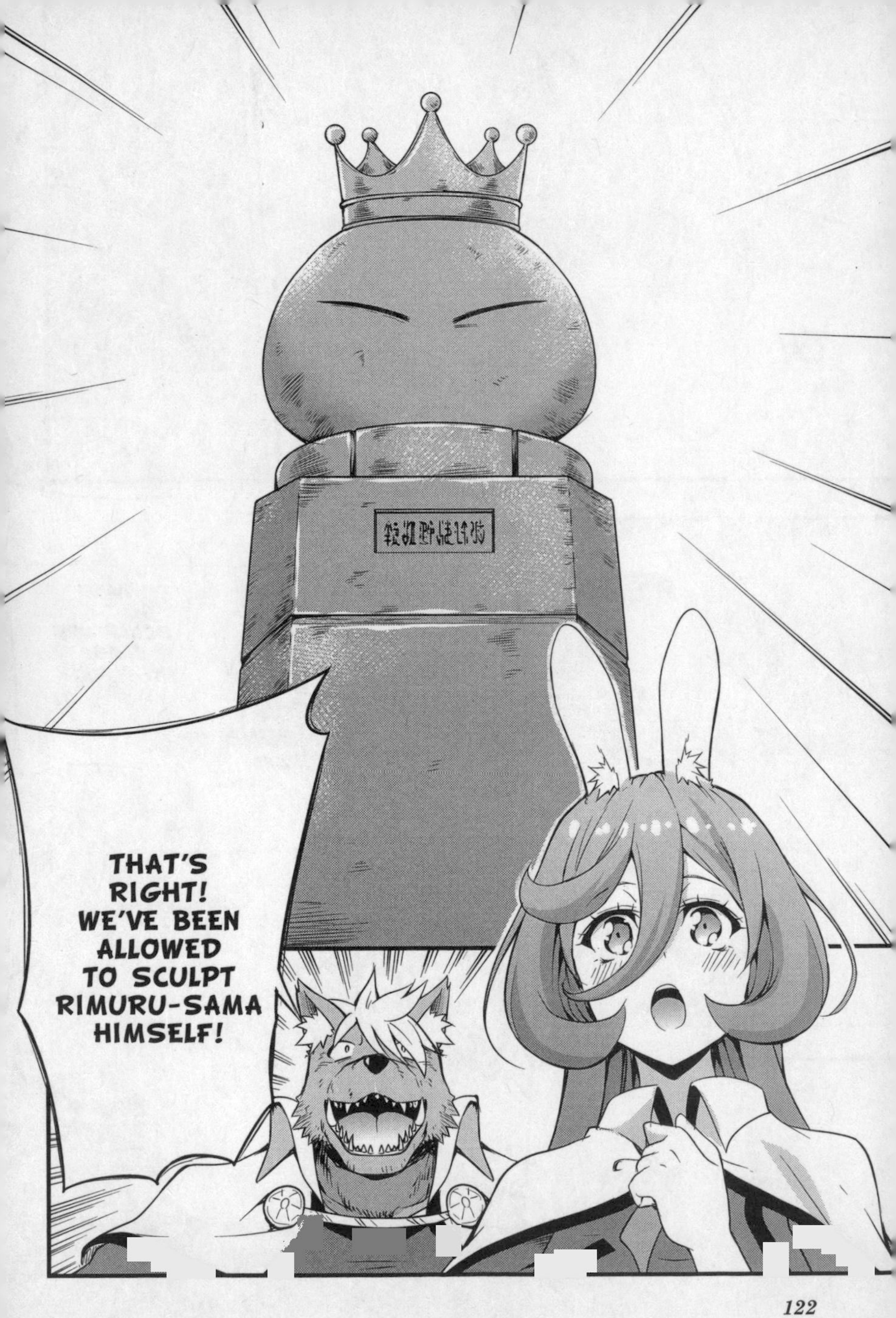
THAT'S RIGHT! WE'VE BEEN ALLOWED TO SCULPT RIMURU-SAMA HIMSELF!

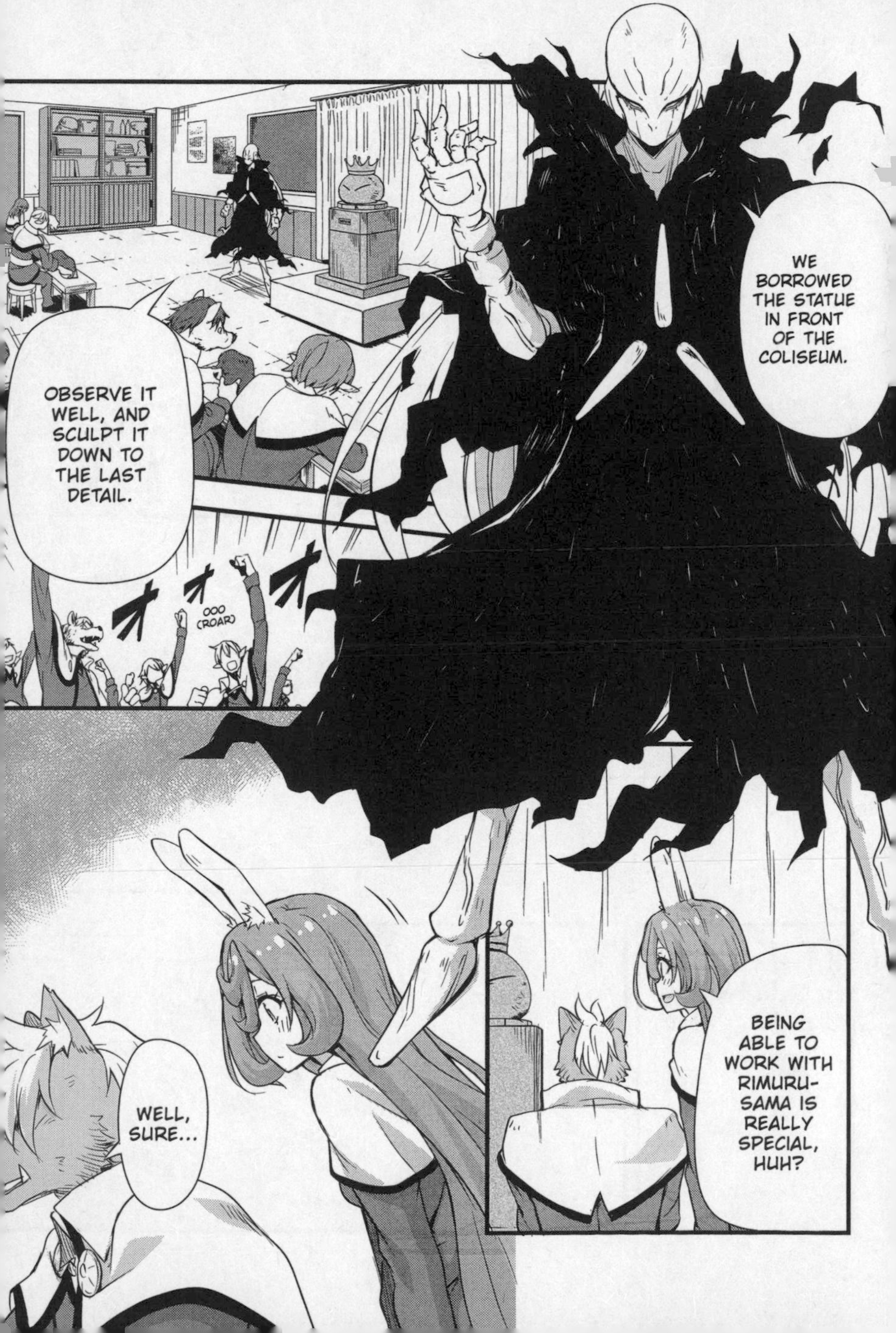
WE BORROWED THE STATUE IN FRONT OF THE COLISEUM.
OBSERVE IT WELL, AND SCULPT IT DOWN TO THE LAST DETAIL.
OOO (ROAR)
BEING ABLE TO WORK WITH RIMURU-SAMA IS REALLY SPECIAL, HUH?
WELL, SURE...

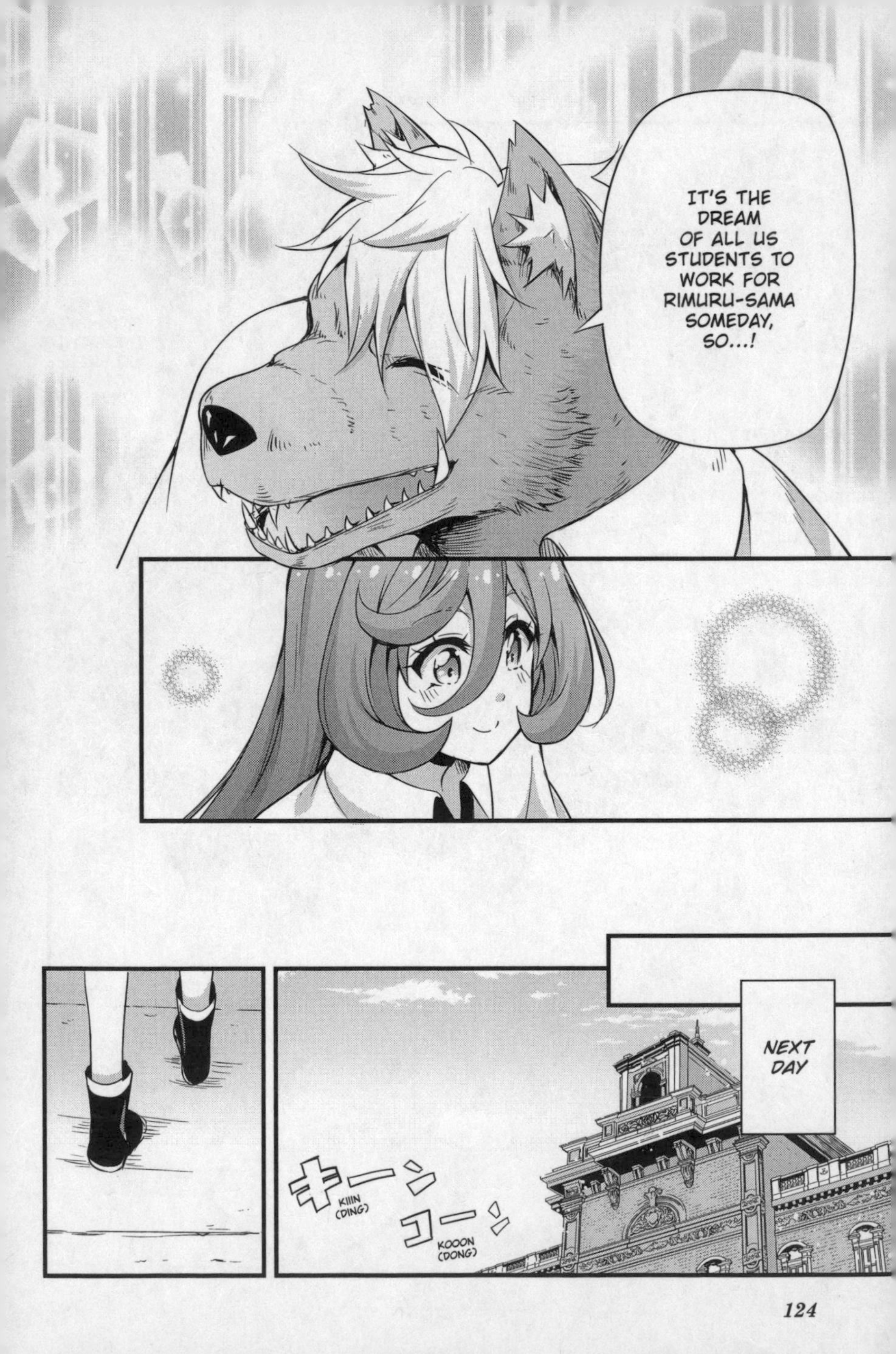
IT'S THE DREAM OF ALL US STUDENTS TO WORK FOR RIMURU-SAMA SOMEDAY, SO...!
NEXT DAY
キーン
KIIN (DING)
コーン
KOOON (DONG)

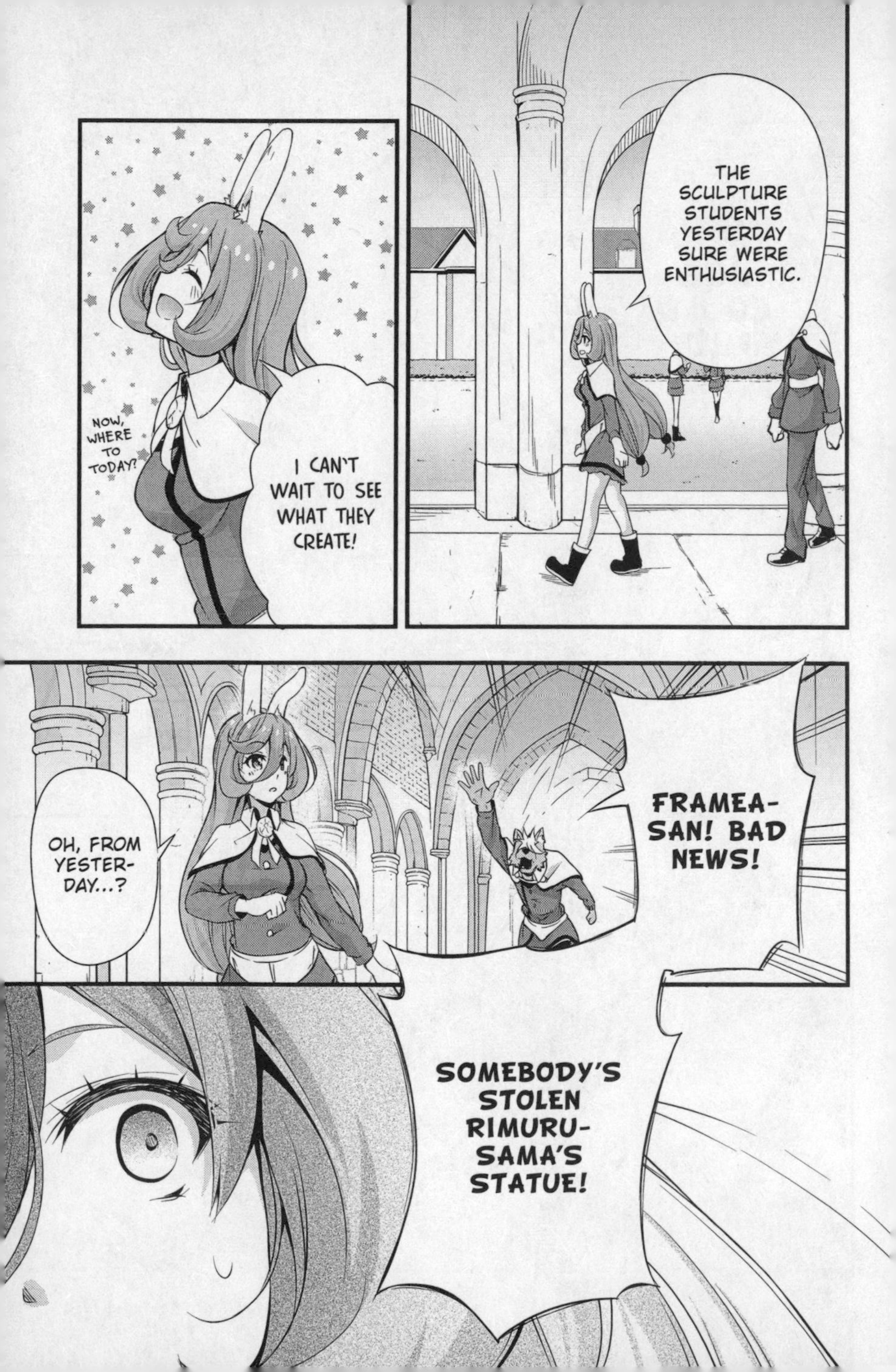
THE SCULPTURE STUDENTS YESTERDAY SURE WERE ENTHUSIASTIC.
I CAN'T WAIT TO SEE WHAT THEY CREATE!
NOW, WHERE TO TODAY?
FRAMEA-SAN! BAD NEWS!
OH, FROM YESTER-DAY...?
SOMEBODY'S STOLEN RIMURU-SAMA'S STATUE!

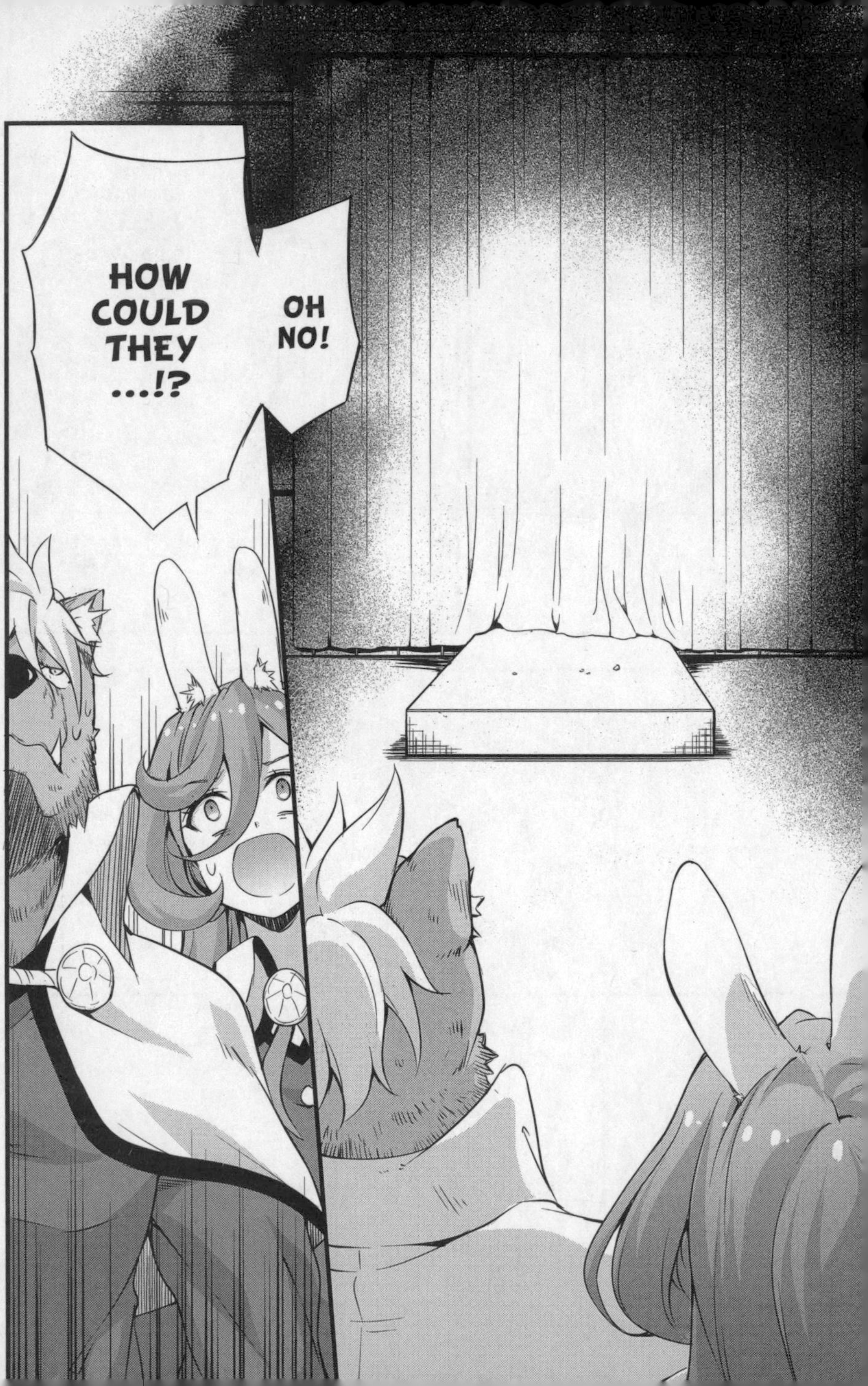
OH NO!
HOW COULD THEY ...!?

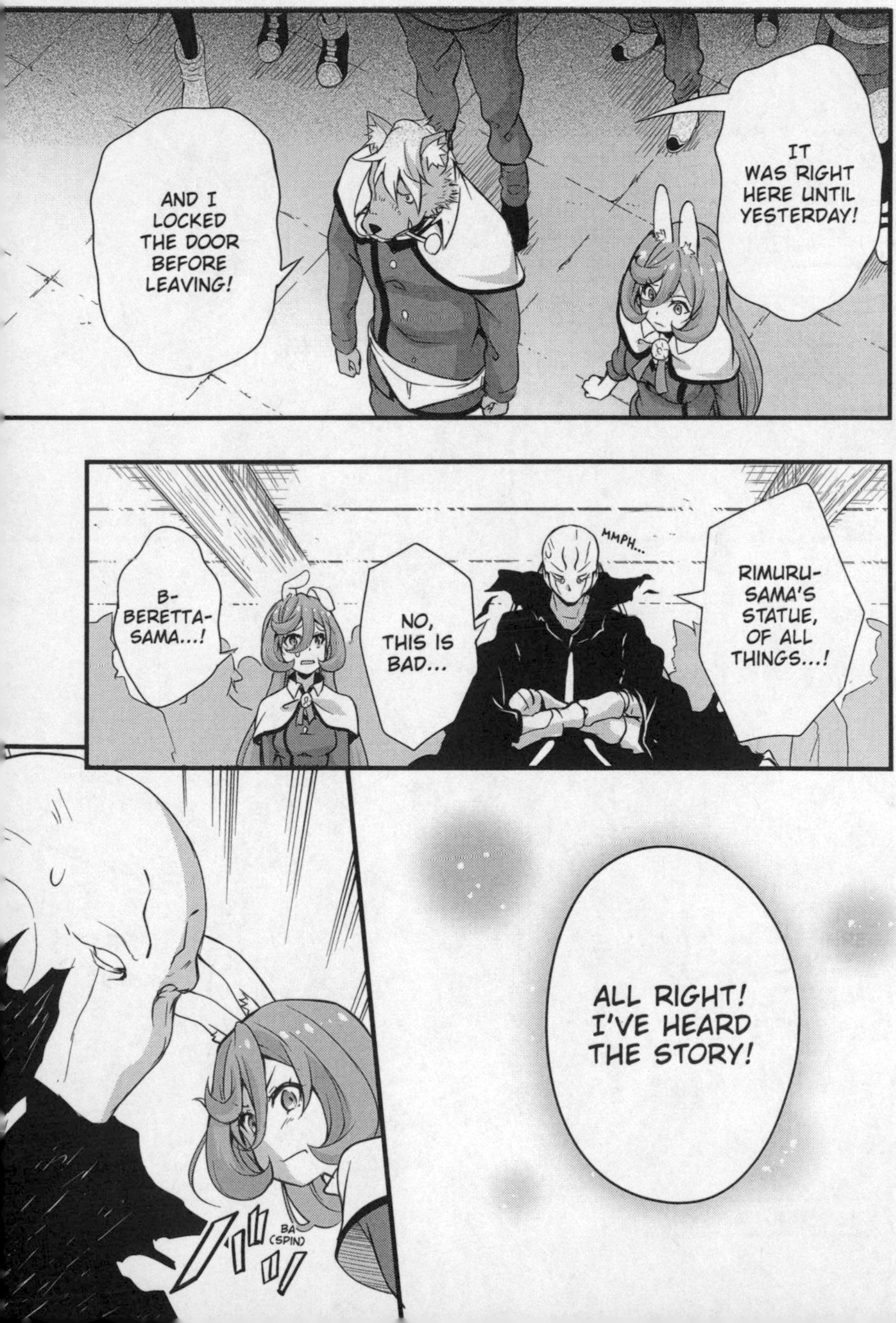
IT WAS RIGHT HERE UNTIL YESTERDAY!
AND I LOCKED THE DOOR BEFORE LEAVING!
RIMURU-SAMA'S STATUE, OF ALL THINGS...!
MMPH...
NO, THIS IS BAD...
B-BERETTA-SAMA...!
ALL RIGHT! I'VE HEARD THE STORY!
BA (SPIN)

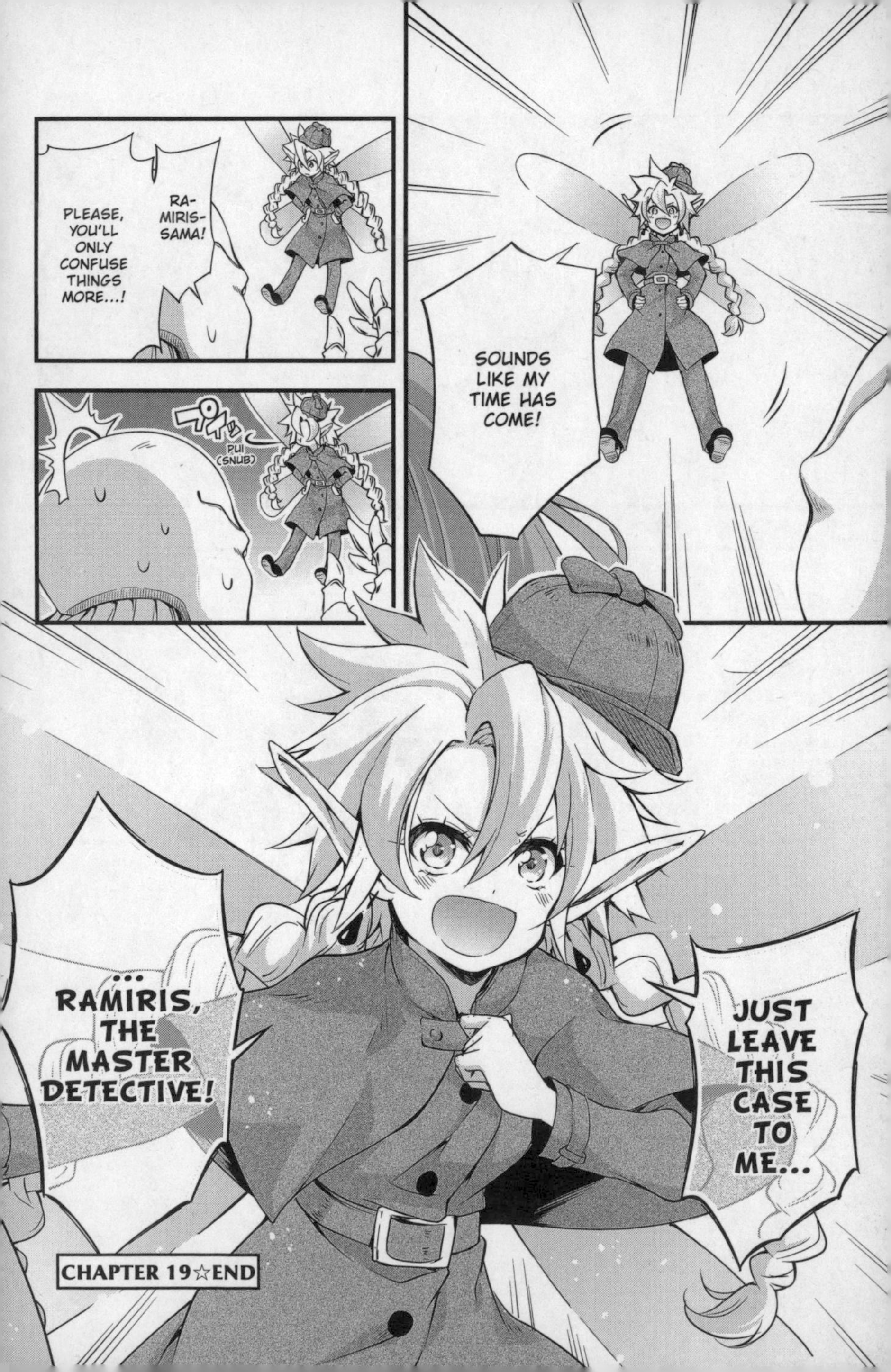
SOUNDS LIKE MY TIME HAS COME!
RA-MIRIS-SAMA!
PLEASE, YOU'LL ONLY CONFUSE THINGS MORE...!
PUI (SNUB)
JUST LEAVE THIS CASE TO ME...
...RAMIRIS, THE MASTER DETECTIVE!

CHAPTER 19☆END

That **Time** I **Got**
Reìncarnated
as a **SLIME**
The Ways of the Monster Nation

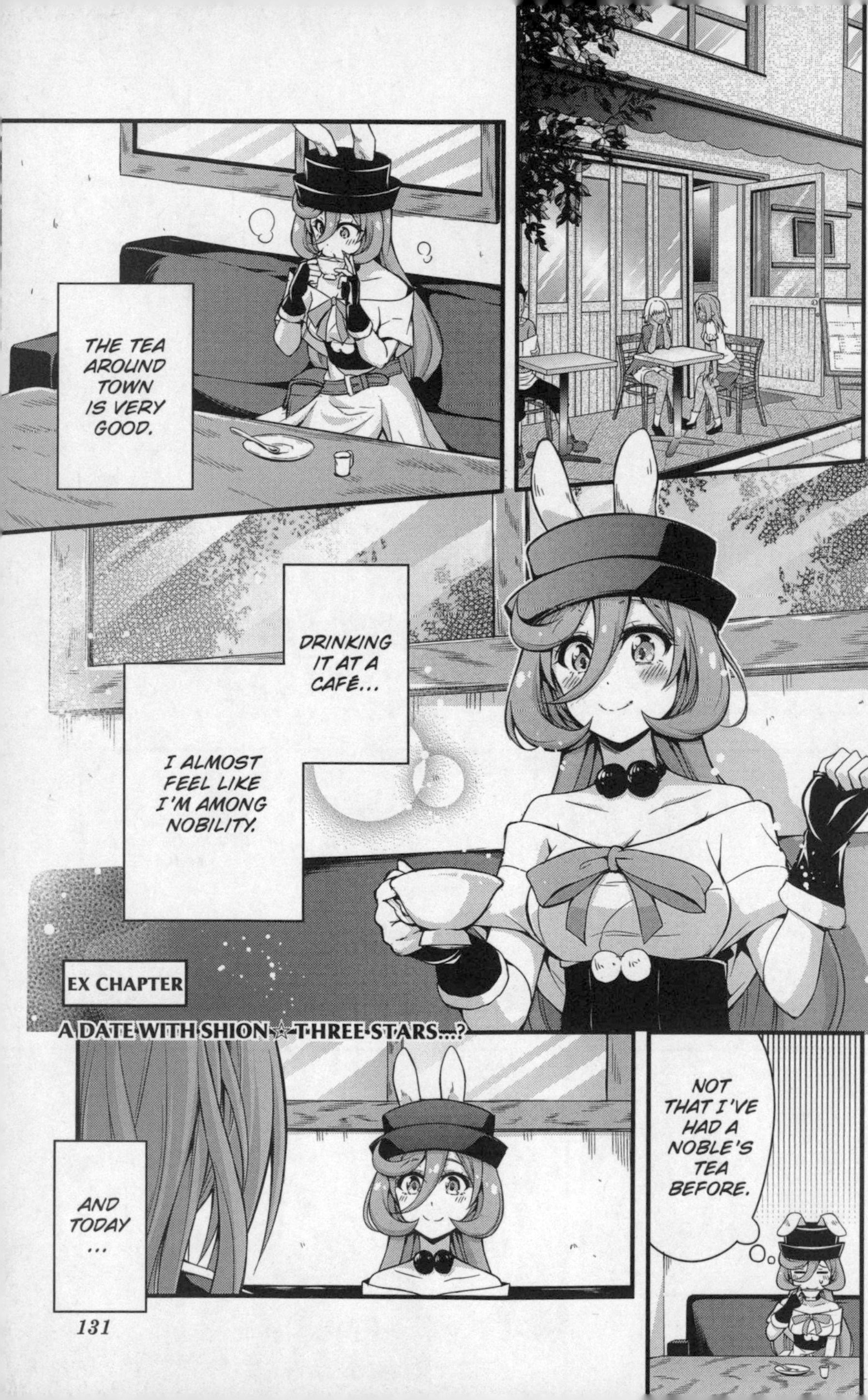
THE TEA AROUND TOWN IS VERY GOOD.
DRINKING IT AT A CAFÉ...
I ALMOST FEEL LIKE I'M AMONG NOBILITY.
EX CHAPTER
A DATE WITH SHION☆THREE STARS...?
NOT THAT I'VE HAD A NOBLE'S TEA BEFORE.
AND TODAY ...

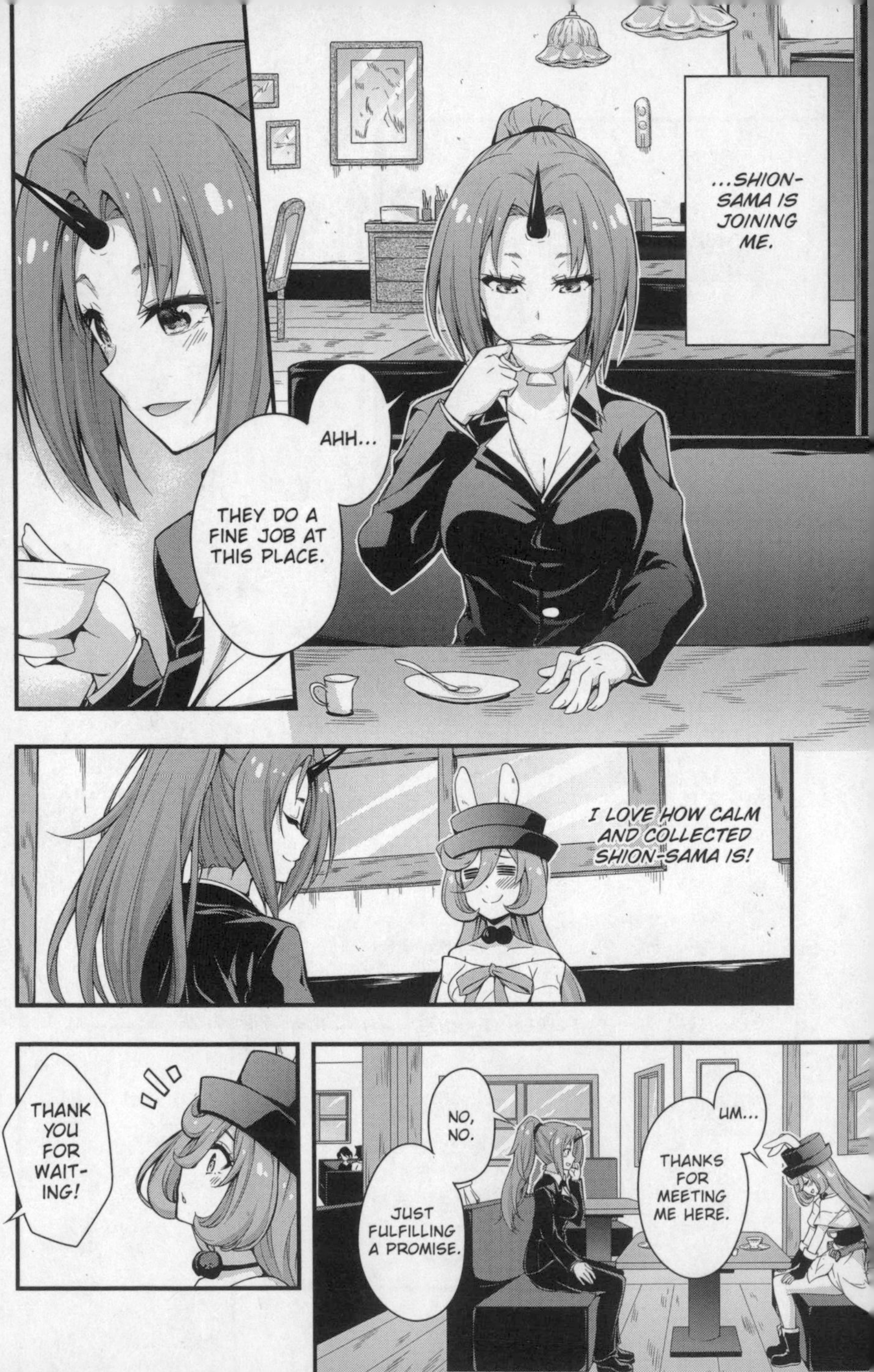
...SHION-SAMA IS JOINING ME.
AHH...
THEY DO A FINE JOB AT THIS PLACE.
I LOVE HOW CALM AND COLLECTED SHION-SAMA IS!
UM...
THANKS FOR MEETING ME HERE.
NO, NO.
JUST FULFILLING A PROMISE.
THANK YOU FOR WAIT-ING!

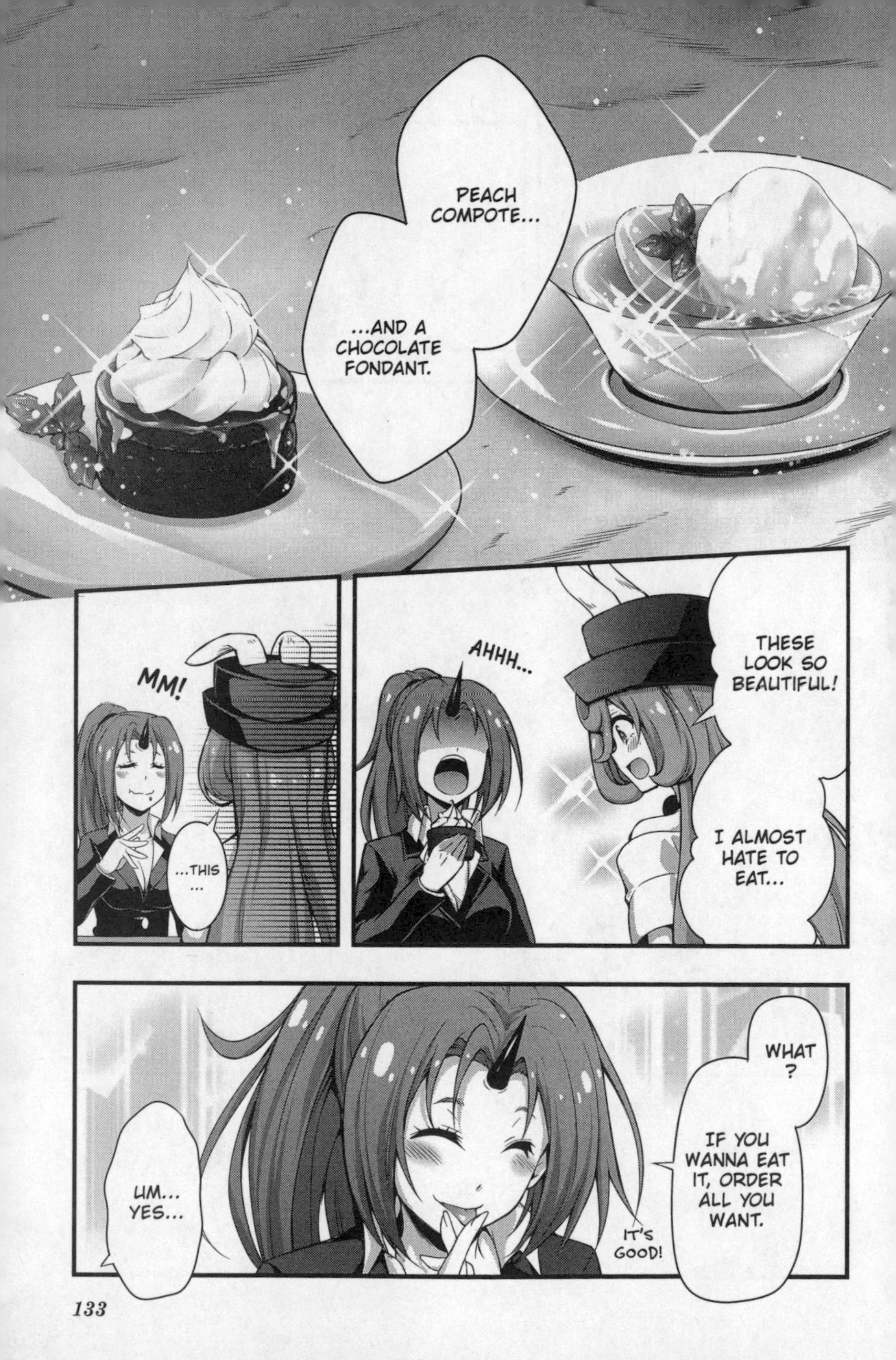
PEACH COMPOTE...
...AND A CHOCOLATE FONDANT.
THESE LOOK SO BEAUTIFUL!
I ALMOST HATE TO EAT...
AHHH...
MM!
...THIS ...
WHAT ?
IF YOU WANNA EAT IT, ORDER ALL YOU WANT.
IT'S GOOD!
UM... YES...

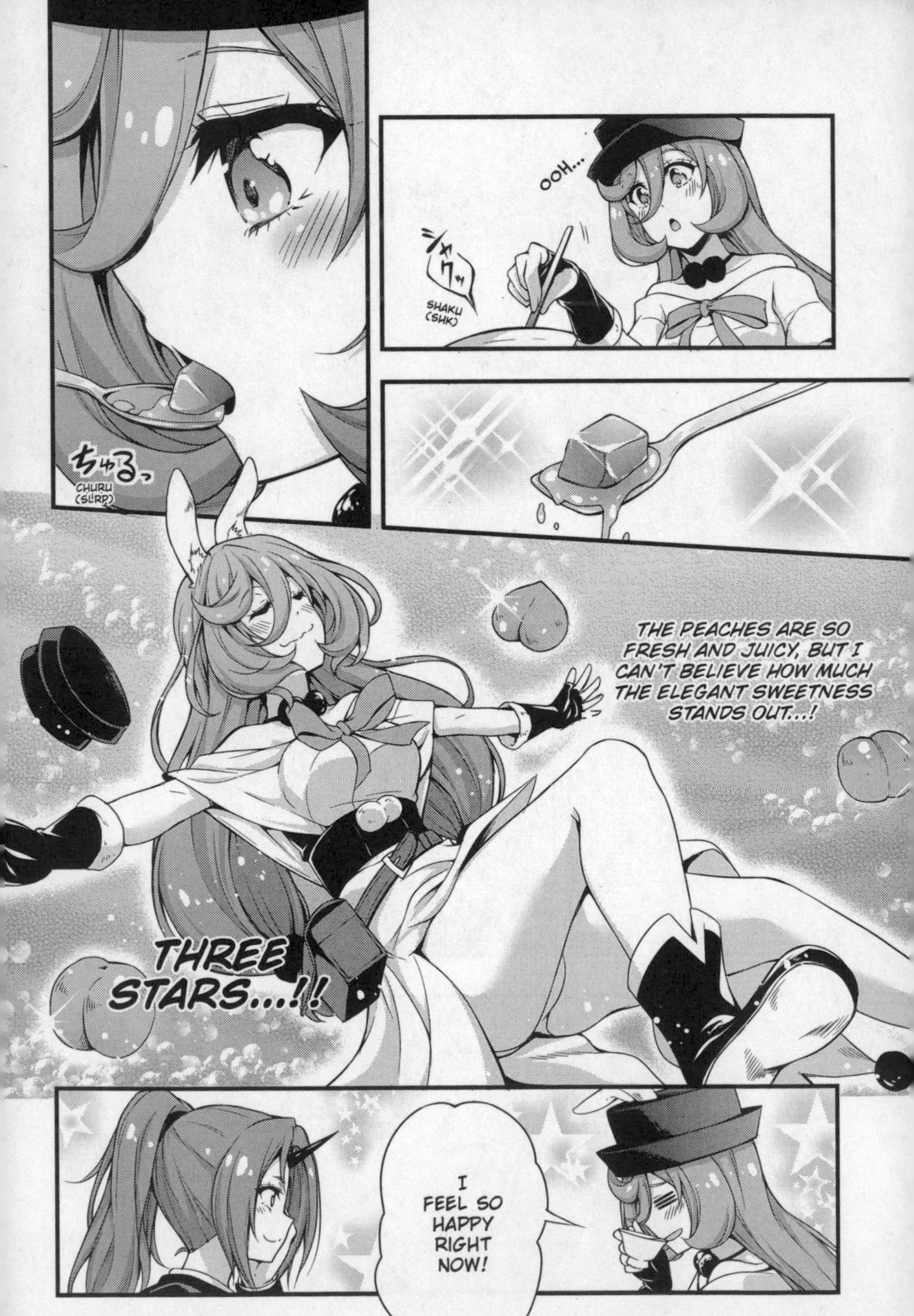
OOH...
シャクッ
SHAKU (SHK)
ちゅるっ
CHURU (SLURP)
THE PEACHES ARE SO FRESH AND JUICY, BUT I CAN'T BELIEVE HOW MUCH THE ELEGANT SWEETNESS STANDS OUT...!
THREE STARS...!!
I FEEL SO HAPPY RIGHT NOW!

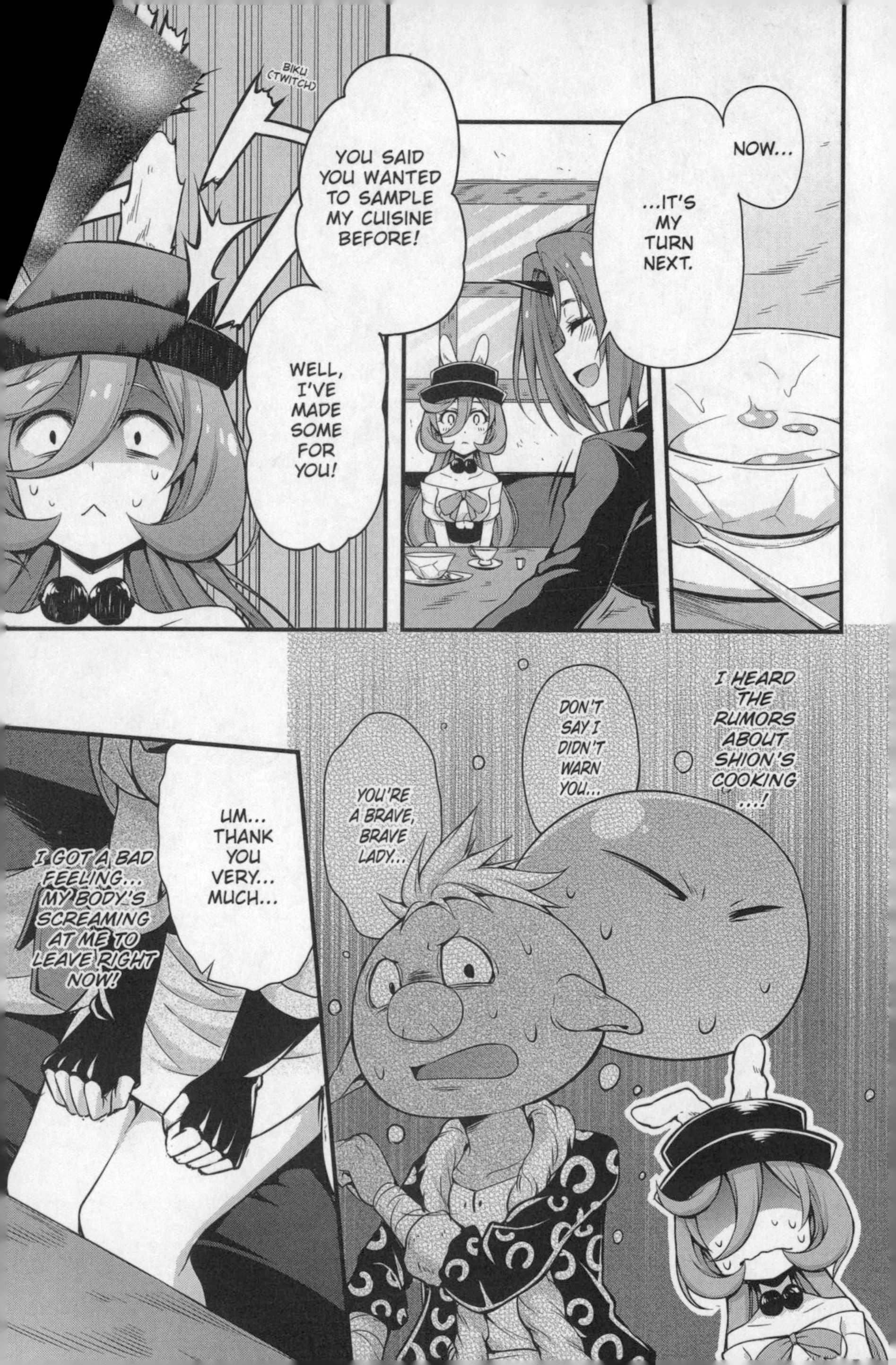
NOW...
...IT'S MY TURN NEXT.
YOU SAID YOU WANTED TO SAMPLE MY CUISINE BEFORE!
WELL, I'VE MADE SOME FOR YOU!
BIKU (TWITCH)
I HEARD THE RUMORS ABOUT SHION'S COOKING...!
DON'T SAY I DIDN'T WARN YOU...
YOU'RE A BRAVE, BRAVE LADY...
UM... THANK YOU VERY... MUCH...
I GOT A BAD FEELING... MY BODY'S SCREAMING AT ME TO LEAVE RIGHT NOW!

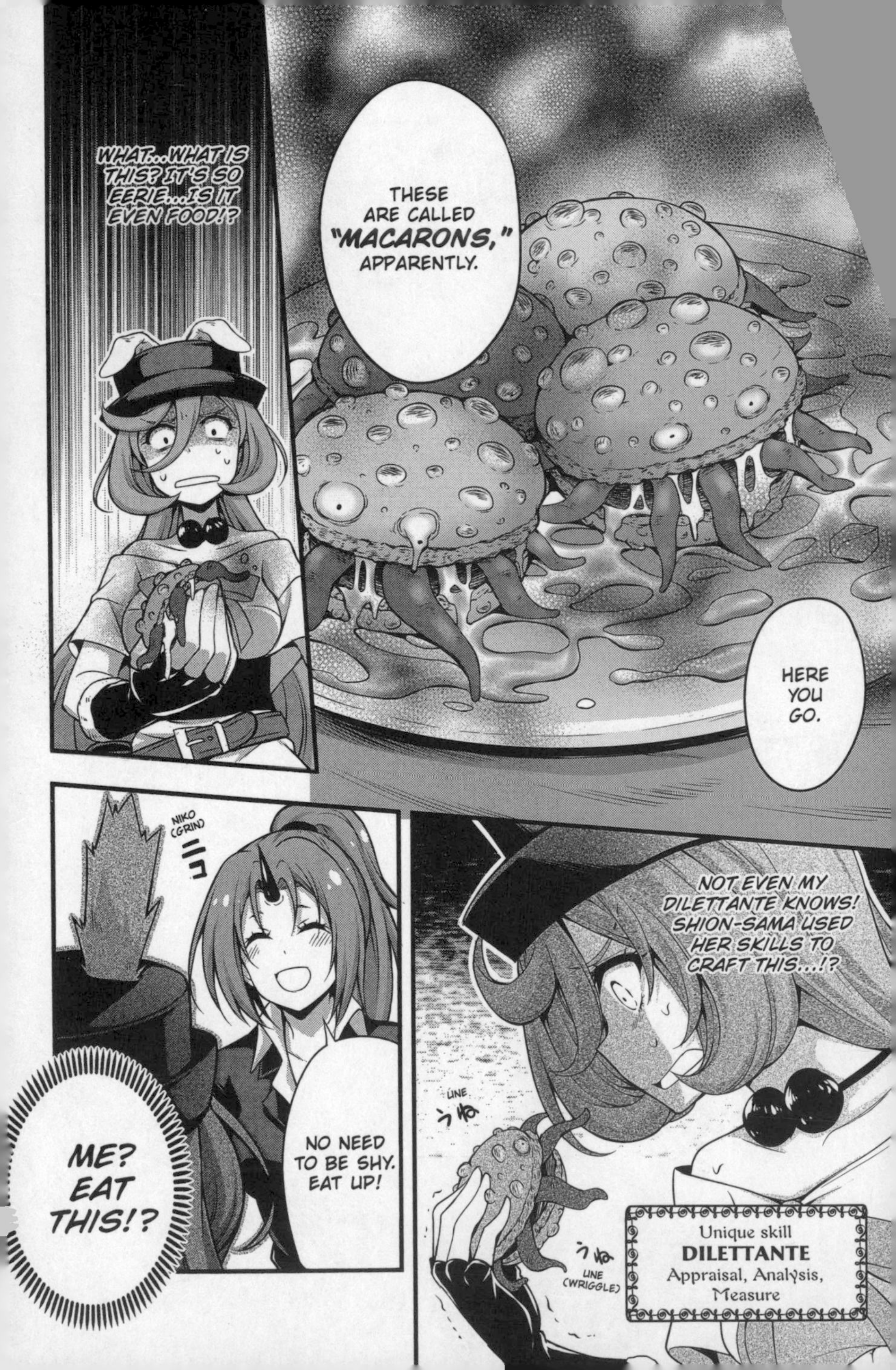
THESE ARE CALLED "MACARONS," APPARENTLY.
HERE YOU GO.
WHAT...WHAT IS THIS? IT'S SO EERIE...IS IT EVEN FOOD!?
NOT EVEN MY DILETTANTE KNOWS! SHION-SAMA USED HER SKILLS TO CRAFT THIS...!?
うね
LINE
Unique skill
DILETTANTE
Appraisal, Analysis, Measure
うね
LINE (WRIGGLE)
ニコ
NIKO (GRIN)
NO NEED TO BE SHY. EAT UP!
ME? EAT THIS!?

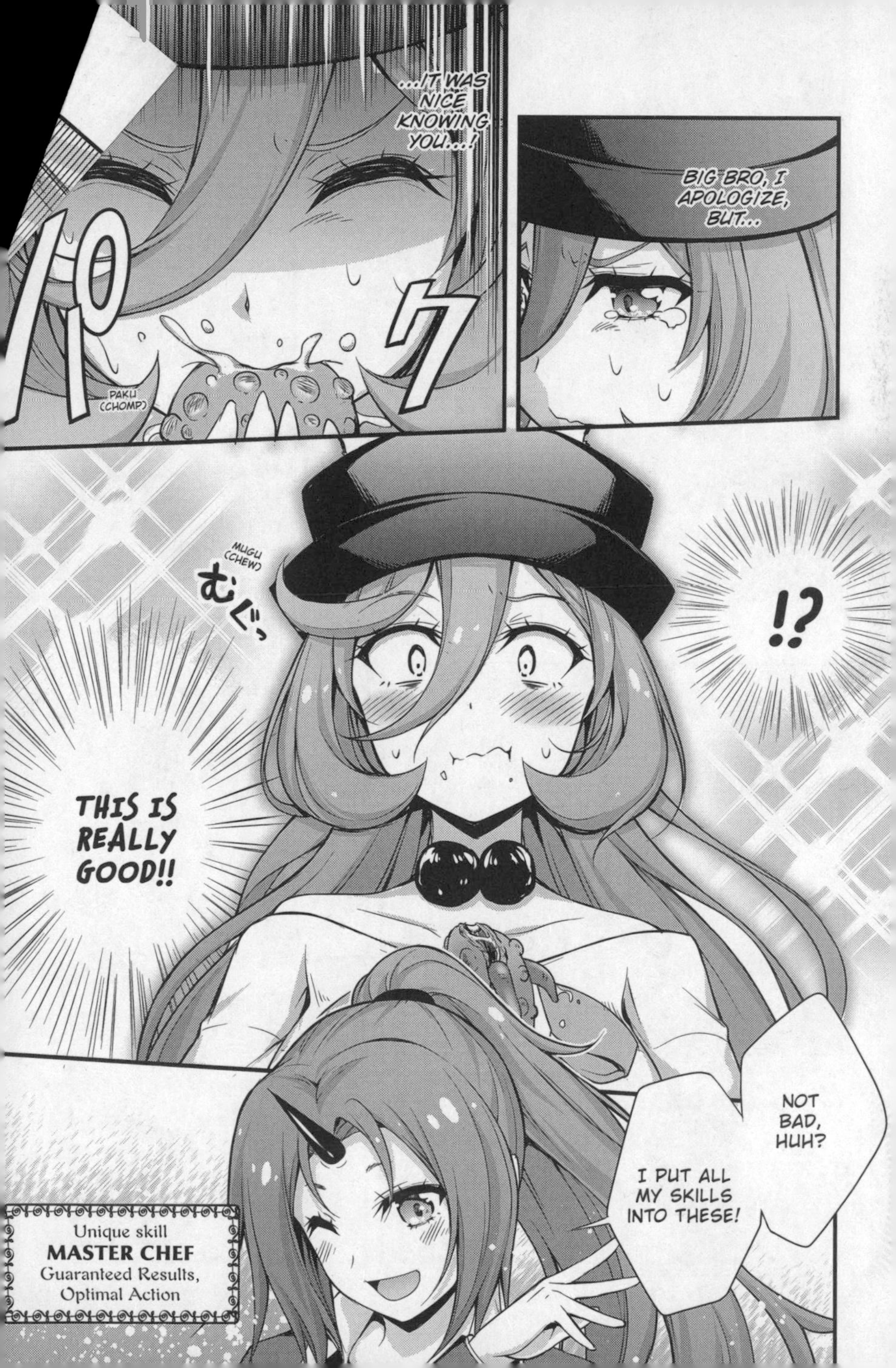
BIG BRO, I APOLOGIZE, BUT...
...IT WAS NICE KNOWING YOU...!
パク
PAKU (CHOMP)
!?
MUGU (CHEW)
むぐっ
THIS IS REALLY GOOD!!
NOT BAD, HUH?
I PUT ALL MY SKILLS INTO THESE!
Unique skill
MASTER CHEF
Guaranteed Results, Optimal Action

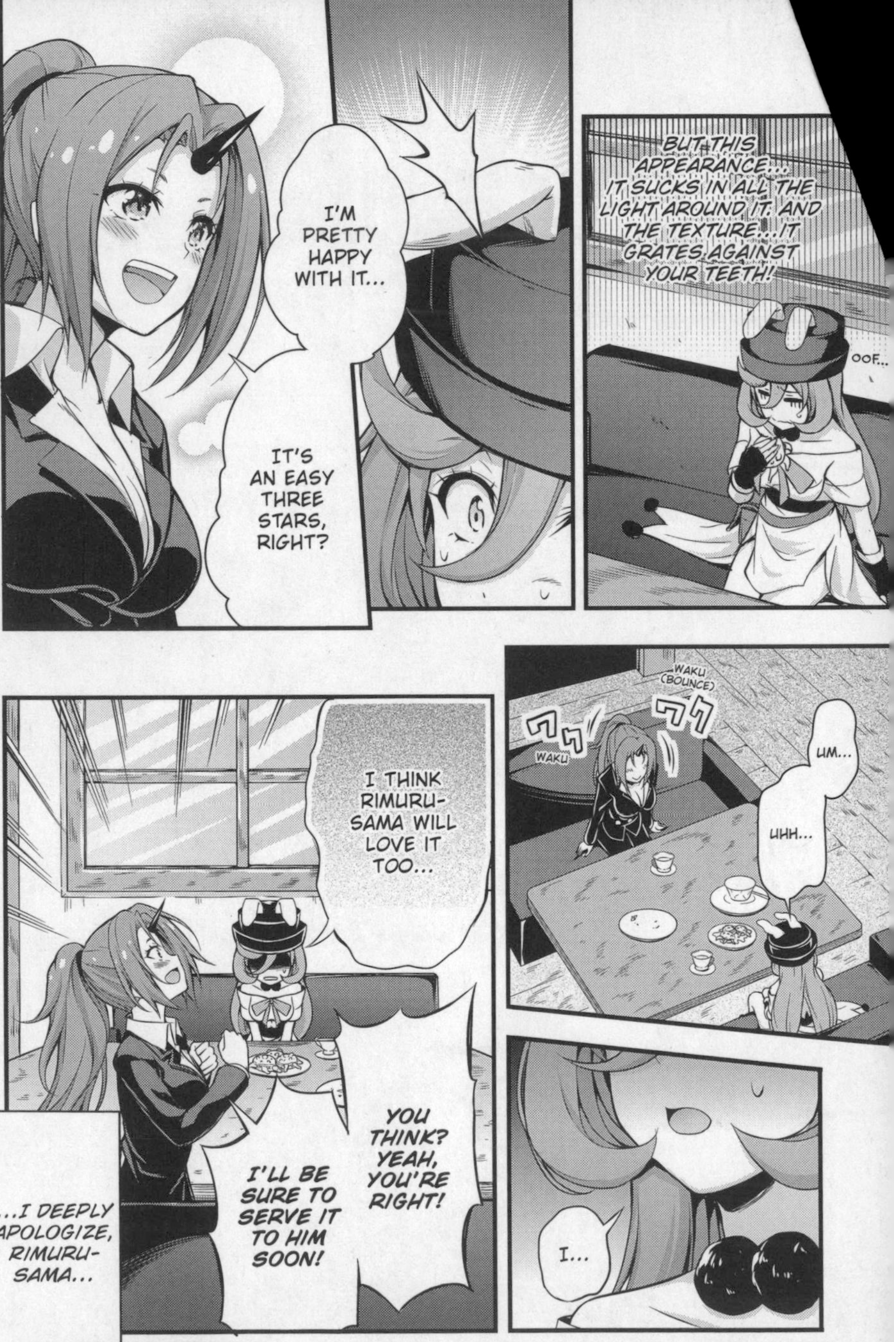
BUT THIS APPEARANCE... IT SUCKS IN ALL THE LIGHT AROUND IT. AND THE TEXTURE... IT GRATES AGAINST YOUR TEETH!
OOF...
I'M PRETTY HAPPY WITH IT...
IT'S AN EASY THREE STARS, RIGHT?
WAKU (BOUNCE)
WAKU
UM...
UHH...
I...
I THINK RIMURU-SAMA WILL LOVE IT TOO...
YOU THINK? YEAH, YOU'RE RIGHT!
I'LL BE SURE TO SERVE IT TO HIM SOON!
...I DEEPLY APOLOGIZE, RIMURU-SAMA...

EX CHAPTER☆END

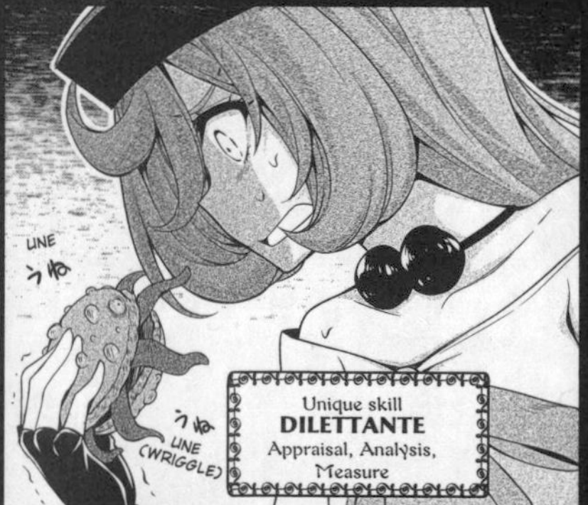

LINE
うね
Unique skill
DILETTANTE
Appraisal, Analysis, Measure
うね
LINE (WRIGGLE)

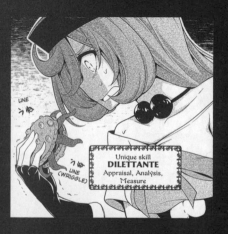

That Time I Got Reincarnated as a SLIME
The Ways of the Monster Nation

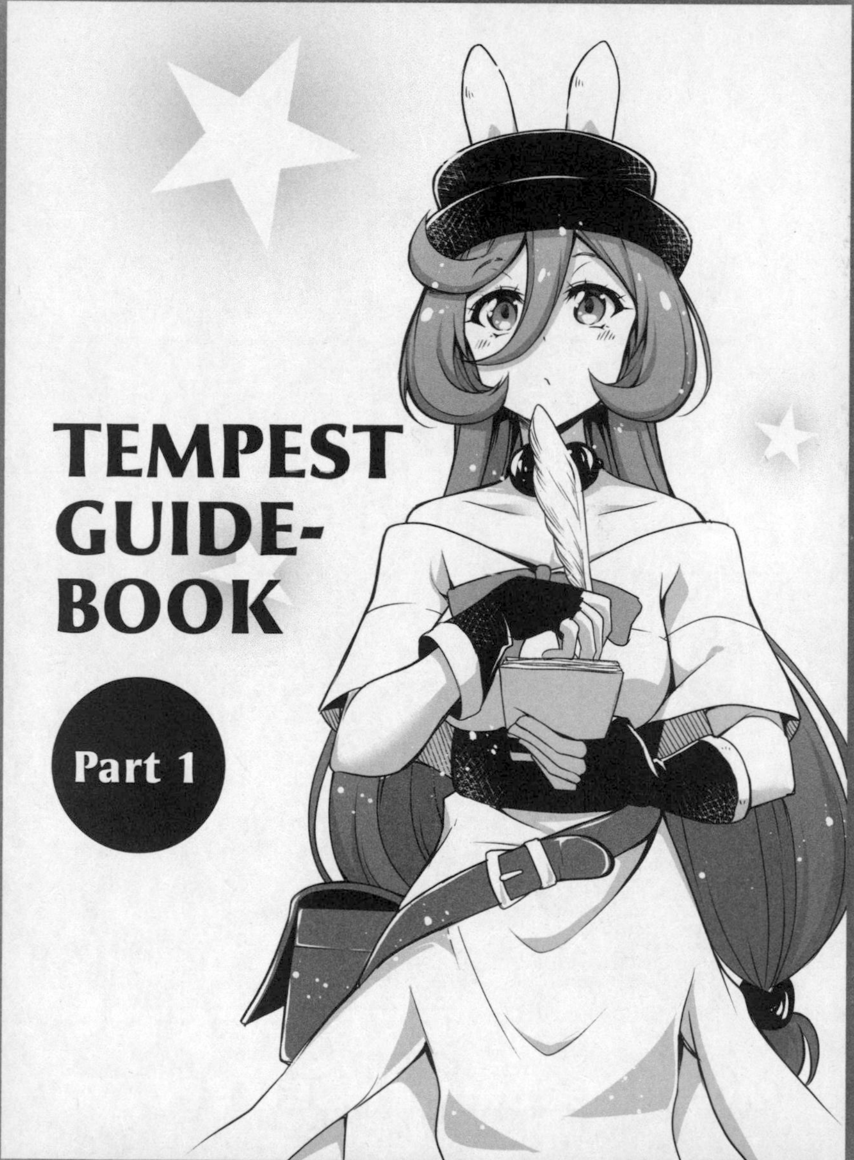
TEMPEST GUIDE-BOOK
Part 1

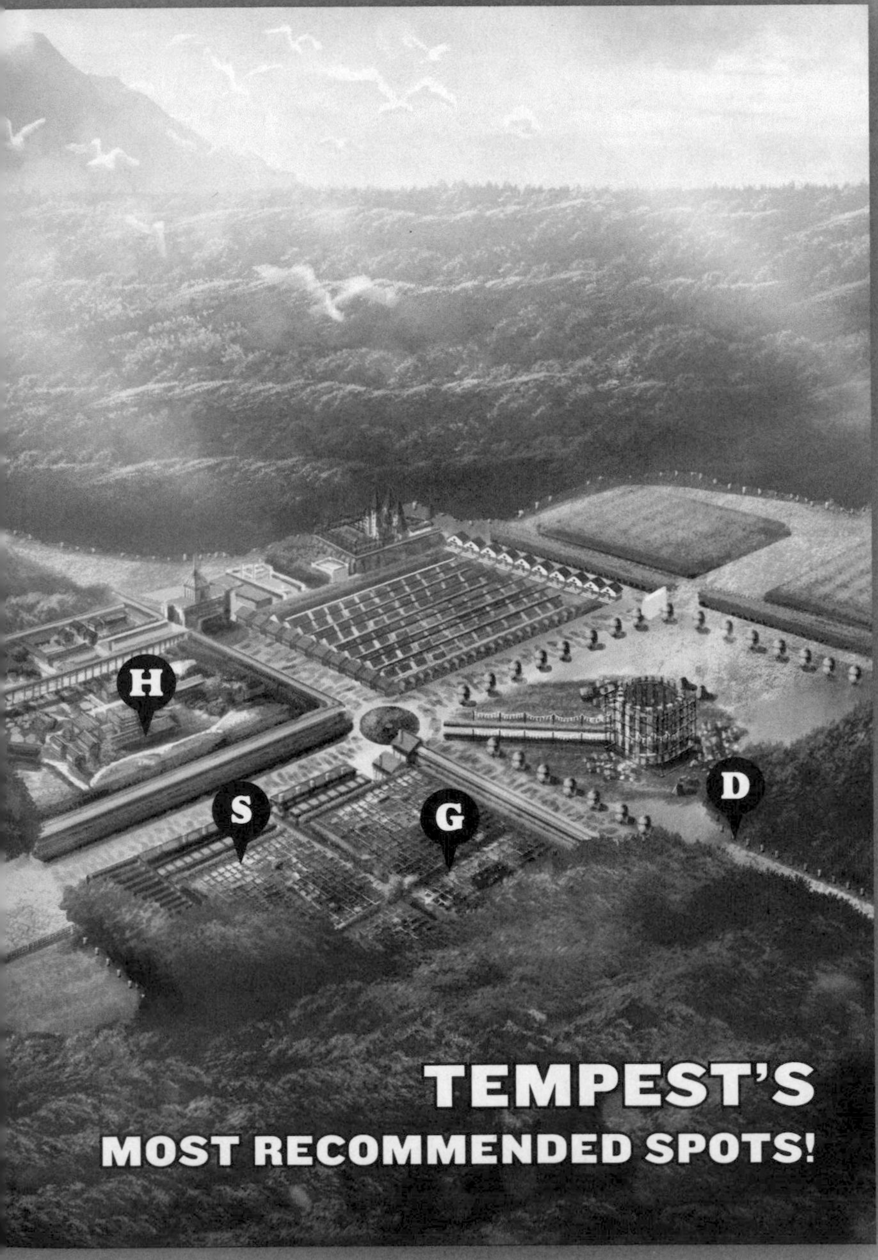
H
S
G
D
TEMPEST'S
MOST RECOMMENDED SPOTS!

TEMPEST GUIDEBOOK Part 1
CONTENTS

GOURMET

GOTTA TRY IT!
GOURMET PICKS

SHOPPING

A MUST IN THE CITY!
SHOPPING GUIDE

HEALING

REST YOUR BONES!
A MOMENT OF SOLACE

DUNGEON

STRIKE IT RICH!?
**CONQUER THE
LABYRINTH**

RUMORS

COULD YOU MEET VELDORA!?
**RUMORS AROUND
TEMPEST**

GOTTA TRY IT!
GOURMET PICKS

Under the guidance of the demon lord Rimuru-sama, Tempest is developing new kinds of food not seen anywhere else. Let's take a look at some of the hottest meals it has to offer!

A Relaxing Break in a Trendy Café

In Rimuru, the capital of Tempest, places called "cafés" that offer light fare are currently popular. The one pictured here features both indoor and outdoor seating, which feels great on sunny days!

The tea served here is very fragrant, with a rich taste that really sticks with you! But while the tea is excellent, the item I'd recommend the most is the cake!

It turns out that the cakes served here are from an artisan who learned the craft from master baker Yoshida-sama, whose work has been praised by nobility from all over!

Peach compote

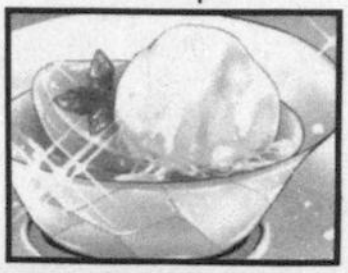

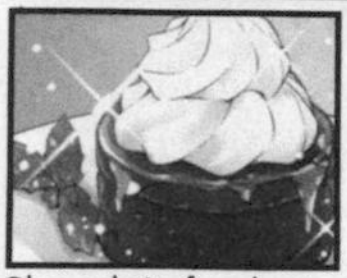

Chocolate fondant

From the "peach compote" that fully showcases the sweetness of their fresh, juicy peaches, to a "chocolate fondant" that grabs you with a rich, sweet flavor and a light, bitter touch...

They're all great, and you'll want to try every variety!

Tackling the Gourmet Road

But Tempest isn't the only place for the latest in haute cuisine! The highway linking the city to Blumund is also lined with delicacies you won't find anywhere else!

"Ramen" and "hamburgers" have become famous, but there's still at least one hidden delight you won't find elsewhere—the "Tempest pizza"!

Made with a crispy bread shell and melted cheese, it's the perfect combination—

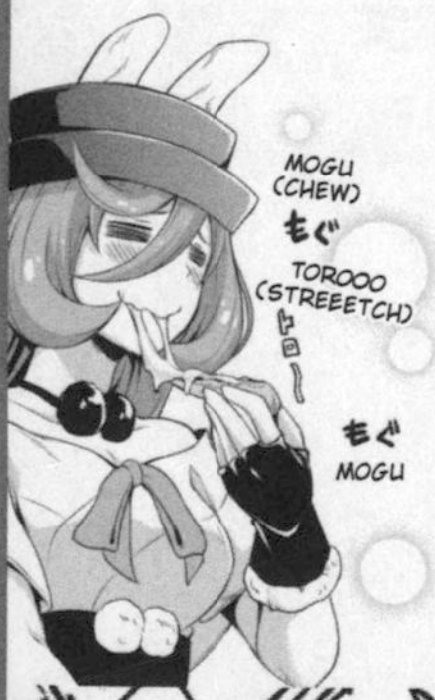
MOGU (CHEW)
もぐ
TOROOO (STREEETCH)
トロ〜
もぐ
MOGU

and it's lovely paired with a nice cold ale!

It's growing more popular by the day, so make sure to grab it while it's hot!

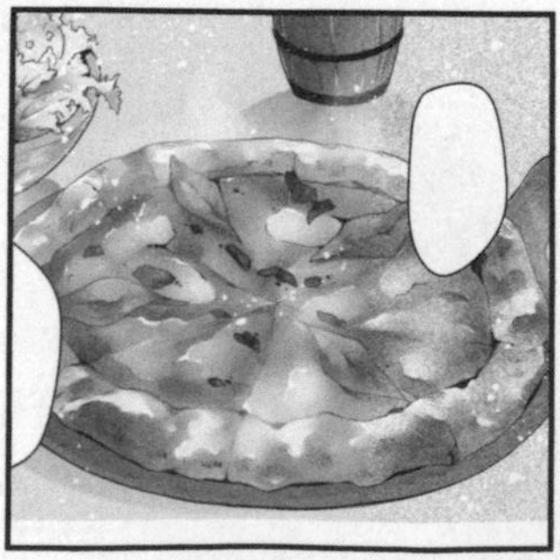

A MUST IN THE CITY!
SHOPPING GUIDE

From adventurers to nobility, people of all classes are coming to visit Tempest. Here's just some of the city's most popular goods, sure to satisfy anyone.

GOURMET

SHOPPING

HEALING

DUNGEON

RUMORS

The Cutting Edge of Fashion

The commercial center of Tempest directly faces the main entrance, ensuring that it's always lively with tourists. My top recommendation is this store, noted for its large windows.

The staff at this boutique consists of not only humans, but also goblinas and representatives from other species, ensuring warm customer service for anyone who visits. Whether you're a human, monster, or demi-human, you'll always feel welcome!

What's more, this shop also occasionally features an exclusive line crafted by the "Oracle" Shuna-sama! I'm sure any woman would want to come here at least once—and if you're in the market for fine silk clothing, this is by far your best option!

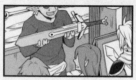

Top Picks for Adventurers!

Tempest's weapon shops offer a fine variety of high-quality equipment. And why wouldn't they? After all, each store is stocked with the latest from the local forges, hammered out by the apprentices of masters like the legendary dwarven smith Kaijin-sama and Tempest's most well-known creator Kurobe-sama!

Weapons from the masters themselves are not for sale to the public, sadly, but you'll still find quality on a level you'd be hard-pressed to track down elsewhere!

That cute, yet imposing form…

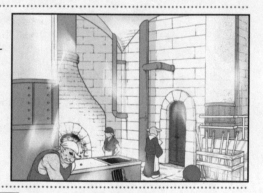

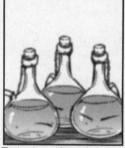

New and Trendy!

Looking for the latest hot souvenir to take home from your stay in Tempest? Look no further! These flasks are modeled after the noble visage of Tempest's leader, the demon lord Rimuru-sama—and what's more, each one contains a dose of healing potion! All this at an impulse-buy price that'll seriously shock you!

REST YOUR BONES!
A MOMENT OF SOLACE

The spa area of Tempest is a hot spot for nobility and wealthy merchants. There's a selection of high-end resorts for them, but the "hot springs" can be enjoyed by farmers, adventurers, and everyone else. What charms can you discover in these relaxing springs?

The "foot bath" is a casual way to sample the springs' healing powers.

The hot springs in Tempest offer more than just a relaxing soak—their waters are also said to provide you with beautiful skin!

Although many readers might not be used to taking regular baths, once you try these springs out, you're guaranteed to become a lifelong believer!

The "yukata" gowns worn by visitors to the springs are also loose, comfortable, and help you get into a relaxing mood. These are available for free at many inns, so ask your innkeeper for details.

Savoring the starry sky at night heals your body and soul!

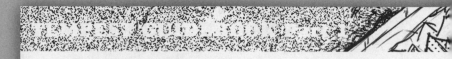

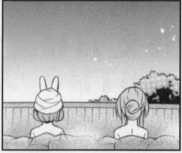

While many springs are available, one particular highlight is the open-air baths. Being outdoors, they offer warm springs, fresh air, and breathtaking views of the outdoors—all at once! Try them, or you'll really be missing out!

Exclusive Gourmet Treats

There's more to enjoy in the hot springs than just the baths! Make sure to scope out the gourmet offerings you won't find anywhere else in town!

One top recommendation: the cowdeer milk available post-bath, chilled near freezing and ready to quench your thirst. Don't forget to put a hand to your hip while chugging it down! Also try the eggs soaked and cooked in the springs themselves—the melt-in-your-mouth taste must be experienced to be believed!

GUIII
(SWIIIG)

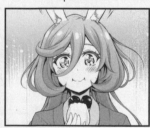

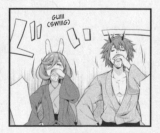

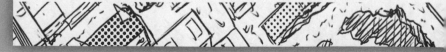

STRIKE IT RICH!?
CONQUER THE LABYRINTH

With fewer monsters roaming the Forest of Jura, adventurers are running out of work—but good news! Why not set up shop in the Dungeon, full of thrills and big profits?

The Dungeon built underneath Tempest is a true master-work, built by the demon lord Ramiris-sama herself! It's a true must for any adventurer in the area. Dangerous monsters lurk within its corridors, so you'll definitely want to form a party to explore it—but conquer those monsters, and you'll earn tons of crystals and parts!

What's more, if you can navigate the monster hordes and tricky traps, treasure chests are waiting for you beyond—magical chests that may contain "Special" or even "Rare" items to loot! Talk about striking it rich!

To those with enough mettle, the Dungeon is a dream come true—don't miss it!

An Oasis in the Labyrinth

The "Explorers' Rest Stop," accessible at Floor 95 via the stairways, is a tad more expensive than typical inns, but offers warm baths and soft beds that're perfect for resting your weary bones after a quest.

The Rest Stop has food and drink too, of course, so whether it's a hearty meal or an ice-cold ale you seek, there's no better place to carouse with your friends and divvy up your booty!

The dungeon floors get trickier and more treacherous as you descend, but the joys waiting at the end can prove addictive!

A Must for All Explorers

Want to hit the Dungeon? Then make absolutely sure to grab a

"Resurrection Bracelet" first. It literally revives you from the dead! Yes, it sounds unbelievable until you try it for yourself, but it really works…

…However! This wonder bracelet only works inside the Dungeon itself, so don't try invoking it anywhere else!

RUMORS AROUND TEMPEST

COULD YOU MEET VELDORA!?

All kinds of rumors, plausible or otherwise, are floating around Tempest. For this column, I tried confirming one of them, only to discover Veldora-sama—surprisingly a gourmet chef himself!

Veldora-sama is very friendly!

Food stalls can be spotted around the Coliseum and everywhere in town. I've recently discovered that Veldora-sama runs one of them himself! It turns out that the Storm Dragon has a foodie side to him after all.

HFF. HFF.

It's really hot, so be careful not to burn your mouth!

Could seeing him in person provide you good luck for the rest of the day?

The "takoyaki" Veldora-sama crafts in his stall is a hot snack cooked on iron plates—warming, fragrant, and lip-smacking good. The sauce on top is packed with flavor—you might get addicted!

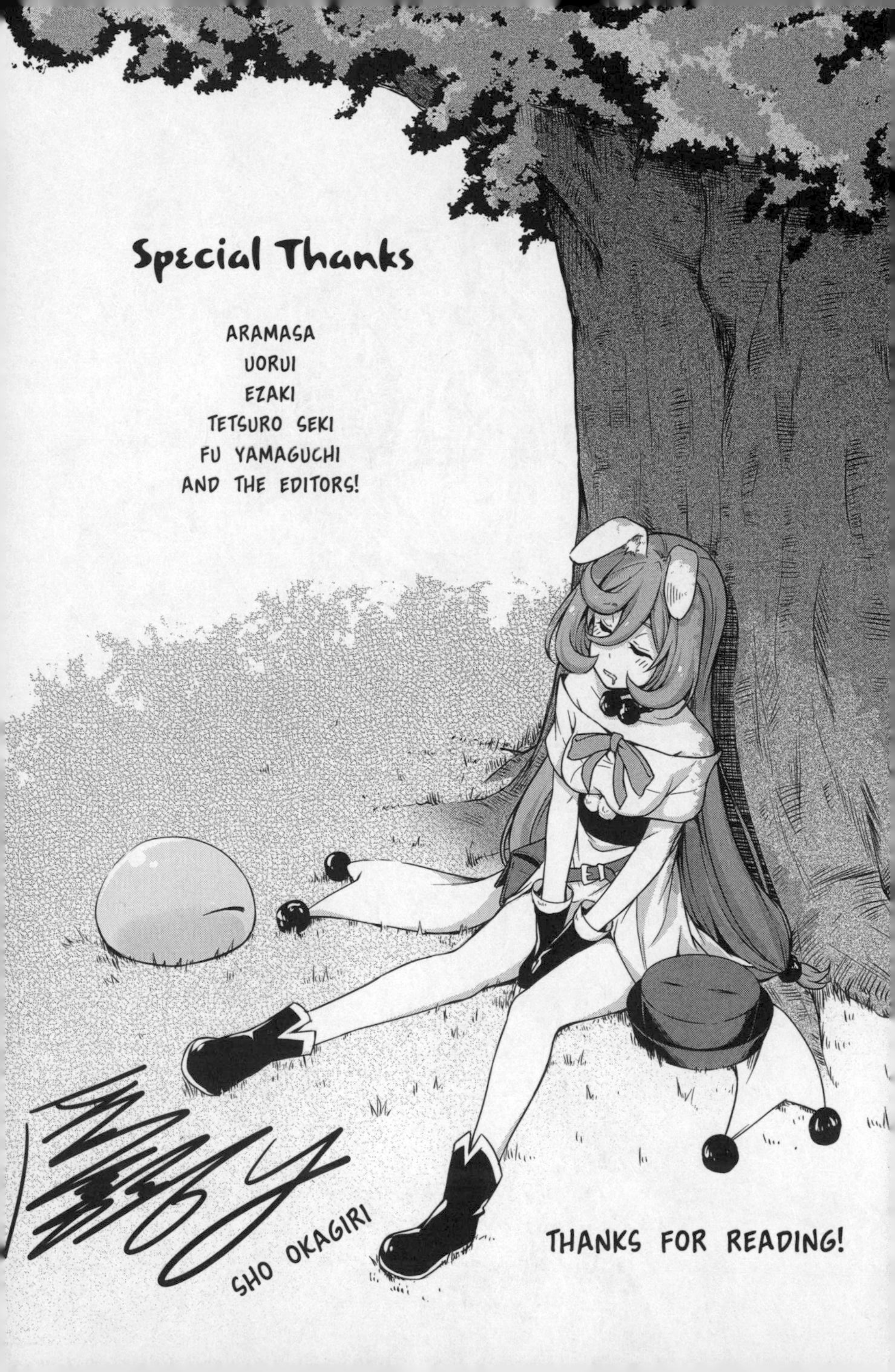
Special Thanks
ARAMASA
UORUI
EZAKI
TETSURO SEKI
FU YAMAGUCHI
AND THE EDITORS!
SHO OKAGIRI
THANKS FOR READING!

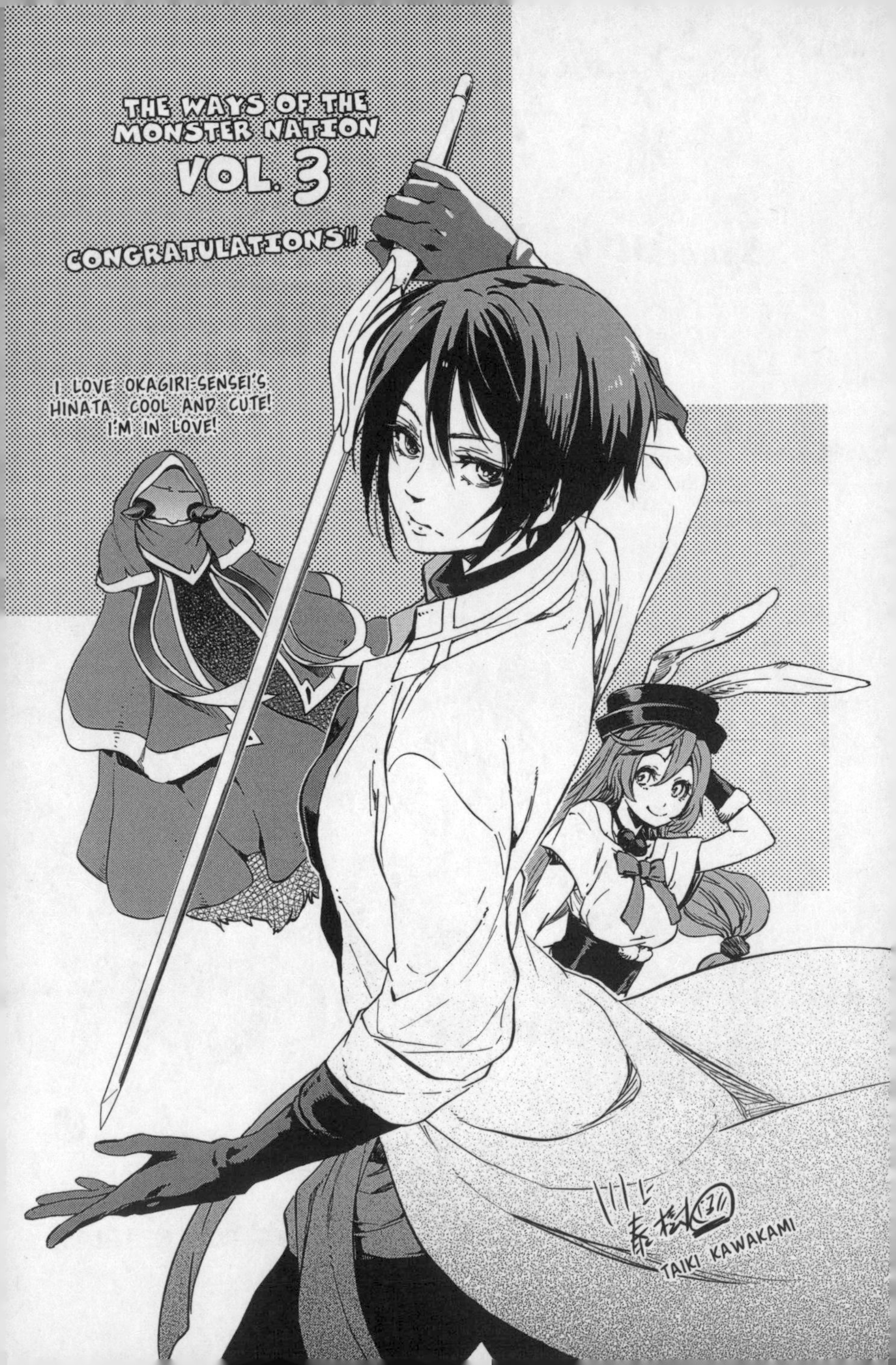
THE WAYS OF THE MONSTER NATION
VOL. 3
CONGRATULATIONS!!
I LOVE OKAGIRI-SENSEI'S HINATA. COOL AND CUTE! I'M IN LOVE!
TAIKI KAWAKAMI

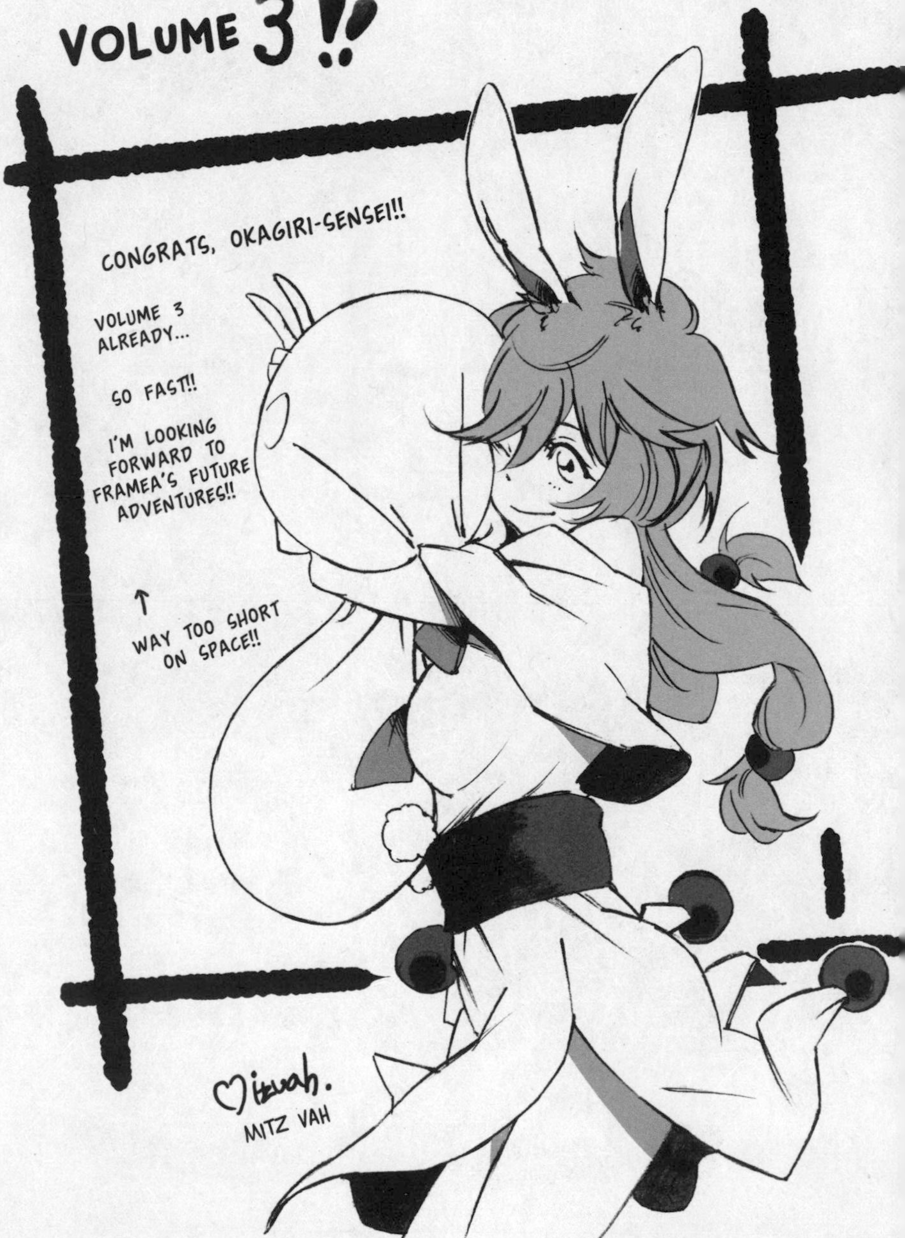
VOLUME 3!!
CONGRATS, OKAGIRI-SENSEI!!
VOLUME 3 ALREADY...
SO FAST!!
I'M LOOKING FORWARD TO FRAMEA'S FUTURE ADVENTURES!!
WAY TOO SHORT ON SPACE!!
MITZ VAH

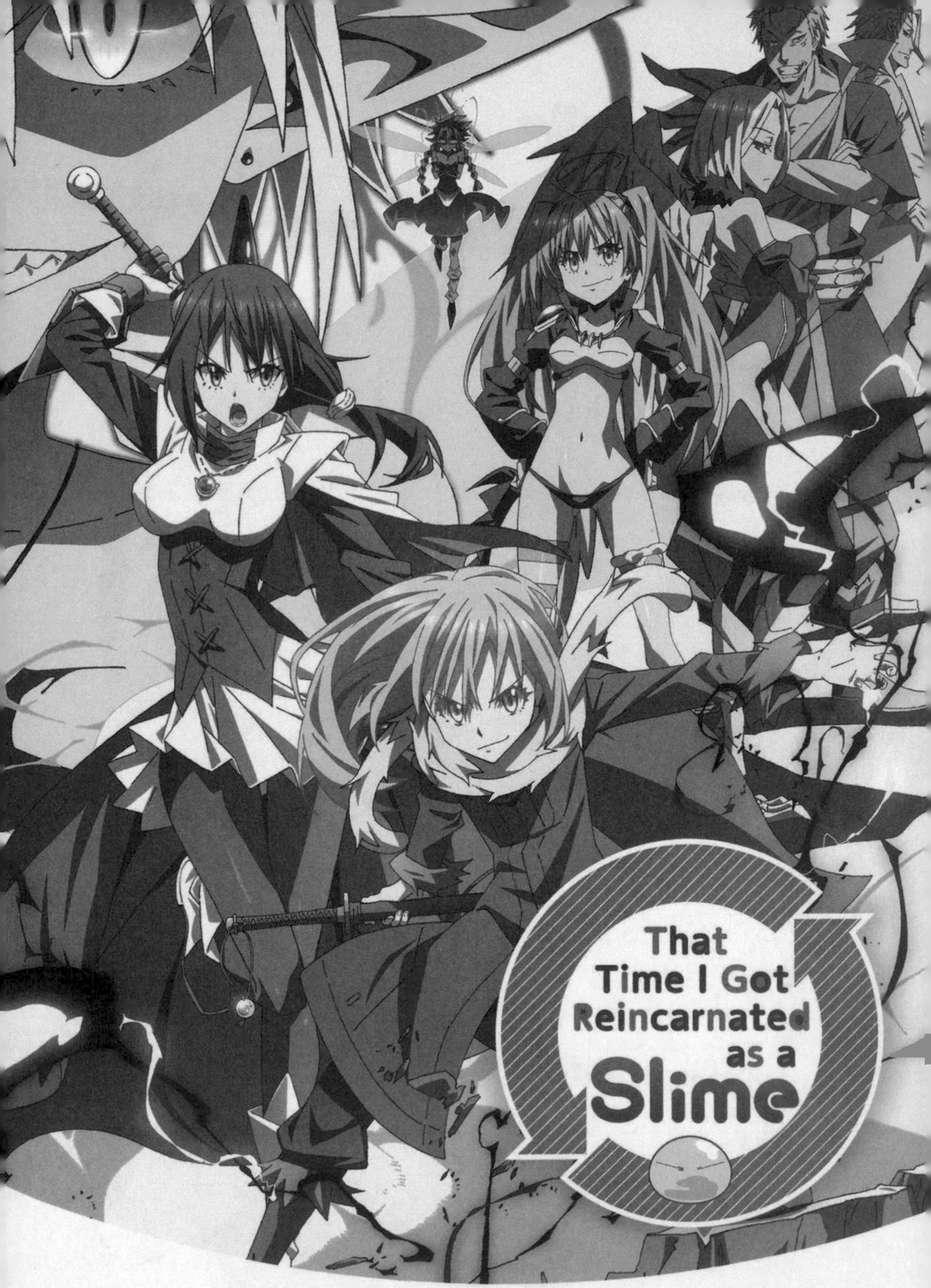
That Time I Got Reincarnated as a Slime

That Time I Got Reincarnated as a SLIME
The Ways of the Monster Nation

Translation: Kevin Gifford • Lettering: Barri Shrager

TENSEI SHITARA SURAIMU DATTA KEN ~MAMONO NO KUNI NO ARUKIKATA~ Vol. 3
©Fuse 2018
©Sho Okagiri, Mitz Vah 2018
First published in Japan in 2018 by MICRO MAGAZINE, INC.
English translation rights arranged with MICRO MAGAZINE, INC.
through Tuttle-Mori Agency, Inc., Tokyo.

English translation © 2020 by Yen Press, LLC

Yen Press
150 West 30th Street, 19th Floor
New York, NY 10001

Visit us at yenpress.com
facebook.com/yenpress
twitter.com/yenpress
yenpress.tumblr.com
instagram.com/yenpress

First Yen Press Edition: December 2020

Yen Press is an imprint of Yen Press, LLC.
The Yen Press name and logo are trademarks of Yen Press, LLC.

The publisher is not responsible for websites (or their content) that are not owned by the publisher.

Library of Congress Control Number: 2020936422

ISBNs: 978-1-9753-1357-9 (paperback)
978-1-9753-1356-2 (ebook)

10 9 8 7 6 5 4 3 2 1

BVG

Printed in the United States of America

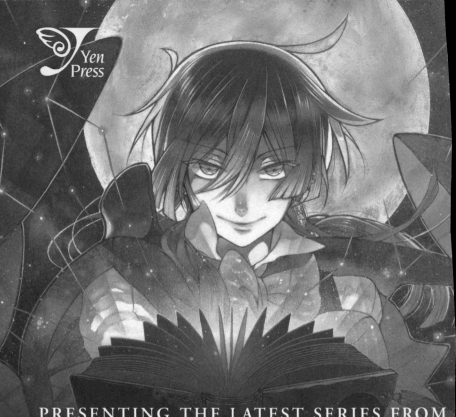